# GOING LOCAL

Going public to gain support, especially through reliance on national addresses and the national news media, has been a central tactic for modern presidential public leadership. In *Going Local: Presidential Leadership in the Post-Broadcast Age,* Jeffrey E. Cohen argues that presidents have adapted their "going public" activities to reflect the current realities of polarized parties and fragmented media. Going public now entails presidential targeting of their party base, interest groups, and localities. Cohen focuses on localities and offers a theory of presidential news management that is tested using several new data sets, including the first large-scale content analysis of local newspaper coverage of the president. The analysis finds that presidents can affect their local news coverage, which, in turn, affects public opinion toward the president. Although the post-broadcast age presents hurdles to presidential leadership, *Going Local* demonstrates the effectiveness of targeted presidential appeals and provides us with a refined understanding of the nature of presidential leadership.

Jeffrey E. Cohen is Professor of Political Science at Fordham University and during 2008–2009 was Visiting Senior Research Scholar at the Center for the Study of Democratic Politics at the Woodrow Wilson School at Princeton University. He is the author of eleven books and monographs – including *The Presidency in an Era of 24-Hour News* – and more than fifty journal articles. Professor Cohen's areas of interest focus on American politics, especially the presidency and public policy.

# Going Local

*Presidential Leadership in the Post-Broadcast Age*

**Jeffrey E. Cohen**

Fordham University

CAMBRIDGE
UNIVERSITY PRESS

CAMBRIDGE UNIVERSITY PRESS
Cambridge, New York, Melbourne, Madrid, Cape Town, Singapore,
São Paulo, Delhi, Dubai, Tokyo

Cambridge University Press
32 Avenue of the Americas, New York, NY 10013-2473, USA

www.cambridge.org
Information on this title: www.cambridge.org/9780521141437

First published 2010

Printed in the United States of America

*A catalog record for this publication is available from the British Library.*

*Library of Congress Cataloging in Publication data*

Cohen, Jeffrey E.
Going local : presidential leadership in the post-broadcast age / Jeffrey E. Cohen.
  p.   cm.
Includes bibliographical references and index.
ISBN 978-0-521-19371-9 (hardback) – ISBN 978-0-521-14143-7 (pbk.)
 1. Communication in politics – United States.   2. Political leadership – United
States.   3. Presidents – Press coverage – United States.   4. Press and politics –
United States.   I. Title.
JA85.2.U6C64   2010
352.23′60973 – dc22        2009025035

ISBN 978-0-521-19371-9 Hardback
ISBN 978-0-521-14143-7 Paperback

# Contents

# List of Figures

# List of Tables

# Introduction

*Some Puzzles*

Since its publication in 1986, Samuel Kernell's "going public" theory has emerged as a leading explanation of presidential behavior. To a large degree, presidential leadership is built upon a going public strategy. However, since Kernell first wrote his book, the political world has evolved. The political parties are now more polarized, the news media highly fragmented, and the public less attentive to news and public affairs than it was a quarter century ago. Presidents have adapted to this changing political context. Although they have not abandoned the going public leadership strategy, presidents have modified their public leadership activities to better fit these new realities. *Going Local: Presidential Leadership in the Post-Broadcast Age* is about the changing nature of presidential going public in an era of polarized parties and fragmented media. This revised going public model better explains recent presidential behavior that seems at odds with our traditional understanding of going public.

For instance, the traditional going public perspective predicts that presidents will build a personal, broad-based following in the mass public, not a partisan one. Consider, however, George W. Bush's behavior in the wake of his narrow election victory in 2000. Bush came to office in 2001 under a cloud, winning the election only after the Supreme Court ruled in his favor regarding the recount of votes in Florida. That, the Court's party line vote on the Florida recount issue, and Al Gore's popular vote lead led to outcry and protest and potentially undermined Bush's legitimacy to assume the office. To heal the nation's divisions, some analysts suggested that Bush should build a bipartisan unity cabinet. Instead, he assembled a highly partisan administration

1

and governed as an ardent partisan throughout his two terms. Going public as traditionally understood does not easily account for Bush's highly partisan governing style.

Second, the going public style also treats major national addresses and national news coverage as critical elements for presidents as they try to build national public support. However, shortly after winning reelection in 2004, Bush announced his proposal to overhaul and reform Social Security. To build support for his reform, Bush embarked on a highly publicized "60 cities in 60 days" tour around the nation. When asked by reporters why he "keeps plugging away on his meticulously stage-managed and strikingly repetitive national tour on Social Security" he responded,

> Part of the reason I'm going around the country ... is because not everyone gets their news from the national news. In all due respect to the national Pooh-Bahs, most people get their news from the local news. And if you're trying to influence opinion, the best way to do it is to travel hard around the country and give the people their dues. (Froomkin, June 3, 2005)

Why did Bush make going local the centerpiece of his campaign to build public support, rather than using the national airwaves and national media?

Third, during the past two decades, most types of going public activities have steadily risen, yet mounting research (e.g., Edwards, 2003) indicates that going public is no longer a very effective method of building public support and influencing public opinion. Why are presidents going public more if they are gaining little from doing so?

In *Going Local: Presidential Leadership in the Post-Broadcast Age,* I address these puzzles by building a new theory of presidential leadership. This theory argues that presidential leadership styles adapt to changes in context. During the past two decades, the context presidents faced has changed as parties have polarized and the news media have fragmented. Instead of "going national," as they did in the era that Kernell studied, presidents now "go narrow"; that is, they focus on mobilizing support from their party base, interest groups, and select localities. Presidents still go public, but now they emphasize a different mix of going public activities compared with a generation ago. In this book

I demonstrate empirically that presidents are reasonably effective in building support, especially local public opinion, among these narrow groups.

## THE ARGUMENT

The rise of polarized parties and a fragmented news media during the past two decades have transformed presidential governing and leadership styles. Going national, a major element of going public, as described by Samuel Kernell (1986, 2006), is not very effective in building public support in the face of polarized parties and a fragmented news media. In place of going national, presidents now go narrow; that is, they focus their public activities on building support in their party base, some interest groups, and select localities.

In *Going Local*, I offer a new context theory of presidential leadership styles. It argues that presidents, as rational actors, adapt to changing circumstances or context because the context affects the ability of presidents to mobilize resources that they can use to affect congressional roll calls. This theory helps explain changes in presidential behavior across two transitions: 1) from institutional pluralism (1950s–1970s) to individual pluralism (1970s–mid-1980s) and 2) from individual pluralism to the current era of polarized parties and fragmented media (mid-1980s–present).

For instance, during the era of institutional pluralism, approximately the 1940s to the mid-1970s, presidents primarily used a bargaining leadership style because of the power of committee chairs to deliver their committee's rank and file membership, and because public support for the president held little sway with these committee leaders. From the 1970s until about the mid-1980s, institutional pluralism gave way to individual pluralism. Committee leaders lost much of their institutional power, whereas individual members of Congress gained greater career autonomy and control. Presidents could not bargain with each individual member of Congress. In place of bargaining, presidents developed the going public approach, in which they would rally public opinion to pressure Congress to support the president's policies. Going public played on members' electoral insecurity. A key feature of going public in this era was the prime-time presidential television address, which aimed to mobilize national public opinion. Through such addresses, among other public presidential activities, going public theoretically would activate opinion across a number of congressional districts, which would make going public more efficient than striking bargains with members of Congress individually.

But in the 1980s, the mass media began to fragment through the rise of cable television and the Internet. The national airwaves did not provide the president with as much access to the public as he had in the 1970s, undermining going national as a leadership strategy. Heightened party polarization erected a further barrier to presidential activation of national public opinion – not as many people would respond to presidential calls as during the previous age. Consequently, from roughly the mid-1980s to the present, presidents have de-emphasized national going public, putting more effort into mobilizing their party base, interest groups, and opinion in localities open to presidential leadership. As in the age of national going public, the president plays on members' electoral motivations, but he does so in a different way, as member's electoral calculations have changed.

In *Going Local*, I show how presidents have responded to the changing context by adapting their leadership style to reflect this new environment. The recognition that presidential leadership styles have changed helps to explain the puzzles posed above – Bush's partisan style, his reliance on going local, and the ineffectiveness of going national.

Furthermore, I show that going narrow is relatively effective in building public support, especially in localities important to the president. Recent research has argued that presidents are not very effective at leading the public (e.g., Edwards, 2003). My argument is that these studies understate the degree of presidential leadership effects. Presidential leadership of public opinion is always problematic. However, the context theory tells us *where* we should look for leadership effects. Rather than look only at national opinion, as most research has done, we need to examine presidents' leadership of their party base and the interest groups, and local communities they target.

In *Going Local*, I spend considerable time looking at presidential influence of local newspaper coverage and the effect of that coverage on public support of the president. That analysis finds that presidents can influence the coverage they receive in local newspapers, which in turn affects the opinions its readers have of the president. The potential to lead may be decreased in the era of polarized parties and fragmented media compared with the era of individual pluralism, but we can detect measurable and meaningful presidential leadership effects.

Rather than try to explain the puzzle of why presidents engage in so much going public activity if it has little pay off, as Edwards (2003) does, I argue that presidents adjust their behavior to maximize their leadership impact given the circumstances they confront. Those circumstances may not be propitious, but presidents rationally exploit them, however limited they may be. Much of what appears so puzzling becomes less so when understood through the lens of the context theory of presidential leadership.

## SOME DATA

In the new era of polarized parties and fragmented media, presidents place more emphasis on narrow groups, like their party base, interest groups, and select localities, and less on influencing national public opinion, a key theme of going public in the era of individual pluralism. I provide evidence that presidents have increased or altered their interactions with each of these three types of "narrow" segments of the political system. Most of the empirical work, however, focuses on presidential targeting of localities, what I call "going local."

Presidents use several methods in their attempts to influence local public opinion, including visits to localities and managing local news coverage. Although management of local news coverage is the spine for going local, it presents two hurdles for influencing local opinion. First, presidents must affect their local news coverage, and second, that news coverage must affect local opinion about the president.

To test for the effectiveness of the going local strategy, I built several specially designed data sets. Two of these data sets look at whether presidents can affect the coverage they receive in local newspapers. I use local newspapers rather than local television data for several reasons. A preliminary content analysis of local television news finds very little coverage of the president in local news broadcasts, and not many local television news stations have their broadcasts archived, a costly barrier to data collection. Many local newspapers archive; they still command relatively large readerships when compared with numerous other news media; and they publish measurable and meaningful amounts of news about the president.

One of these local newspaper data sets consists of a random sample of newspapers across a random sample of days in the calendar year 2000, for a sample of 825 news stories on the president. Other than because of resource limitations, I restricted these data to 2000 in order to match it as closely as possible with the data used to assess the impact of news coverage on public opinion, the 2000 National Annenberg Election Study (NAES). The NAES presents a unique opportunity to assess the impact of local daily news coverage on public opinion, which I discuss more fully below.

To compensate for the fact that the first local newspaper data set looks only at 2000, and thus may be unique or peculiar, I also collected a monthly time series of presidential news from 1990 through 2007 for fifty-six newspapers to look at trends in the *quantity* of presidential news. The results of the analyses of both of these data sets indicate that presidents seem to be able to affect the quantity and tone of their local news coverage.

To look at the impact of news coverage on public evaluations, the second leg of the going local approach, I again use the 2000 NAES. The NAES asked respondents for a feeling thermometer rating on then-President Bill Clinton, as well as to name the newspaper they read. I added information on the tone of news about the president for the respondents' newspaper. The analysis suggests that such news coverage in newspapers that respondents read affects respondents' evaluations of the president. Thus, presidents seem to be able to influence their local news coverage, which in turn influences public evaluations of the president.

**THE PLAN OF THIS BOOK**

Chapter 1 opens with a puzzle: Presidents seem to go public at higher rates now than during the era of individual pluralism, but going public does not appear to be highly effective in influencing public opinion.

To resolve this puzzle, Chapter 1 offers the context theory of presidential leadership, which suggests that the types of going public activities that presidents currently employ differ from those of the era of individual pluralism. In particular, presidents will target narrow groups, putting less emphasis on moving national opinion. The context theory is applied to explain changes in presidential behavior during two transitions, from institutional to individual pluralism and from individual pluralism to the current context of polarized parties and fragmented media.

Chapter 2 presents the first tests of the context theory of presidential leadership by presenting evidence that presidents have increased the attention they pay to their party base, interest groups, and localities, while also documenting declining use of national appeals.

Influencing local public opinion is a key element of going narrow. Presidents can try to influence local opinion by either visiting localities and/or by managing their local news coverage. Because visits are costly and rarely can persuade large numbers of members of Congress to support the president, managing local news coverage appears to provide a more systematic and continuous way for presidents to influence local opinion. In this regard, both local television and newspapers may be important, but I argue for the greater importance of local newspapers. Both local media command relatively large audiences and public respect, but local television does not broadcast much news on the president, whereas local newspapers publish considerable amounts of presidential news. Chapter 3 marshals evidence to support these claims, including a context analysis of local television broadcasts to show their meager attention to the president.

For going local to be effective, presidents must first manage or influence their local news coverage. Chapter 4 presents the theory of presidential news management. The chapter reviews and critiques the literatures on presidential news management and local news coverage of the president. I define presidential news management as the strategy presidents employ to influence their news coverage. Presidents believe that their news coverage will affect their public support. Identifying the specifics of a president's news management strategy, however, is difficult. First, presidents do not announce their news management strategy, and we may not observe some tactics or actions associated with a news management strategy, such as preferences or easier access for favored journalists or news organizations. Perhaps the best that we can do is look at the president's public activities as an indicator of the president's news management strategy. I assume that the president's news management strategy determines important characteristics of these public activities and events, such as their timing, format, location, and content. These activities may be thought of as the public face of the president's news management strategy, an approach similar to Althaus's (2000).

The empirical sections of this book assess the effectiveness of the going local leadership style. Chapters 5 to 7 test the first leg of the going local strategy by looking at whether presidents can influence their local news coverage. Chapters 5 and 6 look at the quantity of presidential news, Chapter 5 using the content analysis of newspapers in 2000, whereas Chapter 6 turns to the 1990 to 2007 monthly time series of local presidential news. Chapter 7 returns to the 2000 content analysis, looking at the tone of local news coverage of the president. Analysis in these chapters shows that presidents can affect the quantity and tone of the coverage they receive in local newspapers.

Chapters 5 through 7 indicate that presidents can manage their local news coverage. Does that coverage affect public opinion? To address this question, I turn to the 2000 NAES in Chapter 8, which asked respondents to name the newspaper they read. I coded each mentioned newspaper for the calendar year 2000 for whether it endorsed Democratic or Republican presidential candidates to measure tone, arguing that these endorsement patterns correlate with tone of presidential news coverage and providing support on this linkage. Analysis indicates that readers of "Democratic" newspapers, with many statistical controls in place, rate Clinton more highly in 2000 than readers of "Republican" newspapers. This finding suggests that if presidents can influence the tone of their coverage in local newspapers, they will realize higher levels of public support among readers of those newspapers.

Chapter 9 recaps the findings, discusses unresolved questions, presents directions for future research, and links this study to the large and growing literature on media bias, with some suggestions for how to study the influence of the news media in modern politics.

The chapter concludes with some thoughts about the nature of presidential leadership. In contrast with other recent studies that suggest limits or slight presidential leadership effects (Edwards, 2003), my study finds potentially significant leadership effects. But to find these leadership effects, we needed to understand the larger context in which presidents find themselves so that we can look for the types of leadership effects that the context allows. Context matters for presidential leadership. Scholars of presidential leadership need to be sensitive to context and how it affects the opportunities and styles of presidential leadership.

## ACKNOWLEDGEMENTS

In writing this book I have accumulated a number of debts. First, several individuals gave me their time and advice, especially Jamie Druckman of Northwestern University, Jeff Peake of Bowling Green State University, and Matthew Eshbaugh-Soha of the University of North Texas. Jamie got me thinking about the deeper meaning of the research reported in these pages, and how to structure and present my argument. Jeff got me thinking on how and why to study presidents and the local media, and his papers on the topic strongly influenced my own research. Matt has helped me in numerous ways, from advice on collecting data and analyzing data, to helping me flesh out conceptual and theoretical issues. Like Jeff, Matt too has done some important work on presidents and localities.

Two institutions provided me with the support to finish this project. My home institution, Fordham University, granted me some funds to employ several students, who collected the bulk of the content analysis data used in Chapters 5 and 7. Fordham also granted me a Faculty Fellowship for academic year 2008–2009, which relived me of my teaching and other university responsibilities, enabling me to devote my energies to finishing this book.

Second, I want to thank the Center for the Study of Democratic Politics (CSDP), of the Woodrow Wilson School, Princeton University, which awarded me a Visiting Senior Research Scholar fellowship for academic year 2008–2009. CSDP provided me with a congenial and stimulating work environment. In particular, I want to thank Michele

Epstein and Helene Wood, who helped me get settled at CSDP and always looked after my needs. Larry Bartels, the Director of CSDP, was a most gracious host. The other faculty and staff at CSDP, the Wilson School, and Princeton University made my visit productive, enjoyable, and one of the high points of my academic career. A special word of thanks goes to Fred Greenstein, with whom I shared many engaging lunches and discussions across a wide variety of topics.

I also want to thank Cambridge University Press, in particular Ed Parsons and Jason Przybylski, who speedily guided me through the review process and offered much cogent advice for revising this manuscript. The two reviewers for CUP, Richard Waterman and Stephen Weatherford made invaluable suggestions.

I also want to thank Christopher Catropa. Chris studied at Fordham University, where he earned his bachelor of arts and master of arts degrees and enrolled in several of my courses. Chris is responsible for collecting much of the data used in Chapters 5 and 7.

Finally, a word of love and appreciation goes to my wife, Phyllis, who puts up with me and my work habits with good grace, tolerance, and a sense of humor.

# CHAPTER 1

# Context and Presidential Leadership Styles

Context shapes presidential leadership styles and the effectiveness of those leadership styles. Presidents select leadership styles that best exploit the opportunities provided by the contexts they face. This perspective on presidential leadership departs significantly from much research on the presidency, which tends to argue that personal and individual factors, such as personality, worldview, and character shape a president's leadership style (e.g., Barber, 2009; Greenstein, 2000, 2008).

I am not the only presidential scholar to emphasize the importance of context in structuring a president's leadership style. For instance, Samuel Kernell's (1986, 2006) "going public" theory argues that the change from institutional to individual pluralism affected the way presidents interact with Congress, transforming a style that emphasized bargaining to one that entailed going public. Kernell rightly points to change in the congressional *context* as a primary causal factor that led presidents to replace bargaining with going public in the 1960s and 1970s. One of the aims of this book is to build on Kernell's key insight about the importance of context in the formation of a general theory of presidential leadership, one that not only explains the factors that motivate presidents to adopt one leadership style over another, but also assesses the effectiveness of each major leadership style.

The going public theory, as described by Kernell (1986, 2006), provides us with one of the most useful and influential accounts of presidential behavior and leadership styles. Since Kernell first introduced the concept, the context that presidents have faced has evolved into one that exhibits greater partisan polarization and more fragmented media. Consequently, the degree to and ways in which presidents engage with the public has also changed. This book offers a revision to Kernell's going public theory that helps us make sense of several puzzles, such as why George W. Bush was such an ardent partisan. Why did he travel around the nation so much when seeking support for his Social Security reform program? More generally, if going public is becoming less effective as a leadership style, why are presidents going public much more now than in the past?

In the context of polarized parties and a fragmented media, going public now entails presidential targeting of narrow groups such as their partisan base, some interest groups, and hospitable localities rather than rallying national opinion. "Going narrow" as opposed to "going national" is now the core of the president's public strategy. This more targeted going public style is a response to important changes in the context presidents face. As stated by Kernell, changes in context have motivated a change in the president's leadership style. Presidents still go public, but going public in the era of polarized parties and a fragmented news media differs in fundamental ways from doing so in the era of individual pluralism.

This book offers a new theory of presidential leadership, one that recognizes the importance of context in shaping presidential leadership styles. Presidential leadership styles adapt to context, as presidents select the leadership style that will maximize their policy objectives within the constraints and opportunities for leadership of a specific context. This theory has implications for the way we study presidential leadership and how we assess its effectiveness. It compels us to look at the conditioning implications of context in shaping presidential leadership and understand that it may have more to do with the context presidents confront than with their individual traits, skills, and abilities.

Several studies (e.g., Edwards, 2003) argue that presidents are no longer effective leaders, especially of public opinion, and even question if they ever were. Clearly, it is not easy to lead the public. Edwards (2003) points out many barriers to effective presidential leadership. But in assessing whether a particular leadership tactic, such as addressing the nation on prime-time television, will be effective, one needs to know how the context affects the potential leadership benefits from any presidential activity. Sometimes a particular context will erect barriers against a leadership tactic, rendering it ineffective, yet at the same time enhance the effectiveness of a different tactic.

If we look at activities inappropriate in a particular context and find few presidential leadership effects, we will mistakenly assume that presidents are ineffective leaders. Thus, we need to match the type of leadership activity to the context to test for presidential leadership effects. Much of the current research on presidential leadership uses the "national going public" leadership style as its reference or baseline. But that leadership style, I argue, was more appropriate in the 1960s and 1970s, the era of individual pluralism, not in the current context of polarized parties and fragmented media. When we look at presidential activities more appropriate in this current context – targeted leadership aimed at the president's party base, interest group, and some localities, as I do in the empirical sections of this book – we find stronger presidential leadership effects on these targets of presidential leadership efforts.

This context theory also tells us something about the potential for presidential leadership. Individual pluralism may have offered presidents relatively potent leadership potential via going public. The current era of polarized parties and fragmented news media heavily circumscribe the amount of influence or impact, especially on public opinion, compared with that earlier era. Regardless of how hard presidents try in the current era, they likely will not match the leadership impacts of presidents of the period of individual pluralism. Today, presidential leadership is even more problematic than it was in the age of individual pluralism.

The next section reviews the findings of studies that have tested aspects of Kernell's going public theory. That review suggests that presidents go public more often now than two decades ago, but going public seems less effective than it once was. This presents us with the question of why presidents go public so much more often given that the effectiveness of such a leadership style has been fading. The answer is that there are different ways for presidents to go public. Presidents have increased their use of some types of going public – for instance, narrow, targeted appeals – while relying less on other forms, such as national televised addresses. The type of going public activities on which presidents now rely flows directly from changes in context, the rise of polarized parties and fragmented media.

After the review of the literature on the going public strategy, I offer the context theory of presidential leadership. The rise of polarized parties and a fragmented media led presidents to alter their going public leadership style because the earlier, nationally focused style had declined in effectiveness. By contrast, a more targeted going public leadership style can be effective in some circumstances.

## GOING PUBLIC: DOING IT MORE, BUT ENJOYING IT LESS

Going public is now the dominant paradigm to explain presidential public leadership.[1] Samuel Kernell, who invented the concept, defines going public as "a class of activities that presidents engage in as they promote themselves and their policies before the American public. . . . [I]n going public, the ultimate object of the president's designs is not the American voter, but rather fellow politicians in Washington." (2006, x). Examples of presidential going public activities include televised press conferences, speeches before select groups around the nation and in foreign nations, and most important, prime-time television addresses.

In the next chapter, I will review in more depth trends in going public, but the focus here is on increases in many types of going public activities, especially narrow, targeted ones. For now, I address the question: Is going public an effective leadership strategy? Can the president shift public opinion by going public, and does Congress respond to presidential going public activities?

### Going Public and the Public Response

For going public to be an effective leadership strategy, presidents must be able to influence public opinion when doing so. Is going public effective in this regard? Research has divided this question into the effects of presidential leadership on the public's *policy preference* versus the public's *agenda or policy priorities.* Arguably, it is more difficult to

---

[1]  Kernell's going public thesis, first presented in 1986, has become so popular that a fourth edition of the book was issued in 2006.

alter the public's preferences than their priorities (see Cohen and Hamman, 2005).

Research generally concludes that presidents have a difficult time altering the public's preferences over policies. George Edwards's *On Deaf Ears* (2003) presents one of the most extensive studies of presidential attempts to influence the public's policy preferences and finds no systematic evidence of public movement to the presidents' policy positions, even when presidents work hard to move the public. However, Edwards generally looks at presidential attempts to influence national opinion in an era of polarized parties and fragmented media, when I suggest we should not expect much presidential impact on national opinion. In contrast to Edwards, Wood (2007) finds that the tone of presidential rhetoric about the economy affects public perceptions of the economy. Yet again, Wood does not address whether presidential leadership effects are lower in more recent than in earlier years of his time series, which spans from the 1980s to the early 2000s.

Somewhat greater evidence suggests that presidents can influence the public agenda, that is, its policy priorities. Cohen (1995, 1997), Hill (1998), and Lawrence (2004) find that presidential policy emphasis in their State of the Union addresses affects public responses to the most important problem question, and Druckman and Holmes (2004) suggest that by altering the public's agenda, presidents may enhance their approval ratings by changing the policy basis on which individuals judge the president.[2]

All of the "agenda setting" studies look at the quintessential broad presidential public activity, delivery of the State of the Union address, which is also now required of presidents. There are some suggestions that the address may be less effective at influencing public opinion in the current era. Baum and Kernell (1999) show that with the emergence of cable television, the audience for presidential speeches has contracted. Young and Perkins (2005) tie these strands of research together and show that in the age of cable, one measure of media fragmentation, the State of the Union address has less impact on

---

[2] Barabas (2008), however, finds that people learn about public policies from watching presidential State of the Union addresses, but it is unclear whether such learning affects presidential ability to influence the public's policy preferences or priorities.

public priorities. Their research also indicates that the address has its greatest impact on public priorities in the age of broadcast television, which roughly corresponds to the age of individual pluralism. This provides some initial evidence that broad going public activities were more effective in the earlier era than in the present.

Finally, Holmes (2008) looks at presidential public support for their nominees to the U.S. Court of Appeals from 1977 to 2004. She finds that presidents increasingly make public statements in support of their nominees and that recent presidents rarely make broad public appeals, instead targeting their comments to narrow audiences, which is consistent with the argument offered here. Given the greater role of interest groups in the judicial confirmation process, Holmes argues that "presidential attention to lower court nominees may be directed not toward influencing public opinion in general, but may be directed at these interested elites" (2008, 112).

Overall, studies rarely compare presidential leadership effects on public opinion in the era of individual pluralism versus the current period of polarized parties and fragmented media, nor do they distinguish the effects of different types of presidential public activities. The one study that makes period comparisons, by Young and Perkins (2005), suggests that national leadership attempts are less effective in the current than in the prior period. Only Holmes (2008) looks at targeted activities in any detail, but she confines her study to judicial nominees and presents no data on the effectiveness of presidential efforts at mobilizing key groups in support of their nominee. Young and Perkins (2005) and Holmes (2008) are suggestive that change in the context has implications for presidential going public activities.

### Going Public and the Congressional Response

Does going public lead to presidential success with Congress? Most of the research on the legislative effectiveness of going public consists of case studies, which raise the issue of generalizability. Canes-Wrone (2001a, 2001b, 2005), Barrett (2004) and Powell and Schloyer (2003) provide more systematic tests of the legislative effectiveness of going public.

Canes-Wrone (2001a) finds that when presidents speak in a nationally televised address in support of a budget proposal, the public salience of the proposal increases, which leads to higher congressional support of the president on that proposal.[3] Barrett (2004) looks at a broader array of presidential public statements in support of issues, and like Canes-Wrone, he finds significant effects of going public on the passage of legislation. Powell and Schloyer (2003) look at whether electorally marginal members of Congress are more susceptible to going public efforts than are more secure members. They report mixed results: Using national televised addresses as their indicator of presidential going public activities, they find that going public is negatively associated with House voting patterns and only positive, as hypothesized, for vulnerable senators.

There are several limitations across these studies for our purposes. None distinguishes the different types of going public. Canes-Wrone and Powell and Schloyer look only at national televised addresses and Barrett condenses all public statements, no matter the source (e.g., major speech, minor speech) into one index. Second, none tests for whether going public is more or less successful in the earlier era or the current one, or looks at the related hypothesis, that different types of going public activities will be more or less effective depending on the time period.

### Summary

Ironically, the literature on going public suggests greater success with Congress than with the public. Rather than affecting policy preferences, going public may operate through agenda setting, in which presidential rhetoric activates existing opinions and Congress responds to the new opinion climate. Still, the research on going public in general fails to take into account the impact of context on the relative effectiveness of different going public activities (but see Young and Perkins, 2005 and Holmes, 2008). Nor has anyone attempted to explain the shift in presidential going public activities, in which presidents now emphasize targeted appeals to narrow groups, rather than aiming to influence national public opinion – whether preferences regarding policies or priorities. The next section addresses this subject.

---

3  Presidents do not alter public opinion in Canes-Wrone's theory. Instead, they only go public on issues on which the public and the president already agree.

## A CONTEXT THEORY OF PRESIDENTIAL LEADERSHIP

The context theory of presidential leadership begins with the assumption that presidents care about policy. This may be the case for many reasons. Policy has important political implications. A president and his party's election chances rest in part on the policies enacted and how well they work. Similarly, policy enactment and outcomes may affect a president's standing with the public and his popularity. Whether the president can get some of his favored policies enacted and implemented may also affect his reputation as a leader. The foundation of a president's legacy to the nation, moreover, depends heavily on the policies enacted during his term of office. Finally, presidents may have a vision for the nation and see policy as a vehicle for steering the nation in that direction. According to the context theory of presidential leadership, it matters little which of these factors induces presidential concern with policy.

Given this policy motivation, presidents spend much of their time and effort ensuring that their policies get enacted and overseeing the implementation of these policies so that they work as intended. Ideally, presidents would probably like to command the enactment of their policies. But in our constitutional system, presidents do not possess such command or decree power.

Presidents have at their disposal two primary avenues for enacting policies: 1) an administrative approach, which relies on issuing unilateral directives like executive orders and 2) a legislative approach, which requires congressional passage of legislation. To a degree, the administrative approach may appear to resemble command authority, but as Howell (2003) and Mayer (2001) have shown, presidents take into account congressional preferences in issuing executive orders. In addition, presidents need a constitutional or legal foundation to issue an executive order. Consequently, the legislative route remains important for the enactment of the president's policies.

It is wellknown that passing legislation is far from easy. More bills die than emerge as legislation. And presidents cannot order members of Congress, even from their own party, to support their legislative proposals. Members of the president's party often bridle against major and high-priority presidential policy initiatives – for instance, George W. Bush's immigration reforms of 2005 and the administration's credit market rescue package of September and October 2008.

To see their proposals enacted by Congress, presidents must build support coalitions (Seligman and Covington, 1989; Edwards, 2000; Cohen, 2006), which is perhaps the overriding task for the president in dealing with Congress. Presidents do not necessarily have to work hard to bring some members of Congress into support coalitions. Those easy targets may agree with the president's proposals and may even have supported the proposals had the president not taken a stand on them. Yet other members have to be convinced to join the coalitions. For these members, supporting the president may be costly. Thus, presidents need to find a way to decrease that cost and/or provide benefits to joining the support coalition that outweigh the disadvantages of membership. This requires that presidents understand what matters to and motivates members of Congress. In formulating a particular leadership strategy to build a support coalition, presidents will apply the resources at their disposal to influence those factors that motivate members on policy issues.

Some of these factors that may motivate members in deciding what position to take on a policy before Congress include desire for reelection, to attain power within Congress, to produce good policies, and party loyalty. These motivations may vary in impact across members of Congress and over time as circumstances change. Moreover, presidents may be more or less able to influence these congressional motivations. As presidents' ability to influence congressional motivations increases, so does the likelihood that presidents will be able to persuade or convince members of Congress to join their support coalition.

The theory offered here argues that context shapes the president's leadership style and context may be a more powerful influence over presidential leadership style than presidential personality, without denying that personality also has a role to play in presidential selection of a leadership style. Context is a powerful influence over presidential leadership style because it also affects the mix of motivations that matter to members of Congress, as well as the president's ability to acquire the resources necessary to influence those motivations.

Context is a necessarily vague and broad-ranging concept. Yet several aspects of the political context may be especially relevant for understanding presidential leadership. For instance, the internal organization of Congress affects the distribution of power within Congress and the factors that motivate members' policy-making decisions. The internal organization of Congress will also affect the success of different types of presidential interactions with the legislature. Similarly, the external political environment may affect members' motivations. For instance, how competitive are congressional elections? What role do parties play in recruitment of candidates and their election campaigns? Both Congress's internal organization and the outer political environment provide context for members. These in turn define the congressional context for the president.

Because presidents cannot command members of Congress to follow their lead, presidents need resources to influence members of Congress. Just as Congress's internal organization and its external environment affect the motivations of members of Congress, the presidency as an organization and the external environment may provide the president with the resources needed to influence members of Congress to join the presidential support coalition. Presidents may receive staff help and information about policy, the preferences of members of Congress, and so on, from the organizational or institutional presidency. These types of resources may be useful to presidents when drafting legislation and bargaining with members of Congress about policy.

From the external environment, presidents primarily raise political capital – that is, public support. Citizen attachment to the parties and the communication system affects presidential ability to generate public support. Ironically, the stronger the citizenry's attachment to the parties, the harder it may be for presidents to generate broad-based public support. Presidents will always have difficulty mobilizing support among voters who identify with the opposition party. Under most circumstances, their partisanship will erect a barrier against supporting the president, whereas voters who identify with the president's party generally will be stable supporters of the president. In the short term, public support levels for the president mostly come from independents and those who weakly identify with either party.

The mix of strong and weak party identifiers, plus independents, will determine whether the president can boost his level of public support and thus whether going public is a feasible option.

Similarly, the communications system also will affect the president's ability to raise public support. Communications systems determine the type of access that presidents have to the mass public and whether the president can expect a large or small audience for his communications efforts. Modern means of mass communication, like radio and television, offered presidents direct access to the public. Presidents could also anticipate a large audience during the age of broadcasting, before competition from cable and the Internet peeled away broadcast television's audience (Baum and Kernell, 1999; Prior, 2007; Cohen, 2008). Going public to mobilize public support likely would be a more inviting possibility during the age of broadcasting than either the era preceding or following it (Young and Perkins, 2005).

This discussion of context and its implications for presidential leadership is necessarily vague and suggestive at this point. The list of possible contextual factors for relevance to presidential leadership can be extended beyond the congressional, party, and communications contexts. Even these three contextual factors would produce numerous combinations. Rather than try to specify all such combinations or list further contextual factors, the next sections look at two transitions, that from institutional pluralism to individual pluralism and that from individual pluralism to the current era of polarized parties and fragmented media, to see how changes in these three contextual factors have affected presidential leadership styles.

### Presidential Adaptation from Institutional to Individual Pluralism
According to Kernell, as the institutional pluralism of the mid-twentieth-century Congress gave way to individual pluralism, presidents found it increasingly difficult to build coalitions within Congress in the manner in which they did before. Neustadt's (1960) bargaining model describes how presidents navigated the political waters of institutional pluralism. Under institutional pluralism, a president needed only to bargain with a relatively small number of committee chairs and party leaders to forge a coalition large enough to win acceptance of his policy initiative. Committee chairs, in particular, could deliver blocs of

votes (the rank and file membership of their committees) for policies that they supported. Committee chairs often played a crucial role in building winning coalitions behind a president's policy. Moreover, as committee chairs earned those posts through seniority, they tended to be relatively insulated from national opinion tides that would, on occasion, sweep from office members representing more competitive districts. Thus, the members to whom presidents turned most often for votes in Congress were among the least attuned to public pressures. Standing with the public under such conditions did not always help a president in his dealings with Congress. Bargaining with congressional power brokers was more important for presidents.

Matters changed radically under individual pluralism. Unlike institutional pluralism, with its centralization of power in the hands of committee chairs in Congress, individual pluralism produced a more decentralized Congress. Committee reforms in the 1970s expanded the number of congressional power centers, while also diminishing the power of full committee chairs. With this dispersion of power, building a support coalition through bargaining became a more difficult task. To construct a winning coalition, presidents had to negotiate with a larger number of legislators, each with their own agenda, constituents, and career ambitions to satisfy. Presidents needed a less taxing method of building coalitions in Congress than bargaining with each member of Congress individually. Presidents also needed to find a resource that they could leverage to convince members of Congress to join the presidential support coalition.

Going public became the solution for the president. By going public, presidents could bring public pressure to bear across numerous members of Congress simultaneously. In this sense, going public reduced the costs for presidents in dealing with an individually plural Congress. By going public, presidents would not have to bargain individually with such a large number of members. Instead, if the president could successfully lead public opinion, a large number of members would follow, feeling public opinion pressure from their districts. The success of going public hinged on the president's ability to influence public opinion. To that end, presidents increased White House resources by adding staff, especially experts in the arts and sciences of publicity.

Kernell identifies several types of going public activities, such as delivering major presidential addresses to the nation on prime-time television broadcasts, offering minor addresses to narrower and more select audiences, traveling around the nation and the globe, and appearing in public (which usually entails speaking to an audience). We can categorize going public activities in many ways. For our purposes here, let's divide them into two sets, those aimed at the nation (e.g., major prime-time presidential addresses and international travel) and those aimed at select audiences and groups (e.g., minor speeches and domestic travel).

Kernell argues that presidents rely less on major addresses than on other forms of going public because addressing the nation too frequently will induce a counterreaction among citizens, causing many to lose interest in what the president has to say (2006, 93).[4] However, major addresses are potentially the most effective form of going public, in part because of their drama and, if used sparingly, their ability to focus the public's attention (2006, 116–121). Finally, major speeches may be a cost-effective method of applying public pressure on Congress because they theoretically tap constituents throughout the nation in every congressional district. Despite these limitations, Kernell finds increases in major speech activity from the 1950s into the 1980s, which is consistent with the going public theory, but he also notices a modest decline for presidents Bush I, Clinton, and Bush II (2006, 116–121, also Ragsdale, 1998, 159–167).

Because of the limitations in the number of major speeches a president may make, presidents turn to minor speeches and other public activities geared at more select and narrower audiences. Kernell argues that minor presidential speeches are especially suited for building coalitions in an individualized pluralism setting, which requires building temporary coalitions among diverse constituencies issue by issue. (1993, 98). Coalition building under individualized pluralism entails a mix of major and minor going public activities, with the choice of going "major-national" or "minor-narrow" a function of the issue at hand, for example, how often the president has already gone national

---

4 The networks have also become increasingly resistant to numerous presidential addresses that preempt their prime-time programming (Foote, 1990).

and the alignment of groups and public opinion on the issue (Cohen, 2008).

### Presidential Adaptation from Individual Pluralism to Polarized Parties and the Post-Broadcast Media

In the late 1980s or early 1990s, a convergence of two factors, polarization of the political parties and the rise of the new media, would make localities and other "narrow" publics the cornerstones of presidential coalition-building efforts (Cohen, 2008). Party polarization would make it nearly impossible for presidents to pursue a strategy of building broad-based and widespread support across the entire mass public. The rise of the new media not only reduced the power of the national news media, but also increased the ability of presidents to target specific publics in their quest to build support coalitions.

*Party Polarization and the Presidency.* Polarization between the parties at both the elite and mass levels has been on the rise for at least the past two decades (Bartels, 2000; Bond and Fleisher, 2001; Hetherington, 2001; Jacobson, 2006).[5] Growing polarization between partisan elites widened the policy gap between the parties and reduced the number of members of either party occupying the policy center (Fleisher and Bond, 2004). In this context, forging a compromise policy position between members of the two parties becomes increasing difficult. Any potential compromise position may be too far away from the preferences of the members of either party to accept. The only sure-fire way to build coalitions when the parties in Congress exhibit as much polarization as they now do is for the president's party to hold enough seats to stymie any filibuster attempt (assuming that the president's party unites behind him). Rarely in recent years has the president's party reached those seat levels.

Partisan polarization at the mass public level also affects presidential coalition building and communications efforts. Mass partisan

5  Skinner (2008–2009) extensively reviews differences in presidential behavior and ties to their parties between the current era of polarization and the earlier time period, when polarization between the parties was less extreme. Skinner, however, is unclear as to whether presidential behavior stimulated party polarization or merely responded to its rise.

polarization, like elite polarization, expands the policy distance between identifiers of each party. In addition, in recent years, the number of voters who identify with one party or the other has grown, as has their loyalty to their chosen party (Bartels, 2000). Consequently, the number of independents has declined. Independents have often been important targets for presidential communications efforts. Presidents could generally count on same-party identifiers to support their policy positions, but with only dim prospects of generating similar support from opposition party identifiers. Thus, independents often were a crucial element in building majority popular support.

Another factor is that many independents tend to be disinterested in politics and public affairs, and thus presidents have difficulty gaining their attention, much less their support (Edwards, 2003). To make matters even more difficult for the president, as polarization has increased, the attitudes of opposition party identifiers have hardened against the president, creating a solid base of opposition with which he must contend.

Presidential coalition building efforts in an age of polarized parties will tend to stress mobilizing the presidential party base and others who might be predisposed to support the president on the case at hand, rather than appealing to the entire mass public and/or using the symbolic appeal of the presidency to muster public support. Presidential public appeals in such a context will often contain a strong strand of partisanship, but not on all issues. Sometimes presidents may try to shift the issue frame away from partisanship and toward patriotism or national security in the hope of overcoming partisan opposition and constructing a rally-like response behind the president.

Both partisan and national security frames have been evident in recent years. The party model is essentially Karl Rove's theory of governing and party building in an age of polarization when the two parties are relatively evenly matched. Recall the example in the introduction in which George W. Bush pursued a partisan approach to governing, rather than a bipartisan approach, as some critics suggested he use because of the controversy over his election in 2000. Bush tried to govern with a slim numerical party majority that was highly loyal to the administration.

The party base provided the foundation for Bush's electoral and governing coalition, but in general there were not enough Republicans in either the electorate or Congress for him to prevail – Republican identifiers rarely constituted more than 40 percent of the mass public and the Republican Party never came close to controlling enough seats to render the Senate filibuster proof. Bush needed to augment his party base with independents and/or Democrats. Finding the issue or frame that would build support among independents or peel Democrats from their party often proved difficult.

For a time, Bush successfully mined the war on terror to attract non-Republicans to support him. When Bush was able to persuade some independents and Democrats of the effectiveness of his leadership on the war on terror, this tactic proved successful. His party gained seats in the 2002 midterms and 2004 presidential elections, and he won a relatively secure 2004 reelection too, some suggest, because he exploited the war on terror issue. But as disenchantment with Bush's foreign policy set in, which was due in part to the length of the Iraq War, his ability to marshal high levels of support within the public diminished. The 2006 midterm election results, in which Democrats took both houses of Congress from the Republicans, could be viewed in part as the waning of the power of the war on terror to rally public support.

With regard to Congress, his party's narrow majority, vulnerable to filibustering in the Senate, often thwarted Bush's policy efforts. Many of his legislative efforts failed, including numerous judicial nominations. Rather than rely on a legislative governing strategy, Bush often turned to an administrative presidency approach, employing unilateral directives, such as executive orders, to implement policy (Aberbach, 2005; Farris, Nathan, and Wright 2004). When he needed to fill administration vacancies but faced opposition in Congress to his nominees, Bush would use recess appointments, when the president waits until Congress recesses to fill the post temporarily. By the end of the next Senate session, the recess appointment must end and the nominee must be confirmed by the Senate (Corley, 2006). By one count, Bill Clinton made 140 recess appointments during his two terms in office. In his first term alone, George W. Bush used recess appointments on 100 occasions (Corley, 2006, 671).

Party polarization created an environment in Congress and in the mass public that made it difficult for presidents to attain support from across the aisle. Going public to move the "median voter" would have little sway for members of the opposition in Congress. Presidents could and would rely on their parties for support, but rarely would their parties provide them with large enough coalitions to prevail on most issues. In an era of high party polarization, presidents would have to find a way to supplement the base of support their parties provided.

*The Post-Broadcast Media and the Presidency.* A series of developments, beginning in the 1970s and extending throughout the next several decades, would transform the news media. This transformation would reinforce the effects of party polarization on presidential leadership, coalition building, and communication styles. We can roughly categorize the history of the news media of the past forty to fifty years into two broad periods. The first, from the 1960s into the early or mid-1980s, has been termed the "golden age of broadcasting" (Baum and Kernell, 1999), and the second, from approximately the mid-1980s, has been called an era of "new media" (Davis and Owen, 1998; Cohen, 2004, 2008; Wattenberg, 2004) or the "post-broadcast" age (Prior, 2007). The age of broadcasting, for reasons that will become obvious, coincides with the era of individual pluralism.

The age of broadcasting can be characterized as one in which a few news outlets, primarily the three major television networks and several national newspapers, the *New York Times* and the *Washington Post*, dominated the news agenda and provided the public with the bulk of its news about national political affairs. Because of limited television viewing choices, the audience for television news and presidential addresses (Baum and Kernell, 1999) was also quite large.

By the late 1970s or early 1980s, this broadcast-dominated news system began to fall apart.[6] First, the arrival of new technologies of communication, such as cable television and the Internet, effectively competed with the broadcast networks, altering the television viewing and news habits of Americans. News audiences shrank as viewers flocked to entertainment and non-news offerings on cable and the

---

[6] Much of the following several pages is developed in greater detail in Cohen, 2008.

Internet. Public opinion toward the news media also began to plum-
met in the 1970s, in part a function of the decline in public confidence
toward institutions in general, as well as a reaction to the news media
in particular. Public confidence in the major national newspapers and
broadcast networks declined more steeply than for other segments of
the news media.

Second, changes in Federal Communications Commission (FCC)
rules and corporate consolidation among newspapers and broadcasting altered news organizations' economic environment. News organizations would become more sensitive to economic pressures, a function of increased competition and corporate insistence on bottom-line
performance. Newspapers and television news broadcasts would thus
adjust their offerings to retain and attract viewers and readers, as well
as slash operating budgets, which included staff downsizings. Soft news
would displace hard news in many venues (Patterson, 2000), and news
niche marketing would develop in which some outlets would target
specific types of news consumers. News niche marketing meant that
a variety of news formats and orientations, rather than the homoge-
nous news product of the age of broadcasting, would be available
to those with an appetite for a special type of news. Thus, we see the
arrival of talk radio in the 1980s, which effectively attracted a relatively
large audience of politically conservative listeners. Cable television
allowed the creation of dedicated around-the-clock news channels like
CNN, MSNBC, and Fox Cable News. Fox in particular branded itself
to build an audience of conservative viewers, whereas in the 2000s
MSNBC took on a more liberal brand. In the post-broadcast era, people could find news tailored to their special needs, interests, tastes, or
desires.

Third, journalistic reporting styles also changed. As noted earlier,
print journalism became increasingly interpretive, and hard news was
replaced with softer fare (Patterson, 2000). Reporters also became
more aggressive in their interactions with the president, as Clayman et al.
(2006, 2007) find in their study of reporters questions in presidential press conferences. And finally, national news about the president
turned increasingly critical and negative (Cohen, 2008). This more
confrontational and critical news environment represented a major
change and challenge to presidents in the late 1980s and thereafter.

These changes affected presidential public communications styles. No longer could a president go on the air in prime time to speak to the nation and attract as large an audience as he had during the broadcasting age. Not only had the audience for presidential speeches shrunk, but the public in general seemed less susceptible to communication effects. Those least interested and informed in politics, when exposed to messages, are more likely to be influenced by political communication than those more interested and knowledgeable, whose relatively well-formed pre existing opinions insulate them from communication influence (Zaller, 1992). But with alternatives to broadcast television, for instance, cable entertainment programming and the Internet, individuals less interested in public affairs and news were less likely to be exposed to presidential communications.[7] The likelihood that a president could move a large segment of the mass public through a prime-time address or other major speech declined with these changes in the viewing and news consumption habits of the mass public (Young and Perkins, 2005).

The growing hostility of the national news organizations and reporters to the president (Clayman et al., 2006, 2007), and to political authority in general, could negatively color the tone of the news presented through these outlets. Presidential communications to the public declined in effectiveness in the face of hostile news. Also, higher levels of public cynicism toward the news media could further blunt the effects of news on public opinion.

*Implications for Presidential Leadership.* A national communications strategy, like that used by presidents in the broadcasting age, would prove of limited effectiveness in building support in the post-broadcast age. With a highly polarized public, a national leadership strategy could rarely rally public support behind the president, except in the special circumstances, like the example of war on terror in the aftermath of September 11. In the post-broadcast age, the audience for news would be comprised mostly of committed partisans, with few

---

[7] Interpersonal interactions may also present less information to these same disinterested individuals, as their friends and acquaintances are also less exposed to presidential speeches and news.

independents or individuals open to presidential persuasion efforts. Thus, this "news attentive public" in general would be highly resistant to political communications efforts. Those already predisposed to the president would stay in his camp, whereas those from the opposition probably would not change their attitudes but potentially could be energized against the president. Political independents and those with less firm political orientations, the primary targets of presidential communications efforts even in the age of broadcasting, rarely watch major speeches and pay attention to the news at much lower rates, in the post-broadcast than in the broadcasting age (Baum and Kernell, 1999; Cohen, 2008; but see Prior, 2007, for a slightly different perspective). Presidents would receive little payoff from employing a national leadership and communication style in the post-broadcast era.

In place of a national leadership style, in which the president tries to build support from the mass public on a larger scale, the polarized partisan atmosphere and the diversity of media outlets have forced presidents to develop a more targeted approach to public leadership and communications. Presidents would target primarily three subsets – their party base, interest groups, and localities – with the hope that these groups would pressure members of Congress to support him. Mobilizing the party base is aimed at keeping congressional members of the president's party in line. However, it is the president's hope that targeting particular interest groups and localities will pressure opposition members (and party mavericks) to support him, supplementing the support that the party base in Congress provides and, in many instances, supplying his margin of victory.

Localities are an especially important element of the presidential coalition-building strategy in the post-broadcast age. Deciding which localities to target for presidential persuasion efforts became relatively easy because of the geographic clustering of partisans. More and more localities became either decidedly Democratic or Republican – the "red-state, blue-state" (or red-county–blue-county) phenomenon (Brooks, 2001; Bishop, 2008).[8] The president has increasingly turned

---

[8]  The contention that the nation has divided into red and blue regions is not without its critics. See Fiorina, 2005 and Ansolabehere et al., 2005.

his communication efforts to the local news media, not merely because of the negative and aggressive turn in the national press, but also because these local media serve as a primary vehicle for reaching local, targeted publics.

Thus, in part because of the rise of party polarization, presidents can count on a significant number of localities to be consistent allies. Presidents target these "naturally friendly" localities in their campaigns to build public support for their policies. Moreover, presidents give special attention to those localities with opposition party representation in Congress but mass public support or potential mass public support for the president.[9] By targeting these types of districts, presidents hope that demonstrations of enthusiastic local support for him and his policy initiatives will pressure opposition party members in Congress, fearful of electoral reprisal, to also support the president's policy initiatives.

This strategy seemed effective for George W. Bush's 2001 effort to secure passage of his tax cut proposals (Edwards, 2008). The president specifically visited districts and states that he won in the 2000 presidential election, but that had Democratic representation in Congress. In many cases, the Democrat in Congress wound up voting for the president's tax cut proposal, providing Bush with the margin of support that he needed for victory (Hacker and Pierson, 2005).

For such a coalition-building strategy to work, presidents not only require a favorable local opinion climate, but also the resources to activate that opinion when needed. Grassroots and local party organizations aided in such opinion mobilization efforts. The George W. Bush administration, with Karl Rove's advice, worked in particular to strengthen these local organizations, as well as allied groups, such as evangelical Christian churches (Balz and Allen, 2004; Bergan et al., 2005; Davies and Newman, 2006; Milkis and Rhodes, 2007; Ubertaccio, 2006).

Ironically, this new era reinvigorated an old form of political mobilization, personal contact. The storied political machines of the 1800s and first half of the twentieth century relied heavily on face-to-face

---

9 A more generalized version of this theory is found in Cohen, 2008, especially Chapter 9.

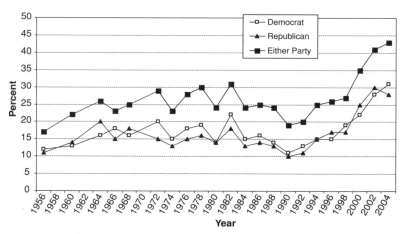

Figure 1.1. Party Contacting, 1956–2004. (*Source:* American National Election Studies.)

contact for building and maintaining their organizations and delivering the vote. Local political leaders and ward and precinct captains knew the residents in their localities personally. These politicians would inform their "constituents" about the issues and candidates for office, pressuring them, sometimes not subtly, to support their organization's candidates in the election. But these local leaders would also help their constituents with personal matters, such as job seeking, short-term financial problems, and the like, in effect serving also as a type of social service agency.

The nationalization of politics and the arrival of broadcast television undermined these local machines and their heavy reliance on large corps of campaign workers. Television provided a relatively efficient way to reach voters compared with the labor-intensive efforts of local political machines. As a result, personal contact between voters and the parties fell off. Figure 1.1, from the American National Election Studies, traces the percentage of respondents who report being contacted by the political parties. Between the mid-1950s and mid-1990s, generally fewer than 20 percent of respondents said that either the Republican or Democratic parties contacted them. Fewer than one-third of respondents reported being contacted by either party.

Matters began to change in the late 1990s, when contacting totals for both parties climbed. Democratic and Republican party contact levels rose to 20 to 30 percent during the 2000s, and 35 to 43 percent of respondents said that either party contacted them. When we look more deeply at these data for the 2000s, we find parties contacting success- fully targeted voters, what has come to be termed "micro-targeting," with the Republican Party generally contacting Republican identi- fiers, and the same being said about the Democrats (Wielhouwer, 2006; Gershtenson, 2003; Panagopoulos and Wielhouwer, 2008). Per- sonal contacting long has been known to stimulate turnout (Rosen- stone, Hansen, and Reeves, 2003; Wielhouwer and Lockerbie, 1994). Research suggests that a significant proportion of the rise in turnout in the 2000s can be attributed to these targeted contacting efforts (Bergan et al., 2005).

New technologies, especially computers and their ability to con- tain and collate vast quantities of information, as well as geographical information systems (GIS), made such grassroots organization meth- ods more efficient and cost-effective (Hillygus and Shields, 2008). But such technologies existed long before the parties and presidents put them into practice. Interest groups began selective targeting of members decades earlier (Walker, 1991). The shift to face-to-face contact between political organizations and voters reflects the polit- ical realities of the times, party polarization and the new media, and as such are relevant to presidential support building and com- munications styles in the post-broadcasting era too. In developing these local and personal contacting methods of support building and mobilization, presidents learned from the parties and parties from presidents.

## CONCLUSION

This chapter has laid out a context theory of presidential leadership styles. As the context changed from institutional pluralism to individ- ual pluralism to the current age of polarized parties and fragmented media, presidential leadership styles have also changed. Presidents alter their leadership style to better match the resources they can generate to the factors that motivate members of Congress. The con- text theory of presidential leadership maintains that leadership style is instrumental to building coalitions of support in Congress. These support coalitions are necessary for the realization of the president's ultimate goal, public policy.

Thus, whereas presidents employed a bargaining leadership style during the age of institutional pluralism, going public became the presidential leadership style during the age of individual pluralism. The style of going public employed in the era of individual pluralism, the broadcasting era, placed great stock in moving national opinion and rising above partisan politics. In the post-broadcasting age, presidents adapted their going public leadership style, targeting select audiences, such as their party base, interest groups, and localities, because of the rise of party polarization and a fragmented media. A key hypothesis of the context theory is that presidents will pay increasing attention to narrow groups, such as their party base, interest groups, and localities, in the age of polarized partiesd and fragmented media compared with the age of individual pluralism. I test this hypothesis in the next chapter.

# Increasing Presidential Attention to Narrow Groups

The context theory of presidential leadership styles argues that in the current age of polarized parties and fragmented media, presidents still go public, but differently than in the age of individual pluralism. Rather than focus their energies on the mass public writ broadly, presidents have shifted much of their leadership efforts to narrower segments of the public, in particular their party base, interest groups, and localities. These segments function much like national public opinion did in the age of individual pluralism; that is, they put pressure on members of Congress to support the president.

Several hypotheses flow from the context theory of presidential leadership. First, presidents will give greater attention to these three segments in the current era of polarized parties and fragmented media than they did during the era of individual pluralism. Second, the relative amount of effort applied to influencing national opinion – for instance, through national prime-time addresses – will decline. This chapter tests these hypotheses.

The context theory also argues that presidents updated their going public leadership style because a nationally based style was declining in effectiveness, but the targeted approach to going public could prove effective. Succeeding chapters will test the effectiveness hypothesis as it pertains to localities. As argued in more detail later, local news media, in particular local newspapers, are an important element in trying to influence local opinion. Can presidents influence the news coverage they receive from local newspapers, and does that coverage affect public support for the president?

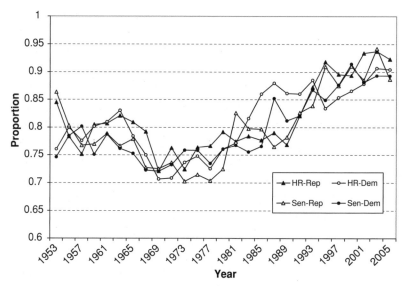

Figure 2.1. Party Loyalty in Congress, 1953–2006 (Percentage of roll calls in which members of Congress voted with their party). *Source:* http://voteview .com/Polarized_America.htm.

## PRESIDENTS AND PARTIES

Presidents had few incentives to pay much attention to their parties during the age of individual pluralism or even during the era of institutional pluralism. In the former, members of Congress exhibited comparatively low levels of party loyalty. Figure 2.1 plots the loyalty rates on roll calls of members of each party for both chambers from 1953 through 2006, defining party loyalty as the proportion of roll calls in which a member votes with the majority of his or her party. We may consider the 1970s as the high point of individual pluralism.[1] That decade exhibits the lowest levels of party loyalty. For example, in the 1970s, House Republicans, traditionally the group most loyal to its party, voted with their party an average of 76 percent of the time. Their loyalty grew slightly, to 79 percent, during the 1980s, but by the 1990s, party loyalty among House Republicans reached 88 percent.

Parties were not irrelevant to presidential coalition building in Congress in the age of individual pluralism. Yet presidents could

---

[1]   The major congressional reforms were enacted in that decade.

expect from one-fifth to one-half of the members of their party to defect and vote with the opposition. The fraction defecting would decline in the 1990s to about one-tenth. With such great potential for party defection, presidents could not rely on partisan appeals to rally co-partisans. Instead, as the theory of going public argues, to build support in Congress, presidents tapped into the members' feeling of electoral insecurity, not party fealty. Presidents could not even rely on rallying co-partisans in the mass public to apply public opinion pressure on members because such a high percentage of the public claimed independence and thus not only was unresponsive to partisan calls, but was potentially antagonistic. A highly partisan presidency in the era of individual pluralism could easily backfire.

Instead, presidents built a personal, not partisan, following in the mass public (Lowi, 1985). Accounts of presidential relations with their parties during this era suggest indifference. Presidents spent little time building party institutions, putting their efforts instead into constructing essentially transient political machines based on loyalty to the president.[2] Neustadt (1990), for instance, suggests that this not only unleashed presidents from their parties but also further weakened already fragile parties.

The rise of polarized parties in the late 1980s altered presidential incentives toward their parties. It was now in the president's interest to build party institutions and resources. Because co-partisans generally composed a ready-made base of support for the president who would support him on almost all issues, there was an incentive to strengthen the parties.

Presidents can help build their parties in several ways. They may be indispensable in fundraising efforts, especially through aiding other candidates in their campaign fundraising efforts. Presidential appearances at party and candidate fundraising events can increase the flow of funds into these organizations, perhaps boosting the likelihood that more presidential co-partisans will win elections. Such efforts can build goodwill between the president and members of his party, as well as an expectation among members that the president may help

---

[2]  A case in point is Richard Nixon's Committee to Re-elect the President in 1972, which had only weak ties to the Republican Party.

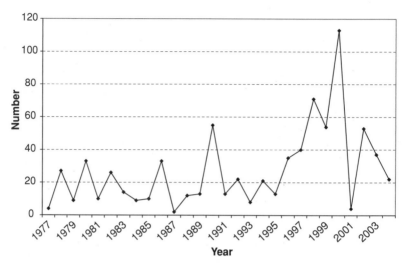

Figure 2.2. Presidential Appearances at Party Fundraisers, 1977–2004. *Source:* Doherty, 2007.

them in their future reelection bids. Furthermore, such efforts may explicitly tie the party to the president, strengthening the incentive for members in Congress to help and support the president.

Doherty (2007, 11) presents information on the number of presidential appearances at party fundraisers from 1977 through 2004, which are plotted on Figure 2.2. In general, these data support the proposition that presidents in the current age have increased their efforts to aid their parties. Unfortunately, Doherty's data do not extend back further in time, which would enable comparisons with presidential behavior in the individual pluralism age. If we view the late 1970s through the mid-1980s as that era, the late 1980s as a transition, and the 1990s and thereafter as the era of polarized parties, we see a definite uptick in presidential fundraising activity in the 1990s.

These data also indicate that some of the rise in such fundraising can be attributed to Bill Clinton, especially during his second term. Rates of fundraising activity dropped during George W. Bush's first term. Only time will tell if this decline in fundraising activity heralds a new trend or is a short-term interruption. We can formally test for whether a trend exists in these data by regressing the number of fundraisers on a year counter, controlling for presidential election years, midterm election years, and a dummy for Bill Clinton.[3] With these controls, each of which is statistically significant, the year counter still reaches statistical significance ($p < 0.05$) and suggests that with each passing year, presidents will attend an additional 0.9 fundraisers for their party. Across this twenty-eight-year period, this accumulates to an additional twenty-four fundraisers. Although not definitive, these data support the notion that presidential activity aimed at building their parties through fundraising is higher during the current age than in the era of individual pluralism.

Presidents may also campaign for congressional candidates. A small body of research has looked at presidential campaigning in midterm elections (Cohen, Krassa, and Hamman, 1991; Hoddie and Routh, 2004; Jacobson, Kernell, and Lazarus, 2004; Keele, Fogarty, and Stimson, 2004; Sellers and Denton, 2006; Herrnson and Morris, 2007). It may seem odd to study such activity. Conventional wisdom held that after Franklin Roosevelt's disastrous efforts to affect the 1938 midterm contests, presidents have been wary of intervening in midterm contests. Not only did almost all candidates whom FDR supported lose, but his midterm activities heightened animosities and soured his relationship with Congress (Nelson, 1988).

Recent research on presidential midterm campaigning has turned the conventional wisdom on its head. Almost all studies of presidential midterm visits during the past forty years show that they helped members of the president's party (but see Keele, Fogarty, and Stimson, 2004). Although it may have been the case during the Roosevelt era that presidential interventions into midterm contests would backfire, such efforts now appear to help members of the president's party seeking election, an incentive for presidents to campaign for co-partisans.

Figure 2.3 displays trends for several indicators of presidential midterm election–related activities. First, both series, mean visits per state (Hoddie and Routh, 2004) and number of states visited (Sellers

[3] The results of the analysis, b (SE), are: Fundraisers = −0.7 (8.2) Constant + 0.89 (0.51) Counter + 16.49 (9.1) Clinton dummy + 16.86 (8.97) Presidential Election year + 24.36 (8.91) Midterm Election year. $R^2 = 48$, Adjusted $R^2 = 0.39$.

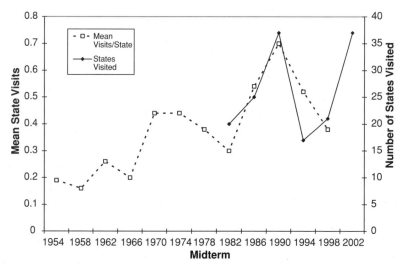

Figure 2.3. Presidential Campaigning in Midterm Elections, 1954–2002.
*Source:* Mean visits per state: Hoddie and Routh (2004); Number of states visited: Sellers and Davis, 2007.

and Davis, 2007), indicate a steady climb in presidential midterm election campaign effort, despite some short-term spikes and dips.

Despite some limitations in these data, the evidence generally points toward increasing presidential involvement and aid for their parties. This trend is consistent with the context theory of presidential public activity, which hypothesizes that the party base is one key element of the presidential support coalition in the current age of polarized parties and fragmented media. Thus, presidents have incentives to build their parties by aiding fundraising efforts and supporting midterm election bids of their party's candidates for office.

## PRESIDENTS AND INTEREST GROUPS

The context theory of presidential leadership suggests that in the post-broadcast age, presidents will pay increasing attention to narrow segments of the population, such as interest groups. Interest groups are perhaps the quintessential narrow group. Given their resources, interest groups have always played an important role in the American policy-making process, including in Congress. The pluralism literature, the dominant explanation for American public policy making in the 1950s and 1960s, explicitly recognized the influence of interest groups in political and policy-making processes. Presidents, too, have always paid some attention to interest groups in their coalition building efforts, even in the era of individual pluralism. Richard Nixon's establishment of the Office of Public Liaison in 1970, which was dedicated to formalizing and building relationships between the White House and interest groups, illustrates the importance presidents attributed to interest groups (Maltese, 1992).

To test the president-interest group connection, we ideally would want data on presidential appearances before interest groups as well as content analyses of these addresses to determine if presidents speak about issues of concern to the interest groups. Collecting such data is difficult. To date, only Holmes (2008) has done so, but for only one type of presidential activity: public support of his nominees to federal appeals courts.

We can, however, gain some perspective on the trade-off of presidential attention to national opinion versus narrower groups with available data on presidential public appearances from Ragsdale's (2009) data. Using these data, Cohen (2008) argues that major prime-time television addresses target the nation, not narrow groups, although presidents may raise issues of concern to certain interest groups in those speeches. Still, the primary target of a major prime-time address is the mass public writ broadly. By contrast, minor speeches may be viewed as presidential attempts to reach interest groups and their members, although we must recognize the heterogeneous quality the targets of minor speeches. Without detailed data on the target or audience of a minor presidential speech, we can suggest only that presidents target interest groups with some of their minor speeches.

Figures 2.4 and 2.5 show the trends in major and non-major presidential addresses, the latter a combination of minor and non–Washington, D.C., addresses for the years 1953 through 2007, with the non-major series serving as a crude indicator of presidential attention to interest groups. Because both series display considerable short-term variation, I have superimposed linear trends lines to give a sense of whether each form of presidential public activity has been increasing or decreasing.

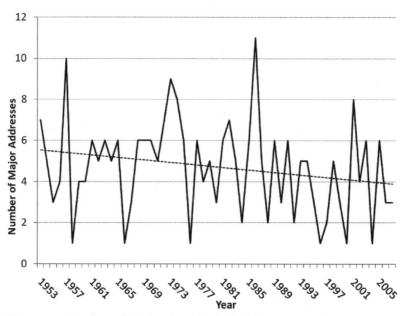

Figure 2.4. Number of Major Presidential Addresses, 1953–2007. *Source:* Ragsdale, 2009.

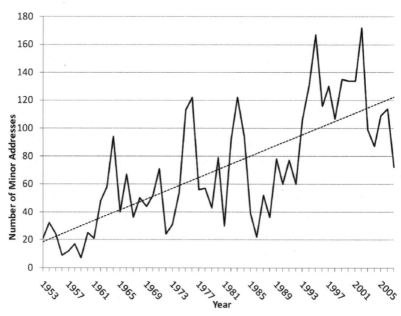

Figure 2.5. Number of Non-Major Presidential Addresses, 1953–2007. *Source:* Ragsdale, 2009: see text for details.

The context theory predicts that we should see a decline in the annual number of major addresses but an increase in the number of non-major speeches from the broadcast to post-broadcast eras. These plots provide support for these hypotheses. Major speeches trend downward, whereas non-major addresses trend upward.

Although it is difficult to see this in the figure, the major address series provide support for another hypothesis: that presidents would use major addresses more during the era of individual pluralism than in the earlier era of institutional pluralism. No definitive dates exist that demark when one of these eras ends and another begins, but we can crudely suggest that the era of institutional pluralism extends from roughly 1953 to 1969; the era of individual pluralism exists for 1970 to 1988; and the current era spans from 1989 to the present. Based on this categorization, presidents addressed the nation in major addresses an average of 4.8 times per year during the era of institutional pluralism, 5.5 times during the era of individual pluralism, and only 3.8 times per year in the current era of polarized parties and fragmented media.[4] Despite the rarity in which presidents make major prime-time addresses, this indicator of presidential public activity appears sensitive to context, as we hypothesized.

The context theory provides a more nuanced hypothesis than the simple trend hypotheses already discussed. Rather than merely predicting declines in major addresses and increases in non-major addresses, we should see a shift in the mix of major and minor addresses. We can define this mix, following Cohen (2008), as the ratio of major to non-major addresses: (number of major address per year)/(number of non-major addresses per year). A decline in this ratio could come about even if the number of major addresses remains the same or increases, as long as the number of non-major addresses increases at a faster rate. Figure 2.6 plots this ratio. As hypothesized, we see the expected drop in the ratio between the individual pluralism era and the following period. The ratio averages 0.22 during the era of institutional pluralism, declines to 0.13 during the

---

4   Even removing the 1986 outlier, in which Reagan made eleven major addresses, the
    average for the remaining years is 5.2.

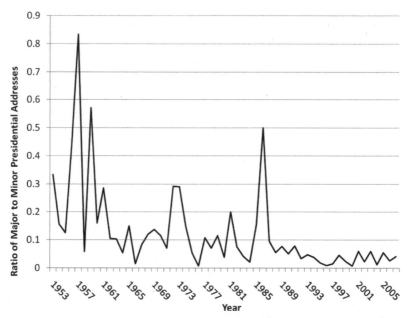

Figure 2.6. Ratio of Major to Minor Presidential Addresses, 1953–2007.
*Source:* Ragsdale, 2009.

individual pluralism years,[5] and plummets further, to 0.04 for the years 1989 to 2007. The large drop in the ratio between the era of individual pluralism and the latest modern era is consistent with our hypothesis.

One issue with the indicators used is that minor speeches only crudely measure presidential targeting of interest groups. Minor speeches may be delivered before a wide or broad-based audience, such as journalists or national dignitaries, with the intention of eventually reaching the nation through national news coverage. Other minor speeches may be targeted explicitly at interest group members, with the intention of mobilizing the interest group behind the president whether the speech receives national news attention or not. Barrett (2007) finds that the national news media report on only a fraction of public presidential comments concerning legislation. Presidents cannot assume that every public utterance will receive national news coverage and they may not want every comment or speech to receive

[5]  If 1986 is removed from calculations, it drops to 0.11.

such coverage, depending on the targeted group. To trace presidential efforts aimed at interest groups requires two pieces of information about a presidential appearance before the group: the nature of the group (the target) and the substance of the comments before the group. In other words, did the president talk about political issues of concern to the group? Presidents, for example, may appear before a group for non-policy reasons, on ceremonial occasions, more with the intention of burnishing their image than in mobilizing the group for policy reasons.

Collecting such data as these, although possible, requires a huge effort on the researcher's part because of the massive number of speeches that presidents make per year. As a consequence, there has been, to my knowledge, only one such effort, that of Holmes (2008), who restricts her data collection to presidential public appearances in support of nominees to the federal appeals courts. Her data confirm the context theory hypothesis regarding interest groups, but one still wonders if her findings generalize to other presidential coalition-building efforts.

In addition to public statements before interest groups, presidents may also aid the establishment of new interests groups who will then become their political and policy allies. Obviously, presidents must be selective with regard to the interest groups they promote. Many will be too small or represent too minor a policy area for presidential effort, whereas others sit on the other side of the political fence and thus do not serve the president's policy designs. Yet, Walker (1983) underscores the importance of government support for the creation and maintenance of interest groups. The Reagan administration, understanding the government–interest group connection, severed those ties, especially financial ones, of interest groups that the administration considered liberal and/or opposed to the president and his policies (Peterson and Walker, 1986).

George W. Bush's faith-based initiative can be viewed in this light. The faith-based initiative aimed to allow church-based groups to deliver public social services, rather than rely exclusively on governmental bureaucracy, the long-standing practice. Bush seemingly had several possible motivations here beyond the policy benefits that he argued would be derived from such a program.

First, the faith-based initiative would organize groups that previously had not been politically engaged. Many of the local organizations that would participate in this effort had no ties to other religiously oriented segments already aligned with the Republican Party. The mobilization of these new groups through the auspices of the faith-based initiative might act as a counterweight to the religious right and its influence within the Republican Party. Second, many groups targeted for the faith-based initiative consisted primarily of Black and/or Hispanic members. The faith-based initiative could be seen as a way for the Republican Party to attract religious Blacks and Hispanics to the Republican fold, making inroads into two groups more traditionally associated with the Democratic Party (Black, Koopman, and Ryden 2004, 11–14; Schier, 2009, 105–107). Compared with other interest groups, those targeted by the faith-based initiative represented possibly millions of individuals, many of whom either had not been effectively organized and mobilized into politics or whose natural loyalties may have resided with the opposition party.

## PRESIDENTS AND LOCALITIES

Localities constitute a third critical element for presidential coalition building in the post-broadcast age. The importance of localities stems from the potential effects of local public opinion on representatives in Congress. Members of Congress need local public support for reelection. A vast literature documents activities that members engage in for those reelection efforts, including the accumulation of office-based resources (Jacobson, 2008). To the degree that presidents can influence local opinion, presidents may further their coalition-building efforts in Congress. In a sense, presidential attention to localities resembles going public nationally, as described by Kernell (1986, 2006), but on a smaller, local scale, with presidents concentrating their attention on a subset of localities, those where presidents think they can affect local opinion and where the member in Congress will be most responsive to local opinion that favors the president.

We should not assume that because presidents increasingly try to influence local public opinion, the task is easy or guaranteed to succeed. Barriers exist to presidential success in moving local public

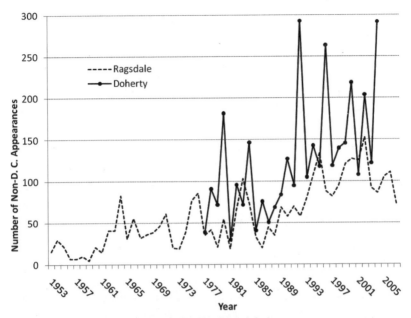

Figure 2.7. Non-Washington, D.C., Presidential Appearances, 1953–2007. *Source:* Ragsdale, 2009 and Doherty, 2007.

opinion. One barrier that we will discuss more fully in the following is the limited coverage of the president in local news media, especially local television. Limited local news coverage constrains the president's ability to influence local opinion.

The electoral security of a relatively large number of members of Congress (Jacobson, 2008) presents the president with a second barrier to overcome. A president may not be able to change local opinion enough to affect the support of the president and his policies among electorally safe members of Congress. Presidential leverage with safe opposition party members may be even more anemic, insofar as they come from districts where local opinion is hostile to the president in most circumstances.

### Trends in Presidential Attention to Localities

Despite these barriers, presidents, consistent with the context theory, have been paying more attention to localities in the current age than during the era of individual pluralism. Figure 2.7 plots two series on presidential travel to localities from Doherty (2007, 11) and Ragsdale

(2009, 202). Doherty's data cover a shorter time span than Ragsdale's but include fundraisers and political events, activities not included in the Ragsdale tally. Despite these differences, the two series tell a similar story – increases in presidential travel to localities in the current era compared with the era of individual pluralism.

Moreover, unlike Kernell's incremental interpretation of data like these, there seem to be two identifiable periods in the Doherty series, 1977 to 1988 and 1989 to 2004. For instance, using Kernell's methodology to eliminate the fourth year of a presidential term because of reelection effects, we find an average of 63.1 local appearances per year for the nine non-election years from 1977 to 1988. By contrast, the average for the twelve non-election years from 1989 to 2004 is 125.9, nearly double that of the earlier set. From another perspective, for the nine non-election years of 1977 to 1988, presidential local appearances ranged from 30 to 90, compared with a range of 84 to 206 for the years since 1989. Of the non-election years from 1977 to 1988, two (1978 with 91 and 1982 with 96) are greater than the minimum number of appearances for non-election years from 1989 to 2004. And of the non-election years from 1989 to 2004, only twice did the number of annual visits fall below the maximum for the 1977 to 1988 period, 1989 with 84 and 1991 with 91.

We can more formally test the incremental versus period effects interpretations. To do this, using the Doherty series, I regress the annual number of visits on a counter (1–28) and a dummy variable for 1977 to 1988 = 0 and 1989 to 2004 = 1, with additional dummy variables for the second and fourth years of the presidential term to account for election effects. If the incremental model is correct, the period dummy variable should not be statistically significant, but the incremental-count variable will be. We will find support for the two-period interpretation if the period dummy attains statistical significance. Incremental processes may or may not exist under the two-period model.

Results support the two-period interpretation (see Table 2.1). First, as expected, the second- and fourth-year dummies are significant, indicating increased presidential attention to localities during election years. The coefficients indicate that presidents make 39 more

TABLE 2.1. *Trends in local presidential travel, 1977–2005*

| Variable | B | SE | t | $p^*$ |
|---|---|---|---|---|
| Constant | 35.70 | 14.87 | 2.46 | 0.02 |
| Yearly Counter | 0.68 | 1.52 | 0.44 | 0.66 |
| Pres. Election Year | 122.22 | 15.41 | 7.93 | 0.000 |
| Midterm Election Year | 39.43 | 15.11 | 2.61 | 0.01 |
| Post-1989 | 71.23 | 24.65 | 2.89 | 0.005 |

* One-tailed tests.
*Source:* Doherty, 2007.

local visits during midterm election years and a whopping 122 additional trips during fourth years. Consistent with the two-period interpretation, the annual counter variable fails to reach statistical significance ($t = 0.44$, $p = 0.66$, one-tailed test). Conversely, the two-period dummy variable is strong and significant. The coefficient indicates that presidents, on average, visit localities 71 times more frequently in period two (1989–2004) than in period one (1977–1988). Further evidence in support of the two-period interpretation is that the $R^2$ of the estimation improves from 0.76 to 0.83 when adding the period dummy to an equation with the other three variables (annual counter, year two dummy, year four dummy).

We need to be cautious in interpreting these data with the prior analysis. That analysis was not meant to be causal but descriptive, merely to demonstrate whether it is better to view the 1977 to 2004 era as one time period or two distinct periods.[6] Analysis of these data indicate that something fundamental changed between the 1970s to the mid-1980s and late 1980s to the present. Moreover, a similar analysis on the longer Ragsdale series does not show the period effects detected in Doherty's data. The fact that the Ragsdale series does not include political events may account for the lack of period effects.

Regardless, both series support the larger argument that the combination of heightened polarization between the parties and a fragmented media altered the political context that presidents face. This

[6] The annual visit series, for instance, exhibits nonstationary properties.

change in context reduced the effectiveness of going public nationally, a primary means for the president in building coalitions in Congress during the era of individual pluralism. In this new context, presidents needed other methods for building those coalitions in Congress. Increasing attention to localities became one such approach for the president.

### Selectively Targeting Localities

Aggregate presidential visits, the type of data used in the prior analysis, provides a blunt way of understanding how presidents use localities for congressional coalition-building efforts. As noted earlier, many members of Congress hold reasonably safe seats, and presidential visits are unlikely to reconfigure local public sentiment enough to alter congressional behavior. Moreover, there is a high cost to each presidential visit. Visiting one locale prohibits the president from visiting another one at the same time or engaging in other activities. Even for the highly active years from 1989 to 2004, presidents visited only about 30 percent of districts.[7] To some degree, it is useful to think of each visit as akin to the president bargaining with individual members of Congress. Presidents may secure additional votes through lone visits and individual bargains, but only one vote at a time. To acquire more than a small number of votes from such individualized interactions with Congress would require extraordinary effort on the president's part.

Consequently, presidents must be selective and strategic in their local appearances. It may make little sense to appear in districts/localities with electorally safe members of either party. Despite the fact that many members represent safe districts, a considerable number of members of Congress may feel political cross pressures that presidents can exploit.

For instance, after winning the 2004 presidential election, which scored seat increases for Republicans in Congress and a stronger vote total for Bush than in 2000, Bush announced his ambitious plan to

---

[7]  This calculation is based on 126 annual appearances on average and 435 congressional districts and assumes that presidents appear in only one district per appearance.

reform Social Security. Rather than put all of his energies into rous-
ing national public opinion, Bush toured the country, making sixty
stops in twenty-eight states from February through April 2005. Bush
strategically targeted localities primarily to visit, states that had
Democratic representatives and senators but that voted for Bush in
2004.

The president visited twenty of the thirty (67%) states that he
won compared with seven of the twenty (35%) that he lost. The ten
states that he won but did not visit elected few Democrats, fifteen in
the House and only two in the Senate. By comparison, the twenty
that he won and visited elected sixty Democratic representatives and
thirteen senators. From another perspective, the average number of
Democrats in the House and Senate per delegation for *unvisited* states
that Bush won was 1.5 and 0.2, respectively. But for the states that
he won and visited, the average delegation contained 3 and 0.65
Democratic representatives and senators. Clearly, Bush stressed visiting states with relatively numerous cross-pressured Democrats – members of the opposition party from states that went for Bush in the
election.

### The Effects of Presidential Visits on the Local Opinion Climate

For this local strategy to work, it must be effective enough to alter local
public opinion, which, in turn, must affect members of Congress.
Evidence in support of the proposition that a presidential trip to
a locality results in public opinion gains for the president and his
policies is slim and far from conclusive.

To date, only two studies look explicitly at the impact of presidential domestic travel on local public opinion. Cohen and Powell
(2005) model the impact of presidential trips to states from 1981
through 1999 on state-level presidential approval as the dependent
variable. With controls for national presidential approval, the partisan
makeup of the state, and national and state economic variables, they
find that a presidential visit will lift state-level presidential approval
by about 1.3 percent, a statistically significant, but not necessarily substantively meaningful amount. The effects of a presidential trip appear
somewhat higher in non-presidential election years and in smaller as

opposed to larger states, but even these effects barely top a 2 percent increase.[8] In a second paper, Cohen (2006) uses SurveyUSA data, which allows him to assess the change in approval associated with presidential trips. Cohen (2006), in contrast to Cohen and Powell (2005), finds no impact on approval change at the state level associated with a presidential trip.[9] These two studies, although far from definitive, do not suggest large-scale or impressive effects from a presidential trip to a locality. Clearly, there needs to be more work testing the effects of local visits on presidential approval, as well as assessment of other opinion indicators, such as opinion on issues.

Perhaps the larger point is that although local travel may assist the president in his coalition-building efforts, it cannot serve as the backbone of such a strategy. Presidents clearly need local support, but traveling to localities can only be used sparingly and strategically. It costs too much for presidents to travel around the country, and initial research suggests only small approval effects from such trips. Moreover, local travel looks too much like bargaining with individual members of Congress, an approach that at best acquires members into the presidential coalition one at a time. Such approaches might be effective in securing an individual member's support, but they are inefficient given the large number of members that presidents require to win. Instead, we need to think of local visits as an element of a larger strategy or approach aimed at localities. Travel to localities thus augments or builds on this larger strategic framework.

Recalling the limitations of addressing the nation on prime-time television, the primary foundation of going public relied on news coverage. As much as the broadcast networks provided the major means of presidential access to national public opinion, local news media

---

[8]  The primary limitation of the Cohen-Powell study is that their data, from the Job Approval Ratings database, http://www.unc.edu/~beyle/jars.html, do not have data for each month for each state. Of 11,400 possible data points (19 years × 50 states × 12 months), they have data for only 929 cases (8%).

[9]  But there are noticeable limits in Cohen's analysis, too. He has data for only six months, August 2005 to January 2006, a relatively short time span. The mix of presidential visits during that short time period may not be fully representative of presidential trips in general. Second, like Cohen and Powell, Cohen does not discriminate among different types of presidential trips, instead treating all trips similarly.

provide the major means of presidential access to local opinion. Presidents may make use of several local media, including local television and newspapers. For a variety of reasons, local newspapers may be the most important means of reaching local residents, although local newspapers are not without their limitations and pitfalls for the president.

# CHAPTER 3

# Presidents and the Local News Media

In response to the rise of polarized parties and a fragmented media, presidents have altered their going public leadership style. Rather than build national public support, presidents in the post-broadcast age pursue a narrower going public style that focuses on their party base, certain interest groups, and select localities. The previous chapter reviewed evidence that presidents engage these narrow groups more in the present age than they did previously. This chapter looks more closely at presidential engagement with localities. As argued earlier, presidents have primarily two means of building public support in localities, by visiting them or through news coverage.

Local visits are costly to presidents, and they can visit only one locality at a time. Presidential activities aimed at the local news media may provide a more cost-effective approach to building local support. Localities present presidents with several news media, local television and local newspapers being the most important. How important are these two local news media to presidential going public efforts? This chapter presents evidence that, despite declining readerships in the late 1990s and early 2000s, local newspapers may be more important to presidents than local television.

Three characteristics of local newspapers make them potentially important to presidents: 1) their comparatively large audience, 2) their relatively high credibility, especially compared with other news sources, and 3) the significant amount of news on the presidency that they report to their readers. In the conclusion, I raise the nagging issue of whether local newspapers will continue to be important to presidents in the near future.

TABLE 3.1. *Percentage of regular users of newspapers, local television, and network nightly news broadcasts, 1994–2004*

| Date | Newspapers | Local television | Network nightly news broadcast |
|------|-----------|------------------|-------------------------------|
| February 1994 | 70 | 71* | 60* |
| April 1996 | 71 | 65 | 42 |
| April 1998 | 68 | 64 | 38 |
| April 2000 | 63 | 56 | 30 |
| April 2002 | 63 | 57 | 32 |
| April 2004 | 60 | 59 | 34 |

* May 1993.
*Source:* Pew Research Center, Biennial News Consumption Surveys.
*Question:* Do you happen to . . . (read a newspaper) . . . regularly or not?

## LARGE LOCAL NEWSPAPER AUDIENCES

Despite declines in readership, a large number of citizens still read newspapers on a relatively frequent basis. The Pew Research Center's Biennial News Consumption surveys have been tracking the reading habits of Americans since the early 1990s.[1] Into the early twenty-first century, according to Pew's estimates, the newspaper audience is as large as the local television audience and much larger than the network nightly news broadcasts. Table 3.1 displays the results of the Pew surveys since 1994 based on the question, "Do you happen to. . . . (read a newspaper). . . . regularly or not?" For 2004, 60 percent of respondents say that they read a newspaper regularly, compared with 59 percent who say that they tune into a local television news broadcast. In contrast, only about one-third claim to regularly watch a national network news television broadcast, and the audience for the cable news networks is even smaller.[2] Whereas the figures on Table 3.1 show a decline of about 10 percent for newspaper readers from 1994 to 2004, a large fraction of the public still claims to read newspapers on a regular basis.[3]

There are several issues with the Pew questions. First, respondents decide how to define what it means to be a "regular user" and may

[1] The Pew surveys were accessed from their Web site: http://people-press.org.
[2] There are two other response categories: "sometimes" and "hardly ever."
[3] Use of most news media has been declining for the several decades (Cohen, 2008).

TABLE 3.2. *Percentage using select news media either "every day" or "several days per week," 1999–2004*

|                              | August 1999 | December 2002 | December 2004 |
|------------------------------|-------------|---------------|---------------|
| Local Newspaper              | 68          | 60            | 58            |
| National Newspaper           | 16          | 16            | 11            |
| National Network Nightly News| 71          | 59            | 52            |
| Morning Network News         | 43          | 39            | 39            |
| Local Television             | 72          | 73            | 70            |
| Public Television            | 43          | 47            | 38            |
| Cable Television News        | 51          | 56            | 55            |
| Talk Radio                   | 21          | 32            | 33            |
| National Public Radio        | 27          | 31            | 29            |
| Internet                     | 14          | 23            | 26            |

*Source:* Gallup Poll.

*Question:* Please indicate how often you get your news from each of the following sources – every day, several times a week, occasionally, or never.

have different understandings of what it means. Some may think that using the news sources on most weekdays would classify them as a regular news user (e.g., three days per week), whereas others might contend that a regular news user must use the news source virtually every day (e.g., six to seven days per week). This lack of specificity may allow people to overstate their degree of news consumption if for no other reason than to keep from embarrassing themselves in a survey situation. Second, the Pew question does not distinguish different types of newspapers, for example, national newspapers, large urban dailies, and weeklies, among others. As an estimator of the readership of local newspapers, the Pew question thus is limited.

The Gallup Poll differentiates local and national newspapers while also asking respondents to be more precise about their news use habits by using the categories "every day," "several times per week," "occasionally," or "never." Unfortunately, these Gallup data exist for only three time points, 1999, 2002, and 2004, presented in Table 3.2.

The Gallup results closely resemble Pew's with regard to newspaper reading, although Gallup finds a larger local television audience than does Pew. According to Gallup, about 60 percent read a local newspaper in 2004 "every day" or "several times per week," which

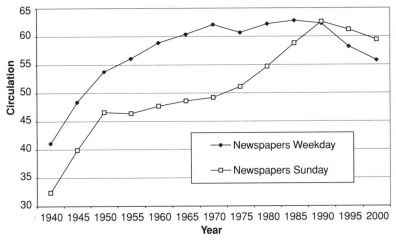

Figure 3.1. Trends in Newspaper Circulation (in millions). *Source:* journalism.org, using data from Editor and Publisher Yearbook, various years.

is comparable to the Pew figure for those who consider themselves regular newspaper readers. Only local television news has a larger audience than newspapers, at 70 percent, although cable news and national network news closely follow, at 55 percent and 52 percent, respectively. Notably, both local television and national network news seem to command larger audiences than in the Pew estimates, which may be a function of the different response categories. Still, both Pew and Gallup indicate a large, albeit declining, local newspaper readership.

Rather than rely on surveys, we can look at circulation figures. The virtue of circulation figures is that because they determine advertising rates, a major source of revenue for newspapers, they must be verified by independent auditors, like the Audit Bureau of Circulations and BPA Worldwide. Figure 3.1 plots trends in newspaper circulation from the 1940s to 2000 for weekday and Sunday editions. The weekday editions combine morning and afternoon newspapers; the figure does not show the decline in afternoon newspaper circulation and the rise in morning newspapers.

Newspaper circulation increased from the 1940s until about 1990. A decline in circulation for both newspaper editions started about 1990 and continued into the early 2000s. According to these aggregate

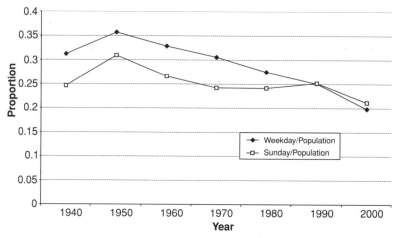

Figure 3.2. Newspaper Circulation as a Proportion of Population Size.

figures, from the 1990s to 2000s, newspaper circulation hovered in the range of 55 to 62 million. These aggregate circulation figures do not taken into account growth in population. Figure 3.2 plots weekday and Sunday circulation as a proportion of the total U.S. population by decade from 1940 through 2000. This figure tells a somewhat different story. As a proportion, newspaper circulation has been in decline since the 1950s, when it peaked at nearly 36 percent for weekday newspapers and 31 percent for the Sunday edition. By 2000, the proportion for weekday and Sunday editions dropped to 20 percent and 21 percent, respectively, a 50 percent decline.

As with the survey data, we must be careful in interpreting these circulation proportions. Newspapers are shared within family units. Each circulating newspaper may be read by more than one individual. U.S. census figures in 2000 estimate that the average household contained 2.6 individuals, for a total of 105.5 million households. With households as a base, newspaper circulation as a proportion of households in 2000 stood at about 53 percent and 56 percent for the weekday and Sunday editions, respectively.[4] According to these estimates, roughly one-half of the adult population has access to a newspaper, but the

4  Further complicating estimates of newspaper exposure is that we do not know how many people have stopped their newspaper subscription but continue to read the

aggregate circulation figures do not provide us with a way to deter-mine how faithfully each household member reads the newspaper or even how many members of the household read the newspaper. Still, both surveys and circulation totals indicate declines in newspaper use. Using either of these indicators, we see that newspapers continue to have a large audience at the turn of the twenty-first century, if not as large as it once was.

Neither of the above indicators of newspaper use measures the types of stories consumers read or how much time per day they spend reading the newspaper. Newspapers contain a variety of stories, from international, national, and local hard news to features, sports, and entertainment. If local newspapers are to be an important element of the president's leadership strategy, they not only must attract a large number of readers, but readers also must turn to local newspapers for news about the president. Again, survey results suggest that readers use newspapers for news as well as for other types of information (e.g., sports, weather).

Pew surveys suggest that people turn to newspapers primarily for local news. The summer 2006 Pew survey found that 53 percent of respondents turn to newspapers for news about local government, compared with 45 percent who turn to television (but the Pew ques-tion did not distinguish local from network or cable television). By contrast, people are more likely to turn to television for Washington and international news by large margins. Whereas 68 percent and 67 percent turn to television for Washington and international news, respectively, only 27 percent and 24 percent, respectively, turned to newspapers for such news.[5] Thus, there seems to be a division of

newspaper online. For instance, the Pew Internet and American Life Project esti-mates that in December 2005, nearly 70 percent of the public has gone online for news at some point, and 30 percent claimed to do so "yesterday." These Pew surveys do not tell us which news sources people are using on the Internet, but Internet news users appear to spend little time looking at news online. On average, those who went online yesterday spent only six minutes looking at news, compared with thirty min-utes spent watching television news, fifteen minutes reading a newspaper, and sixteen minutes listening to news on the radio. These figures come from journalism.org, the State of the News Media 2007 (online).

5 The report accessed from the Pew People and the Press Web site: http://people-press.org/reports/display.php3?PageID=1066.

TABLE 3.3. *What people read in the newspaper of those who read a newspaper "often" or "sometimes," 1985 and 2006*

|  | 1985 | 2006 |
| --- | --- | --- |
| Local Government News | 91 | 91 |
| National News | 84 | 88 |
| International News | 81 | 84 |
| Editorial/Opinion Page | 60 | 60 |

*Source:* Pew Research Center for People and the Press, "Online Papers Modestly Boost Newspaper Readership, Maturing Internet News Audience Broader Than Deep," Released, July 30, 2006.

attention, with newspapers being used for local information and television for national news.

Although people prefer television to newspapers for national news, nearly all who say that they read newspapers "often" or "sometimes" use newspapers for more than just local news coverage (see Table 3.3). Whereas 91 percent of these "consistent" readers read newspapers for local news, 84 percent and 81 percent read them for national and international news, respectively. Also, the editorial and opinion pages attract large numbers of newspaper readers (60%). Moreover, these figures show little change among newspaper readers during the past twenty years. Assuming that about 60 percent of the public reads newspapers on a fairly regular basis and 80 percent read them for Washington/national news, much of which is about the president, then a president may potentially reach nearly one-half of the public (60% × 80% = 48%) through local newspaper coverage. Overall, the local newspaper readership may be large and attentive enough to merit the president's desire to want to reach it.

## RELATIVELY HIGH LOCAL NEWSPAPER CREDIBILITY

The public holds positive attitudes about local newspapers, making these outlets a credible source for news. Credibility is important in affecting attitudes; research indicates that credible sources have greater impact on attitudes than less credible ones (Miller and Krosnick, 2000).

TABLE 3.4. *Favorability of select news media, 2001 and 2005*

| News Medium | 2001[*] | 2005[*] |
| --- | --- | --- |
| Local Television | 79 | 73 |
| Local Newspapers | 75 | 72 |
| Network Television | 72 | 68 |
| Cable Television | 78 | 67 |
| *Washington Post/New York Times* | 52 | 38 |

[*] Percent "Very Favorable" and "Mostly Favorable."
*Source:* Pew Research Center for the People and the Press.
*Question:* Now I'd like your opinion of some groups and organizations in the news. (First) would you say your overall opinion of . . . is very favorable, mostly favorable, mostly unfavorable, or very unfavorable?

Generally, people have favorable opinions about their local newspapers, but also tend to feel favorable to most forms of news media. Table 3.4 presents results from Pew Research Center polls in 2001 and 2005 that compare the favorability of several types of news media outlets, including local newspapers.[6] Although local newspapers ranked third in favorability in 2001, just a shade behind local and cable television, local newspapers almost were tied for first with local television in 2005, with a 72 percent rating (73% for local television). Almost all media, with the exception of local newspapers and network television, show some slide in favorability from 2001 to 2005. Specifically, local television witnessed a 6-percent drop, cable television 9 percent, and the major national newspapers a massive 14-point decline from 52 to 38. In contrast, local newspapers held relatively steady, with a 75 percent rating in 2001 and 72 percent in 2005, whereas network television slid 4 points, from 72 percent to 68 percent.

It is not entirely clear why people feel favorable or unfavorable toward certain news media. Perhaps more important than favorability is whether a person thinks the news source provides mostly facts or opinion. Such an orientation would be especially important for news sources to which people traditionally turn for information about the world, rather than interpretation, like talk radio or blogs, or even editorial and columnist pages in newspapers.

[6] These results were accessed from www.journalism.org, State of the News Media, 2006.

TABLE 3.5. *Percentage of respondents seeing select news media as primarily factually versus opinion oriented, 2005*

| News medium | Mostly facts | Mostly opinion | Both | Don't know |
|---|---|---|---|---|
| Local Television | 61 | 25 | 6 | 7 |
| Daily Newspapers | 54 | 31 | 6 | 8 |
| Network Evening News | 53 | 31 | 6 | 9 |
| Major National Newspapers | 45 | 30 | 6 | 19 |
| Network Morning News | 39 | 33 | 5 | 22 |
| News Blogs | 20 | 32 | 2 | 45 |
| Talk Radio | 10 | 68 | 5 | 17 |

*Source:* Pew Research Center for the People and the Press, "Public More Critical of Press, But Goodwill Persists," June 26, 2005.

*Question:* As I read a list, tell me if you think these organizations mostly report the facts about recent news.

People seem quite discriminating in assessing whether a news outlet presents mostly fact or opinion, and their assessments seem quite reasonable. As shown on Table 3.5, based on a Pew Research Center poll in June 2005, respondents see talk radio primarily as an opinion forum. Moreover, those familiar with blogs also see this new form of communication as more opinion than fact. By contrast, respondents see daily newspapers as primarily conveyors of fact: 54 percent feel this way compared with 31 percent who view daily newspapers as primarily opinion forums. This compares favorably with the network evening news broadcasts. Only local television receives a higher proportion, with 61 percent seeing it as a factual medium and 25 percent perceiving it as more opinionated. Major national newspapers do not fare as well as the other news outlets, although pluralities see them as factual (45% vs. 30%). The network morning news programs receive the lowest totals perceiving them as a factual rather than an opinion medium (39% vs. 33%).

The major blemish with regard to local newspaper credibility is evident when the public is asked to assess whether they can believe what the news media reports. Believability is central to the notion of credibility: If the public disbelieves what the press reports, then in no way can we consider the press to have credibility. Table 3.6 presents results of Pew surveys since the mid-1980s on the believability of several news media.

TABLE 3.6. *Believability of select news outlets, 1985–2006*\*

| | 1985 | 1989 | 1993 | 1996 | 1998 | 2000 | 2002 | 2004 | 2006 |
|---|---|---|---|---|---|---|---|---|---|
| Daily Newspaper | 80 | 67 | 63 | 61 | 63 | 61 | 59 | 50 | 55 |
| Local Television | 81 | – | – | – | 73 | 69 | 65 | 69 | 60 |
| CNN | – | – | 76 | 71 | 72 | 65 | 66 | – | 60 |
| Fox | – | – | – | – | – | 47 | 53 | 54 | 51 |
| ABC News | 83 | 75 | 76 | 74 | 71 | 62 | 65 | 58 | 59 |
| CBS News | 84 | 74 | 75 | 72 | 69 | 63 | 64 | 57 | 54 |
| NBC News | 82 | 79 | 73 | 74 | 70 | 63 | 66 | 61 | 60 |

Now, I'm going to read a list. Please rate how much you think you can believe each organization I name on a scale of 4 to 1. On this 4-point scale, "4" means you can believe all or most of what the organization says, "1" means you believe almost nothing of what they say. How much would you rate the believability of . . . (name news organization) on this scale of 4 to 1?

\* The figures in the cells represent the combined percentage answering 3 and 4.

*Source:* Pew Research Center and Princeton Survey Research Associates.

All of these news outlets show very high levels of believability in the mid-1980s, with declines thereafter. Starting in the 1980s, typically 80 percent of respondents give each outlet a score of 3 or 4 on a 4-point scale, with 4 meaning that the respondent can believe all or most and a 1 meaning that the respondent can believe almost nothing. Each news outlet believability score deteriorates almost in lockstep with the others, so that by the mid-2000s, only from 50 percent to 60 percent will rate the outlet a 3 or 4 on the 4-point scale.

Daily (local) newspapers fare no better, and perhaps slightly worse, than most of the other outlets. They scored a 55 in 2006, 4 to 5 points behind local television, ABC, NBC, and CNN, outscoring only two outlets, CBS at 54 and Fox Cable News at 51, both small differences. Fox Cable News was somewhat disadvantaged because a slightly higher percentage of respondents said they could not rate it, presumably because they either did not watch it or because it was not offered by their cable service.

The fact that each outlet's level of believability has eroded at a similar pace suggests that responses to this question have less to do with the outlet itself and more with general orientations toward the news media.[7] General Social Survey and Harris Poll data, asking about confidence in people who run television and the press, show a similar secular decline dating to the mid-1970s (see Cohen, 2008, ch. 8). Similarly, American National Election Study data from the mid-1980s onward find increasing cynicism toward the news media in general. It is somewhat odd that believability in local newspapers and local television would erode in similar fashion to the broadcast networks given the great diversity of the local news outlets. Moreover, Pew reports a partisan gap in believability across news outlets, with Republicans generally less believing of the news, regardless of the outlet, than Democrats, with the exception of Fox. This reinforces the notion that something other than assessments of each specific outlet is shaping the public's believability in the news.

The erosion in believability covaries with the secular decline in news attention. Each news outlet, again excepting Fox and CNN, has suffered a long-term decline in audience size. Perhaps the decline in

---

[7]   For more detail on the points of the next several paragraphs, see Cohen, 2008.

believability is merely a rationalization for why some individuals have stopped reading newspapers or watching news broadcasts.

Finally, these believability ratings are somewhat at odds with the high favorability ratings for the news media noted earlier and, for the local press, a strong sense that they report facts more than opinion. Regardless, the 55 percent believability score for local newspapers corresponds to the percentage who say that local newspapers are more inclined to report facts than opinion. Yet, despite the decline in news outlet believability, generally more than half of respondents say that the news is believable, especially the media of concern here, local newspapers.

## SIGNIFICANT AMOUNT OF NEWS CONTENT IN LOCAL NEWSPAPERS

As detailed earlier, local television differs little from local newspapers in terms of audience size and public attitudes toward them. In fact, local television generally receives slightly higher marks than local news-papers and possesses a somewhat larger audience. Why study local newspapers, then, instead of local television? Primarily because local television contains little news on the president, and studies suggest that local newspapers set the news agenda for local television, not vice versa (Kaniss, 1991). By contrast, local newspapers carry a con-siderable, if not overwhelming, amount of presidential news. Without much news about the president, local television cannot affect attitudes toward the president, much less information levels. Thus, for the pres-ident, local television will not be a feasible conduit toward reaching the mass public, but many local newspapers willbe.

Few systematic studies of the content of local television currently exist. Extant studies tend to focus on the amount of crime reporting and the characteristics and effects of crime reporting, topics generally of little relevance to this study (Dixon and Azocar, 2006; Dixon and Linz, 2000; Dowler, 2006; Gilliam and Iyengar, 2000; Poindexter, Smith, and Heider, 2003).

A few more general studies exist. For instance, Klite (1995) con-tent analyzed local television broadcasts in the 10:00 or 11:00 P.M. slots for fifty stations across twenty-nine cities for one day, Wednesday,

January 11, 1995. He found that an average of 50 percent of the broadcast news concerned crime and disaster. Government news, which did not distinguish level of government, accounted for 12.5 percent of broadcast time, or about three to four minutes in a typical thirty-minute broadcast. Kaniss (1991, ch. 4) provides a similar assessment of local television news in her content analysis of Philadelphia stations for a two-week period in the mid-1980s.[8]

The Project for Excellence in Journalism (PEJ) has done some of the most extensive content analyses of local television news broadcasts. According to its 2006 State of the News Media report, crime tops the list of the most commonly reported type of story, amounting to more than 40 percent of stories in the local evening and late news broadcasts; whereas the combination of government, elections, foreign affairs, and defense account for 19 percent of evening and 17 percent of late broadcasts.[9]

Somewhat more effort has focused on election campaign reporting. Stevens et al. (2006) find that local television stations in Minnesota report more news about the presidential election than about the Senate or local elections and that news reports tended to be about the horserace, with little time devoted to issues. Focus group interviews found frustration with the brevity and superficiality of election stories (Stevens et al., 2006), and a study by Just, Crigler, and Buhr (1999) of the 1992 presidential election found that local television offered less substantive news coverage of the campaign than did newspapers or network television.

Fowler (2007) conducted the most extensive content analysis of local news broadcasts, but she, too, focused on election coverage. Using the University of Wisconsin NewsLab, Fowler was able to digitally download entire news broadcasts across several months of the election campaign for three election cycles, 2002, 2004, and 2006.[10]

---

[8] PEJ's study is limited, to one day, eight stations, in three cities. A useful overview of content analyses of local television news can be found in Riffe et al., 2005.

[9] May 11, looking at twenty-four newscasts across eight stations in three cities- Houston, Milwaukee and Bend, Oregon- from the Web site: http://www.stateofthenewsmedia.com/2006.

[10] She tracked news in 112 stations in 50 markets in 2002, 44 stations from 11 markets in 2004, and 35 stations from 9 markets in 2006 (p. 42).

She found very little election coverage, with about two minutes given to the presidential election per night in 2004, and around an hour to nonpresidential elections across the entire campaign. Government news, including foreign affairs, commanded about one to two minutes per day (45).

Fowler did not present breakdowns for presidential news within the government or foreign affairs categories. Clearly, the president will not occupy all of that news time, but we do not know which fraction. Nor do we know from her study how much of the time given to election reporting was at the expense of government/foreign affairs reporting or other types of stories. Still, the amount of news given to political and governmental affairs, even during the election cycle, is meager.[11]

Because of the lack of research on the president in local television news, I content analyzed all local evening news broadcasts for June 1, 2000. I selected this day for comparison purposes; it is one of the days selected for the content analysis of local news on the president used later in this study. This was a potentially newsworthy day with regard to the president. President Clinton met with Israeli Prime Minister Ehud Barak in Portugal as one leg of a trip to Europe; a federal judge ruled that Elian Gonzales had to be returned to his family in Cuba; Attorney General Janet Reno, who was fighting the return of Elian Gonzales, made a comment about it that day; and reporters accompanying President Clinton on his European trip asked him about the ruling.

I used the Video Monitoring Service (VMS) archive on LexisNexis to search for all stories on local television broadcasts in the early evening, using "President and Clinton" as the search term. VMS abstracts all broadcasts for the fifty largest U.S. media markets. With at least four network affiliates per locality, there are a minimum of two hundred local television stations covered by VMS, yet I was able to find only sixty-nine news segments[12] from fifty-six stations reporting any news on the president. The vast majority of local television stations did

---

[11] She also tests for the effects of local television news exposure on political behavior, such as turnout and voting, and fails to find an effect, which she attributes to the low quantity of such news.

[12] There may be several items within a news segment.

not broadcast any news in which the president appeared or was even
mentioned.

Furthermore, when presidential news stories were broadcast, they
tended to be quite short, averaging slightly less than two minutes
(115 seconds). By contrast, three presidential stories appeared on the
NBC network broadcast on the same day, averaging two minutes and
fifteen seconds each, for a total of six minutes and forty-five seconds
of presidential news. Of the local news segments on the president,
forty-three (62%) lasted for two minutes or less and thirty (43%)
lasted for one minute or less. Only four of the local news broadcast
segments lasted longer than five minutes; after they were eliminated
from the count, the average local television news broadcast containing
a reference to the president spanned not quite ninety seconds.

Additionally, all of the longer story segments referred to the Elian
Gonzales case. The long segments tended to be in localities with interested populations, such as in South Florida, where large numbers of
Cuban Americans reside. Stories about the President's European trip
tended to be quite brief, merely noting that he met with Ehud Barak,
the Israeli Prime Minister, or was in Europe.

Although we should not try to generalize from this small sample,
when we consider other studies of local television, we can say that presidential news on local television is occasional rather than consistent,
and brief, containing little detail because of its brevity.[13] By contrast,
as detailed subsequently, local newspapers provide readers with more
frequent and more detailed news stories on the president than local
television news.

[13] It is difficult to compare television and newspaper reporting. Later chapters rely on
an extensive content analysis of newspaper reporting on the president. That sample
consists of twenty-four newspapers across twenty days, both randomly selected from
LexisNexis. On June 1, 2000, excluding the *Washington Post*, which is in the sample,
fourteen of the remaining newspapers reported thirty-one stories on the president.
The *Post* alone contained 12 presidential stories. The thirty-one stories averaged
777.6 words, ranging from a low of 106 to a high of 4,214. Linguists estimate the
normal speaking rate for formal presentations, like news broadcasts, to be from two
to two and a half words per second. Using this standard, and average television story
duration of two minutes, yields a word count of 240 to 300 words per average local
television news cast on the president. This figure is likely overstated too because most
of the longer presidential news stories contained much nonpresidential information.
Still, this 300-word average falls far short of the approximately 750 to 800 found for
the typical newspaper story.

## CONCLUSION

Going public in the post-broadcast age entails presidential targeting of narrow groups, such as their party base, interest groups, and select localities, instead of trying to reach national public opinion. Local public opinion may be an especially important resource for presidents in the post-broadcast age. Presidents can reach local public opinion either by visiting localities or by generating news coverage. Because visiting is a relatively costly activity, local news coverage is the preferred or more useful avenue for influencing local public opinion.

This chapter has reviewed data on the two most important local media, local television and local newspapers. Both local television and newspapers possess relatively large audiences, and the public views them as equally believable, especially compared with the national news media. Yet, presidents are likely to find local newspapers more important to the leadership efforts than local television because of the dearth of news on the president on local television.

Will local newspapers continue to be important to presidents? Most of the empirical analysis for this study is for 2000. Since then, local newspapers have been hemorrhaging revenues and readerships. Readership declines are especially heavy among younger people, who have increasingly turned to the Internet for news. Consolidation of local newspapers into chains and cutbacks in news production budgets have reduced the amount of news produced locally. Many wonder whether newspapers as we know them will exist in the future.

As readership declines, local newspapers may become less important to presidents in their attempts to build local support. Regardless, local newspapers may remain important because their readers tend to be the most politically active and aware. By reaching these potential opinion leaders, presidents may still be able to influence the shape of local public opinion, albeit indirectly. Moreover, if newspaper readers migrate to the Internet, they will not necessarily cease reading their local newspaper. They will just read it through a different medium. We can make a parallel argument here. In the 1950s, movies lost audiences to television, but the Hollywood studios remained the dominant producers of entertainment. Instead of solely producing movies for theater release, they became producers of television programs, using essentially the same production system for television that they used for movies. If we make an analogy of the news organization to Hollywood production companies, what we may be witnessing is the transformation of the medium of communication, not the substance of communication – in this case, news.

The second trend, the decline in local production of news, may actually be beneficial to presidents. In trying to manage the news they receive in local newspapers, presidents confront a great number, variety, and heterogeneity of local newspapers. As local newspapers consolidate into chains and produce more news elsewhere, coverage of local events and concerns may recede, but other types of news, such as coverage of the president, may occupy a greater proportion of the news hole. Concentration in the news industry, as was the case in the 1960s and 1970s, when the broadcast networks dominated the provision of news transmission to the public, may also have been the heyday of presidential leadership of public opinion (Young and Perkins, 2005). If local newspapers consolidate into chains, with more news produced nationally for all of them to share, the attendant danger to the president is that reporters covering the president for the chains of local newspapers will adopt the confrontational style so prevalent among reporters and editors of the major national news media (Clayman et al., 2006, 2007).

The larger point for this study is that the era of going public nationally has ended. Because of high levels of party polarization and a fragmented news media, presidents currently focus their public support–building activities on their party base, interest groups, and localities. If presidents are less able to influence public opinion through local newspapers, they will either have to find a replacement or will see declines in their ability to rally segments of the public behind them. This does not undermine the usefulness of the theory developed and tested in these pages, but rather affects only the specific behaviors of presidents. We can only speculate about the future of local newspapers and their continued relevance for presidential leadership.

# A Theory of Presidential News Management and Local News Coverage

The previous chapters argue that local newspapers have become increasingly important to presidential communications and support building efforts in the late twentieth and early twenty-first centuries. In the post-broadcast age, presidents found that the national leadership style, used with some success from the 1950s into the 1970s, was no longer as potent at mobilizing mass publics support and building support coalitions. Hence, presidents developed a revised going public style to accommodate to the realities and constraints of the post-broadcast age. This revised or updated going public style targets the president's partisan base, specific interest groups, and select localities.

Local newspapers may be especially important to the president in targeting localities. As argued in Chapter 3, local newspapers are attractive to presidents because they still command a relatively large audience; they are still highly respected, especially compared with the national news media; and they present measurable amounts of news on the president, especially in comparison to local television. Local newspapers may be the most potent medium for presidential communications efforts targeted at localities.

But local newspapers will be useful to presidents only if they are able to affect the news that is published about them. Whether presidents can "manage" their local news is an empirical question; the next several chapters test the ability of presidents to affect certain important characteristics of presidential news in local newspapers. This chapter presents the theoretical foundation for the analysis that follows. Before turning to theory, it is instructive to review the literature on

71

presidential news management and local news coverage of the president, both of which are limited in several regards.

## PRESIDENTIAL NEWS MANAGEMENT AND THE PRODUCTION OF PRESIDENTIAL NEWS

There are several limitations of past research on presidential news management. First, existing research does not present a clear definition of presidential news management. Instead we find a variety of definitions and even variance in terminology. Second, existing research rarely specifies the causal relationship between the president's news management and either relations with the press or news about the president. Third, most of the research focuses on relations and interactions with the press. Little attention is given to the impact of news management on news itself. The research that does exist is either anecdotal and/or relies on interviews with either White House staffers or journalists.

### Defining News Management

Research on presidential news management has yet to present a clear definition for the concept and even uses varying terminology. Consider the array of terms used – spin (Maltese, 1992; Kurtz, 1998; Rozell, 1993), image control (Rozell, 1995), news management (Zeidenstein, 1984), and strategic communications (Althaus, 2001). Are these merely synonyms? If not, what are their differences? Specifically, what is news·management?

Althaus (2001) offers a clear definition of strategic communications, one type of news management activity, so this is a useful place to start (also Manheim, 1994). Strategic communications, according to Althaus, consist of public communications from the president through two channels, public speeches of various kinds and press briefings. Althaus argues that the president can manipulate or regulate the content and timing of his speeches and press briefings, which he does to affect news coverage of presidential public activities and statements on issues. In this way, presidents are strategic not only about going public, but also in how they go public.

By increasing his attention to an issue or topic, Althaus argues, presidents signal to the press that the topic is important to him. Similarly, when the president focuses his attention on one topic and fails to speak about others, he again signals the importance of that topic. These "tactical moves" may affect the news media's agenda if the news media are more likely to publish stories on more important than less important issues and the news media in part take cues on importance from the president. Presidential success in influencing the media hinges on the press's ability to find alternative sources for information. Althaus has taken a key step in conceptual clarification. Yet strategic communications, by his definition, constitute only one aspect of presidential news management, albeit the most observable.

I define "presidential news management" as all activities that presidents engage in to affect the content and other characteristics of their news coverage. These activities may be targeted toward the press in general; to subsets of the press, like local newspapers; or to individual journalists. In studying presidential news management, we need to identify the particular presidential action, the target, and the aspects of news coverage the president aims to influence. In some cases, presidents want to restrict or limit news coverage because of controversy and/or the potential for negative coverage. Presidents do not always want news coverage.

Moreover, although many presidential news management activities may be readily observable because they are performed in public, some presidential activities cannot be observed easily or systematically because they are done out of public view, behind the scenes and in private. For instance, the administration may leak information to a pliant or friendly journalist who may not be able to inform other journalists that the president or the administration is the source of the leak. Presidents sometimes use leaks as trial balloons to test the public reaction to a possible action or policy. By hiding the administration's ties to the leak, the president can minimize the damage of being associated with a proposal that proves unpopular or politically costly.

Similarly, presidents may provide information to journalists on "deep background," as FDR sometimes did in his many interactions with journalists. FDR's tactic did not allow those reporters who were privy to the information to associate it with the administration in their news reports. The goal of this strategy was not so much to affect coverage on the specific topic, but to create cordial relationship with reporters and make them allies of the administration (White, 1979; Winfield, 1990). Presidents may not even keep documents on certain activities relevant to news management. The nonpublic nature of some aspects of presidential news management forecloses the ability to study them systematically.

Furthermore, unless the president explicitly announces his news management strategy, we have no idea whether or not an activity was part of that strategy. To speak of a presidential news management strategy assumes conscious or purposeful behavior and that the administration possesses an underlying rationale or strategy for acting as it does in public. An administration may not have a specific or well-defined news management strategy. Activities that we assume are elements of the larger presidential news management strategy need not be systemic or thoughtful. They may be haphazard and reactive and made up on the spot, and may not even have been elements of the president's news management strategy.

Given these limitations in identifying presidential activities aimed at affecting news coverage and the specifics of the president's overall news management strategy, if in fact one exists, the best we can do is follow Althaus's lead and look at the impact of public activities on presidential news coverage, noting the limitations of such a research approach. This will enable us to test which types of presidential public activities, as well as which attributes of public presidential activities, affect presidential news coverage.

## Causally Linking News Management to News Coverage

The literature on presidential news management also often fails to specify the causal mechanism linking news management activity to the two key dependent variables, relations with the press and impact on news content. Much of the relevant literature assumes the newsworthiness of presidents.[1] Presidential newsworthiness serves as the

---

[1]  On newsworthiness, see Graber (1997, especially 118–122) and Groeling (2008).

often unstated causal factor in much of the literature; that is, presidents can successfully manage the news about them because journalists think that what presidents do is newsworthy. The inherent newsworthiness of presidents provides presidents with a key asset. However, although newsworthiness may provide presidents with an advantage in their relations with journalists, the assumption that presidents and their activities are inherently newsworthy, and more newsworthy than other events, is debatable.

Paletz and Entman (1980) argue that presidents possess advantages over journalists because they can regulate both reporter access to them and the flow of information about their activities and decisions to journalists. Journalists, in turn, produce the kind of news that presidents want because they place a high value on news about the president. Newsworthiness, in effect, provides the basis for the effectiveness of specific presidential actions. Yet, it is not clear that presidents are as advantaged as Paltez and Entman contend. Others (Cook, 1998; Cook and Ragsdale, 1998) argue that journalists have resources that they can use to their advantage, such as access to news media outlets and influence over how stories are written. Reporters are not hapless in their relationship with the president; thus, presidents and the press "negotiate the news."[2] But the underlying premise, as in the work of Paletz and Entman, is that presidents are newsworthy.

Zaller's (1998) product substitution model presents a well-developed hypothesis about the effectiveness of a certain type of news management technique – tight control of information. Although his model pertains to presidential election campaigns, it has relevance to governing. Zaller contends that strict candidate control of the access and the flow of information may prove to be counterproductive, in contrast to the arguments of Paletz and Entman (1980). According to Zaller, journalists, for professional reasons, want to play an active part in news production, to "co-produce" the news with candidates. When relegated to a passive role, they will seek other sources for news and begin to write stories critical of the candidate's relationship with the press. Grossman and Kumar (1981, 253–273) make a similar argument in the context of presidents in office, although the dynamic for

[2]  Also see Grossman and Kumar, 1981.

the deterioration in president–press relations differs from Zaller's. Still, the underlying assumption in all of the aforementioned studies is that presidents are newsworthy.

Although it may be the case that presidential election campaigns are inherently newsworthy, presidential actions in office vary in newsworthiness. Barrett (2007), for example, finds that not all presidential public statements regarding legislation receive coverage, and Cohen (2008) finds temporal variation in the amount of presidential news. Presidential newsworthiness is not a constant, but a variable. Presidents may be able to affect the degree of newsworthiness of their public activities. The market model developed in the following assumes that presidential newsworthiness is variable and identifies several factors that affect the newsworthiness of presidential public activity.

### Little Research on the Impact of News Management

Most research on presidential news management focuses on president–press relations rather than on the impact of news management activities on news coverage (Rozell, 1990, 1993, 1995; Zeidenstein, 1984). Much of this is anecdotal (e.g., Maltese, 1992; Kurtz, 1998) and/or relies on interviews with White House staffers (Rozell, 1990, 1993, 1995) or journalists (Zeidenstein, 1984). This research assumes that president–press relations affect news coverage – when the relationship is harmonious, presidents will receive positive news coverage, but when the relationship sours, presidential news will turn negative, too (Grossman and Kumar, 1981). But it is not clear that the president–press relationship affects presidential news so strongly. For instance, in his interviews with White House staffers, Rozell (1995) finds that the context, such as party control of Congress and the nature of the issue, may affect presidential news coverage more than president–press relations.

Several relevant studies attempt to assess the impact of news management on news coverage. Hertsgaard's (1988) content analysis of news coverage during the Reagan years attributes the president's favorable news coverage to the administration's deft handling of the news media, but his design does not compare the relative efficacies of different news management approaches. Wanta and Foote (1994) look at how presidential communications affect evening news broadcasts.

They find that presidential communications are most effective in setting the news agenda when no credible news sources other than the president exist, which is often the case in international affairs.[3] Finally, Althaus (2001) looks at several aspects of presidential communications on news coverage of the first Gulf War. He found that when President George H. W. Bush focused attention on the Gulf Crisis, the evening news tended to broadcast stories favorable to the president, but that Bush's public statements and appearances had little impact on the number of Gulf Crisis stories or the amount of coverage that Gulf Crisis policy issues received. Research on news management effects is scant and none addresses the issue of this study, local news coverage of the president.

## RESEARCH ON LOCAL PRESIDENTIAL NEWS COVERAGE

Only a scant literature has studied local news coverage of the presidency, focusing instead on either election coverage or topics other than election contests. Generally, relevant studies suffer from limited samples of local news, with little attention to news management effects, either empirically or theoretically.

## LOCAL NEWS COVERAGE OF PRESIDENTIAL CAMPAIGNS

Although several studies of presidential campaign news look at local newspapers, only three include a relatively large number of local newspapers.[4] Graber (1976) content analyzes twenty newspapers for presidential election campaign news in 1968 and 1972 and the three network broadcasts for 1972. Her sample includes some national, as

---

[3] See the related agenda setting studies of Edwards and Wood (1999), Eshbaugh-Soha and Peake (2006), Wood and Peake (1998), and Peake (2001). They look not at presidential communications strategies, but at the impact and responsiveness of presidential attention to policies on the congressional and news media agendas. This research finds presidential responsiveness to the congressional and news media agendas, but presidential attention only weakly affects their agendas. However, Peake (2001) shows presidential attention effects on less salient foreign policy issues.

[4] Other presidential campaign studies, but with limited samples of newspapers, include Aday and Devitt, 2001; Davidson and Adams, 1961; Farnsworth and Lichter, 2005; Just, Alger, and Kern, 1996; Kiolbassa, 1997; Patterson, 1980; Stempel, 1961; and Wasserman, 1999.

well as smaller, regional newspapers, but most are major urban dailies. Although she compares press and television coverage, she does not compare across the newspapers, nor does she look at whether campaign activities affect the quantity and quality of local news coverage. Stovall (1984) content analyzed fifty randomly selected newspapers, coverage of the 1980 campaign, asking whether the incumbent, Jimmy Carter, received more coverage than the challenger, Ronald Reagan, but he did not compare coverage across the fifty newspapers or assess which types of campaign events garnered more news coverage. Shaw and Sparrow (1999) analyze approximately twelve thousand articles from forty-one newspapers during the 1992 election campaign, focusing on whether the elite press affected the campaign news agendas of the non-elite press, often finding such agenda-setting effects.

Each of these studies is useful in demonstrating a data collection effort across a relatively large number of local newspapers and, at least in Stovall's case, a conscious effort at building a random sample of newspapers. But none looks at variation in campaign coverage across local newspapers; the studies consider local newspapers as a homogeneous set, which implies uniformity or lack of variance in local newspaper coverage of presidential election campaigns, a questionable assumption. Other than Stovall's, none looks at differences in news coverage of candidate campaign events, which we can take as an aspect of a candidate's news management strategy. But Stovall does not assess which types of campaign events receive more or better coverage or what kind of coverage different local newspapers give to which types of events other than the simple comparison between Carter's and Reagan's events.

**Local News Coverage of the President**
Several recent studies explicitly look at local news coverage of the president.[5] Farnsworth and Lichter (2005) present information on presidential news coverage in four local newspapers for three years, 1981, 1993, and 2001.[6] They find that the four local newspapers

[5] Older studies include Cornwell, 1959; Balutis, 1976, 1977; and Kernell and Jacobson, 1987.
[6] The *Austin American-Statesman, Des Moines Register, San Jose Mercury News,* and *St. Petersburg Times.*

report less news on the president than national newspapers, but it is not clear that the four newspapers are representative of local newspapers in general. Moreover, they only include front-page news stories and do not count stories from wire services, which may understate the quantity of presidential news in local newspapers.[7]

Conventional wisdom contends that presidential travel to localities will be covered in local newspapers and that coverage generally will be positive.[8] Eshbaugh-Soha and Peake (2006) and Barrett and Peake (2007) test whether the conventional wisdom is correct, with Eshbaugh-Soha and Peake (2006) looking at local reporting on G. W. Bush's public campaign in support of his Social Security reform proposal in 2005, whereas Barrett and Peake (2007) looked at local coverage of all presidential trips in 2001. Both find that characteristics of newspapers and the local context may affect local news reports on the trip, but such coverage is not uniformly positive. These studies suggest limits to the effectiveness of presidential travel to localities, but both investigate trips involving relatively controversial policy. Trips associated with less controversial topics might be more effective in generating positive press.

Peake (2007) content analyzed the front pages of one hundred newspapers on twenty-one randomly selected days in 2006, finding 841 presidential news stories. It is important to note that Peake grounds his study in market and sociological theories of news production, finding that President Bush received more and better news from newspapers that endorsed him and that newspapers with larger circulation and from areas with Democratic representation in Congress tended to offer more presidential news. In contrast, rather than using newspapers as the sampling unit, Eshbaugh-Soha (2008a, 2008b) used presidential speeches or public remarks by Clinton and Bush in 1995 and 2003, their third years in office. He then searched seven newspapers for news about those speeches, locating 288 such stories. Large-circulation newspapers oddly publish shorter stories on the president,

---

[7] By only looking at first years in office, they may overstate the amount of local news coverage. Cohen (2008) finds higher coverage levels during the first year.

[8] Cohen and Powell (2005) and Cohen (2006) look at the impact of presidential travel to localities on presidential approval, with mixed results.

but do so more frequently than do smaller newspapers.[9] Stories emanating from Washington, D.C., have a higher probability of coverage than those from elsewhere.

This small literature should be applauded for its sensitivity to sampling issues and testing of hypotheses derived from several theoretical traditions. Their results indicate systematic variation in news coverage of presidents across local newspapers, in contrast with the consonance hypothesis, which argues that news agendas about national affairs across newspapers are quite similar because of the agenda-setting power of the *New York Times* and other elite press (Comstock and Scharrer, 2005, 180).

Still, this literature is limited in assessing the effectiveness of presidential news management on local coverage. First, Eshbaugh-Soha and Peake (2006) and Barrett and Peake(2007) consider only one type of presidential news management activity, travel to localities. And although Peake (2007) roots his study in concerns of presidential news management (53), his aggregation of stories by newspaper obviates the ability to assess whether different news management activities affect the amount and tone of presidential news. Eshbaugh-Soha (2008a, 2008b), by contrast, provides an initial glimmer of the impact of differing presidential activities, the decision to stay in Washington or not, on presidential news. Yet, none of the existing research develops a theoretical foundation for studying the impact of presidential news management on local coverage. The next section takes a step in that direction.

## PRESIDENTIAL NEWS MANAGEMENT AND LOCAL NEWS

This study focuses on presidential news management as a factor in the production of local news about the president, asking: "What are the causal mechanisms through which news management activities affect local news coverage of the president?"

It is useful to begin by specifying some common assumptions about news and news production. First, events are the primary stuff or raw material of news. Presidential activities can be thought of as one type

---

[9]   These findings may result from the small sample size.

of potentially newsworthy event. Second, the news hole is finite in size. News organizations need a minimum amount of events on which to report. On "slow news days," news organizations may find it difficult to fill the news hole, but for most days, there are more potentially newsworthy events than space available to cover all of them. Consequently, events compete for news coverage, and presidential events compete with nonpresidential events for news coverage.[10] Finally, the news production process is complex, and many factors affect whether or not an event is covered (Shoemaker and Reese, 1996). For present purposes, three factors will affect presidential news coverage: the economics of news production, journalist news values, and news organizations' "political" agendas. Presidential news management affects news coverage of the president through its impact on news production economics, journalists' news values, and news organizations' "political agendas."

## The Economics of News Production

Economic or market models have been found especially useful in integrating a large number of factors that affect news production (Cohen, 2008; Hamilton, 2004). Such models begin with the observation that newspapers in the United States are primarily private enterprises and, thus, must make a profit in order to survive and prosper. The major product that news organizations produce, obviously, is news. Thus, it is useful to think of news as a commodity produced in a competitive market, with presidential news as one type of news. Following from this model, news stories with greater profit potential will be more likely to be published than those with less profit potential, all else being equal.

Profit is a function of the revenues that news organizations collect minus the costs of production. Revenues come from two sources: consumer purchases and advertising. Advertising revenue depends on the size and characteristics of consumers. Thus, consumers affect revenues directly through their purchases and indirectly through advertising. The market model suggests that newspapers will be sensitive to consumer tastes in news; that is, they will offer news that consumers want.

---

[10] Multiple presidential events may compete with each other for news coverage, too.

News production costs have fixed and variable components: physical facilities necessary to produce the newspaper or broadcast; personnel, such as reporters, editors, and other production staff; and the delivery or distribution system. News organizations can employ standard techniques of cost control to lessen their production costs, like increasing efficiency and productivity, subcontracting parts of the production process, and shifting the costs of production to others.

Consider two types of news media content, presidential news and nonpresidential content.[11] In equilibrium, the profit derived from a presidential news story will be equal to the profit from a nonpresidential media content story. If the profit associated with one type of news story increases, we expect news organizations to increase their provision of that type of news story and decrease their provision of the other type, all else being equal.

### Presidential News Management and the Economics of News Production

Based on the market model, presidential news management will influence the local production of presidential news insofar as presidents affect the profit potential of presidential news, either by reducing the costs of news collection or by stimulating demand for presidential news. This perspective on presidential news management differs from that usually found in the literature.

Consider how presidential activities may affect the costs of news production. Presidents may make it easier for reporters to collect news about him, thereby reducing the costs of news production. For instance, the White House provides reporters with a place to work, which it has done since the McKinley administration (Kumar, 1997). The press secretary holds twice-daily news conferences, providing reporters with a steady stream of potential news. Press releases, the president's schedule, and advance notification of presidential announcements also aid reporters in gathering news about the president. The expectation of regular and easy-to-collect news about the

---

[11] Studies often characterize media content as informative (news) or entertaining. Here, nonpresidential news content may be either news that is not concerned with the president or entertainment. This simplification is useful for isolating the factors that affect the production of presidential news.

president creates incentives for news organizations to assign a reporter to the White House beat. Investing in such resources also creates incentives for news organizations to publish news about the president, lest their investment go to waste. Such services subsidize the collection of presidential news, thereby reducing the cost of collecting news about the president.

Such activities may be especially consequential for local newspapers, which often lack the resources to collect news about the president on their own. They may not be able to afford to detail a reporter to the White House or staff a Washington news bureau. Resource-limited newspapers may be especially dependent on White House services and activities for news about the president, as well as on other intermediary news collection services, like the wire services and news syndicates.

Presidential news management activities may also stimulate demand for presidential news among consumers (citizens). As such demand rises, we may witness an increase in the amount of published news about the president. For instance, presidential travel to localities may stimulate local demand for news about the president's trip, piquing curiosity about why the president decided to visit the locality and boosting local pride as a result of presidential attention to the locality. Thus, we would expect higher-than-usual amounts of presidential news coverage when the president visits a locality.

**Implications of the Market Model of News Production**
Presidential news management may stimulate demand and/or reduce the costs of news collection for local newspapers, which the market model suggests should affect the production of news on the president in local outlets. Yet, factors associated with nonpresidential news production may also affect the production of presidential news. Under some conditions, even if presidential news becomes more profitable, the amount of presidential news produced may decline because nonpresidential news has become relatively more profitable. For instance, assume that the cost of producing presidential news declines. Everything else being equal, we would expect an increase in presidential news production. But if the cost of producing nonpresidential news declines by an even greater rate, the amount of presidential news will decline, while the production of nonpresidential news will increase.

The same dynamic holds if revenue associated with presidential news increases, but revenue from nonpresidential news increases at a higher rate. Then we should see a decrease in the amount of presidential news and an increase in nonpresidential media content.

This model has important implications for understanding the provision of presidential news. Theories of presidential news that look only at revenue and cost associated with presidential activities overlook the dynamics that the market model of the presidential news reveals, which will sometimes lead to incorrect predictions about the provision of presidential news. Decisions to run a story on the president are not independent from decisions to run nonpresidential news stories. The comparative profit potential of both types of stories determines how many of each type appear in the news. To understand more completely the provision of presidential news requires that we take into account the factors that affect the profitability of presidential news *as well as of nonpresidential news*, as the market model outlined here does.

### Journalistic Professionalism

Journalists may want to publish a story not because of its profit potential but because their professional judgment tells them that the story *should* be published, that it is newsworthy. In reaction to the yellow journalism of the late nineteenth and early twentieth centuries, which tarnished the reputation of the press, journalism transformed itself by professionalizing. Schools of journalism were established to provide prospective journalists with academic training; professional norms and ethics were developed and agreed on; and national and regional societies were organized to disseminate these norms and reinforce professional behavior among journalists.

Through these practices and institutions, journalists began to view themselves as professionals. Consequently, they developed a template for writing news stories, the inverted pyramid and objective reporting, and established norms for deciding on the newsworthiness of events. Objective reporting entailed the presentation of facts and balance and offering both sides of a story, and importance became a prime criterion for newsworthiness (Graber, 2001; Groeling, forthcoming). Presidents increasingly were thought to be important and, thus, newsworthy.

Professional judgment about newsworthiness need not always run counter to economic considerations. Economic and professional criteria may converge, for instance, when readers demand news about a presidential activity and when journalists deem that presidential action is important and, thus, newsworthy. But sometimes economic and professional judgment about newsworthiness diverge, for instance, when readers think that some stories are "boring" but reporters push for their publication because of their importance. Newspapers may decide at times to publish stories that undermine the bottom line, but limits exist as to how much they can do so lest the financial health and survival of the newspaper be damaged. Resource-laden newspapers may be better able to absorb such professional-based publication costs than those that that are less well endowed.

By heightening the sense among reporters that an action is newsworthy, the president may be able to affect the production of news about him. For instance, presidents may appear important – and more important than other politicians – when engaged in foreign affairs. Presidential travel to foreign nations may be designed in part to take advantage of the impact of foreign affairs on journalists' perceptions of importance. Journalists, thus, will desire to publish stories about the presidential visits to foreign lands because they think such trips are intrinsically important.

Or, when access to the president is restricted and information about the president limited, journalists may increasingly value each additional access venue and piece of information. For instance, if presidents appear at press conferences regularly and frequently, their value to journalists may decline because of the ease of availability. By reducing the frequency of presidential press conferences, the value of any one press conference may rise because of its scarcity and infrequency. Through the regulation of presidential activities, presidents may affect the importance journalists ascribe to them. Journalists' perception of presidents and their particular activities as more or less important is one way presidents may affect their news coverage.

## "Political" Agendas and News Production
Newspapers may have political, policy, and/or ideological agendas that may affect their production of news. By saying that a newspaper has

such an agenda does not mean that the newspaper merely has a point of view about political, policy, or ideological matters, but that it aims to affect debate, and perhaps even outcomes, on such matters. Hence, a newspaper may desire that a particular candidate win an election, that a policy is enacted, or that people's thinking about government is changed.[12] When the newspaper aims to promote its agenda through its pages, it may do so at the expense of economic and professional considerations.

It is important to distinguish the concept of political agendas from media bias, although the two are closely related. Entman (2007) identifies three ways in which the term "media bias" is used: distortion bias, content bias, and decision-making bias. Distortion bias refers to the distortion or falsification of reality. Often those who argue that their side of an issue or debate is not receiving "fair" treatment make this kind of charge, such as conservatives who view the news media as liberal. It is difficult to measure distortion bias, except when facts have been misreported, because no agreed-on standard of "objectivity" exists to serve as a baseline (D'Alessio and Allen, 2000; Druckman and Parkin, 2005; Gilens and Hertzman, 2000; Groeling and Kernell, 1998; Kahn and Kenney, 2002). Content bias refers to the equal treatment of two sides of a debate. Studies of bias in election reporting look mostly at content bias, asking whether the competing candidates receive the same treatment in the news (see D'Alessio and Allen, 2000).

The concept of political news agendas most closely resembles decision-making bias (Entman, 2007), in which the motivations and mindsets of news personnel lead them to produce news of a certain cast. One should not, however, look at the content of the news product to determine if a newspaper has a political agenda. Different decision-making processes may produce the same type of news

[12] In other words, the newspaper has a policy to promote its agenda. When identifying a newspaper as having such an agenda, we usually point to the owner as the source, with the owner requiring the news organization to implement the agenda. For instance, Fox Cable News is often said to pursue a conservative agenda in many of its news broadcasts because of the insistence of Rupert Murdoch, the leading shareholder and founder of the network. But a political agenda can arise from the negotiation among important news personnel, including editors and reporters as well as owners.

product.[13] To say that a newspaper has a political agenda, one must identify a conscious policy to pursue that agenda in its pages.

Viewing the political agenda of a newspaper from this perspective, though admittedly difficult, has important implications for the effectiveness of presidential news management. Basically, a newspaper with a political agenda will, to some degree, be immune to presidential news management activities. Such a newspaper will interpret presidential actions and decisions through the lens of its agenda, not through the perspective promoted by presidential news management activities. Assume, for instance, a Democratic president and a newspaper with a Republican agenda. Almost nothing this president does will affect how this newspaper reports on him. The newspaper will probably report news in a way unsatisfying to the president, but the same president will probably receive more favorable or satisfying treatment from a newspaper with a Democratic agenda. The greater the spread of political agendas across news outlets, the less effective presidential news management activities will be.

## SUMMARY

Presidential news management strategies work through two primary mechanisms, the economics of news production and journalistic professionalism. By contrast, when a news outlet possesses a political agenda, activities associated with the news management strategy will lose their effectiveness. The next chapter begins the empirical analysis of presidential news management on the production of local news

---

[13] For example, a newspaper may be said to be conservative in its news. That conservatism may arise from the political beliefs of news personnel, as they put their ideological stamp on the news. Or the conservative leanings of the news product may come about as the newspaper tries to make the news product appealing to an underserved market. For instance, early talk radio may have possessed conservative leanings to lure conservative listeners, who were alienated from other media outlets, which they felt were "biased" against their conservative proclivities. Third, conservative leanings in the news product may reflect the political orientations of the newspaper's existing readership: Where there are many conservatives (or liberals), the newspaper serving the area may lean in a conservative (or liberal) direction as well.

by focusing on the quantity of presidential news in local newspapers. Succeeding chapters will look at the tone or valence of presidential news in local newspapers, as well as the prominence of the president in local news. The next chapter also introduces one of the major data sets used in this study, the local presidential news database.

# CHAPTER 5

# The Quantity of Local Newspaper Coverage of the President

This chapter addresses the question, "Do presidential public activities affect the amount of news coverage that presidents receive in local newspapers?" The argument here is that local newspapers have become important for presidential public leadership. Presidents have increasingly turned their attention to gaining coverage in local newspapers because those newspapers have credibility with their readers, they have relatively large readerships, and presidents believe that they will generally garner better and more positive coverage from them than from the national news media. This chapter uses the Local Presidential News Database to assess the amount of news that presidents receive in local newspapers.

Before gauging the impact of presidential public activities, we need to assess the amount of local news coverage of presidents. Do local newspapers actually cover the president with enough frequency and regularity for presidents to view them as important complements in their public leadership strategy? If local newspapers do not report much news on the president, presidents cannot rely on them in their attempts to lead public opinion. The Local Presidential News Database indicates considerable presidential news coverage in local newspapers.

## HOW MUCH NEWS COVERAGE DO PRESIDENTS WANT?

How much coverage do presidents seek from local newspapers? On the one hand, the more news there is about the president, the less news there will be about his competitors, such as leaders in Congress. The public may come to view the president as comparatively more important than other political leaders if there is a larger quantity of news about him. By looking less important than the president, these competitor leaders will have a harder time rallying public support behind their efforts and against the president. But when competitors appear less important than the president, the president still cannot be guaranteed that his public leadership efforts will work (Edwards, 2003); however, the prospects of presidential leadership improve when competitors do not look important. As Miroff (1982) reminds us, insofar as the president can "monopolize the public space," his capability to lead the public rises.

This implies for the president that more media coverage is better. Presidents may not, however, always desire high or intense levels of news coverage. During difficult times or when dealing with contentious issues, presidents may prefer less press coverage. Intense media scrutiny may increase public expectations and pressure on the president to resolve an issue or force a president to act when he prefers not to. For instance, during the mortgage crisis of 2008, President George W. Bush initially preferred limited or no government action, thinking that the market could correct the problem in a more timely and efficient manner. Yet, high levels of news coverage on the issue, such as on Bush's lack of involvement and leadership, forced not only greater presidential engagement but also some support for government action to deal with the crisis.

My assumption is that presidents prefer to regulate the amount of news coverage they receive, sometimes seeking greater news coverage and at other times wanting to limit or even avoid being covered in the news, depending on the current circumstances and their goals and agendas. A presidential news management strategy, to be effective, must take into account both the benefits and costs of news coverage.

As noted, there are limits to our ability to empirically assess the effectiveness of presidential news management strategies. First, we are rarely privy to the goals and operational details of a president's news management strategy. We cannot always see the news management strategy in action, and we can never be certain that presidents faithfully and systematically implement their news management strategy. The best we can do is test the impact of presidential public activities on news coverage. Doing so assumes that public activities provide us with a reasonable indicator of the president's news management strategy (Althaus, 2001; Waterman, St. Clair, and Wright, 1999). Variation in the amount and type of public activity thus indicates presidential attempts to regulate their news coverage. Before we can test these ideas, we need to know something about the amount of news coverage that presidents receive in local newspapers. The next section describes the Local Presidential News Database.

## THE LOCAL PRESIDENTIAL NEWS DATABASE

The variety and volume of news erects a high barrier to collecting news on the president, much less on other topics. Studies of newspaper content rely on several data collection or sampling designs, each with its own pitfalls: purposive, convenience, and random and stratified random samples (Long et al., 2005).

Purposive samples select news outlets based on specific characteristics. For instance, the *New York Times* is often studied for national news, with the assumption that the *Times* is representative of national news providers, or more important, that it sets the news agenda for other major news outlets to mimic. Although they are popular for news content analyses (Riffe and Freitag, 1997), purposive samples raise issues of generalizability.

Convenience samples, using whichever media outlet is available, are the least desirable. For instance, in his groundbreaking work of historical trends in presidential news, Cornwell (1959) used the *Providence Journal* as an example of a local newspaper to compare with the *New York Times*, because Cornwell taught at Brown, located in Providence, Rhode Island. In his replication of Cornwell's study, Balutis (1976, 1977), based in Buffalo, New York, replaced the Providence newspaper with the *Buffalo News*. Resource limitations sometime force convenience samples on research.

Random sampling overcomes the limitations of purposive and convenience sampling, allowing generalization from the sample to the population. Randomly sampling newspapers may be problematic because of the great number of very small newspapers with small circulations. Larger newspapers, which are smaller in number but greater in impact because of their circulations, and which often set the agenda for smaller newspapers (Long et al., 2005, 205), may become underrepresented in pure random sampling designs. Thus, Long et al. (2005) argue for stratified random sampling, stratified along important newspaper characteristics, like circulation. The research question should determine the sampling design. Because content analysis of local news on the president is in its infancy, particular attention needs to be paid to these sampling issues. At the same time, feasibility of collecting relevant data also must be kept in mind.

### Data Collection Procedures

The questions posed here require a relatively large number of news stories about the president across a wide variety of newspapers and days, the latter being important to ensure variance across presidential activities. Thus, the Local Presidential News Database content analyses a random sample of local newspapers across a random sample of days in 2000. The year 2000 is used to correspond with the National Annenberg Election Study (NAES), used later in this book to assess the impact of presidential news in local newspapers on public evaluations of the president. Thus, this data set is temporally limited. Insofar as 2000 differs from other years, we may be unable to generalize. For instance, 2000 was a lame duck year for the sitting president. Yet, it is likely that the processes that lead to certain characteristics of presidential news will be similar in other years.

I began with the LexisNexis Academic Universe newspaper database. From the U.S. news menu, I developed a preliminary list of all newspapers from the four regions – Northeast, Midwest, Southeast, and West, for a total of 268 newspapers. From this list, weeklies, specialty, and professional publications (e.g., *Chicago Lawyer*), and those not in the archive in 2000 were eliminated. From the remaining set, twenty-four newspapers were randomly selected for inclusion in the database.[1] Although it contains fewer newspapers than some other studies, like those of Shaw and Sparrow (1999) and Peake (2007), the newspapers here were not selected on any characteristics other than their inclusion in the LexisNexis newspaper archive.

---

[1]   Budget limitations restricted me to 24 newspapers.

How representative is the LexisNexis database? As far as I am aware, there are no intentional factors that would bias the LexisNexis archive, other than the fact that larger newspapers are somewhat overrepresented. Others have used LexisNexis as a population base to draw their samples (e.g., Arnold, 2004). I follow this tradition, trading off some potential but unknown sampling error for access and ability to easily and reliably retrieve presidential news stories.[2]

Table 5.1 lists the newspapers and some of their characteristics. They come from all four regions, some serving large urban centers and others smaller communities. For instance, the *Capital* of Annapolis, Maryland, served a Standard Metropolitan Statistical Area (SMSA) of approximately 35,000 in 2000, compared with the *New York Daily News* and *Chicago Sun-Times*, which circulate in areas of 21 million and 9 million people, respectively. The newspapers also vary in their circulations, with the smallest, the *Capitol Times* of Madison, Wisconsin, having a circulation of about 18,000 compared with the *Washington Post* at 700,000. The average newspaper here has a daily circulation of just below 200,000. Six maintain Washington, D.C., bureaus, whereas two others have access to Washington, D.C., bureaus through the chains that own them. Some are locally owned, including several smaller papers; some belong to regional chains, like Lee; and a number are members of larger national chains, like Cox, McClatchy, and Scripps. The newspapers also represent communities of varying political leanings. Although the average newspaper comes from an SMSA that gave George W. Bush 50.1 percent of the vote in 2000, their vote varied from a low of 33 percent for Bush for the *New York Daily News* and *Providence Journal* to a high of 77.5 percent for the *Idaho Falls Post Register*. This variance in newspaper characteristics will provide us with analytic leverage in understanding the processes by which the president figures on their pages.

Selecting when to sample newspaper content is as important as selecting which newspapers to sample. As Tidmarch and Pitney (1985, 465) so aptly caution with regard to Congress, but also of relevance

---

[2]   An alternative would be to use a true population of newspapers and search their own archives on the Web, but many newspapers charge for such access, and they are not uniform in archiving back issues. Like many previous studies, practical considerations constrained my sampling design.

TABLE 5.1. *Characteristics of newspapers used in the analysis*

| Newspaper* | Circulation | State | Distance to D.C. | SMSA POP. | Bush, % 2000 | D.C. Bureau | Owner |
|---|---|---|---|---|---|---|---|
| Madison, WI Capital Times (4) | 18068 | Wisc. | 848.65 | 426526 | 34.7 | No | Capital Newspapers |
| Chicago Sun-Times (74) | 481000 | Ill. | 702.52 | 9157540 | 39.4 | Yes | Hollinger International, Inc. |
| Lincoln, Journal Star (12) | 77376 | Neb. | 1208.89 | 250291 | 55.4 | No | Lee Enterprises |
| Milwaukee Journal Sentinel (59) | 235704 | Wisc. | 794.92 | 1689572 | 51.3 | Yes | Journal Comm. |
| South Bend Tribune (22) | 71738 | Ind. | 612.62 | 265559 | 50.0 | No | South Bend Tribune |
| St. Louis Post-Dispatch (8) | 277842 | Mo. | 835.94 | 2603607 | 45.9 | Yes | Lee Enterprises |
| Boston Herald (31) | 227583 | Mass. | 442.37 | 5819100 | 35.7 | Yes | Boston Herald Media |
| New York Daily News (71) | 708477 | N.Y. | 228.25 | 21199865 | 33.1 | Yes | Daily News (New York) |
| Providence Journal-Bulletin (29) | 159896 | R.I. | 407.32 | 1188613 | 33.3 | No | Providence Journal Co. |
| Bergen County, N.J., Record (51) | 179634 | N.J. | 233.9 | 884118 | 43.0 | No | North Jersey Media Group |
| Augusta Chronicle (21) | 72894 | Ga. | 555.95 | 477441 | 59.9 | No | Morris Comm. Corp. |
| Annapolis, MD Capital (10) | 42847 | Md. | 32.96 | 35838 | 53.8 | No | Capital-Gazette |
| Charleston (S.C.) Gazette (36) | 51150 | W.V. | 363.19 | 251000 | 51.3 | No | Daily Gazette Co. |
| Raleigh News and Observer (14) | 178210 | N.C. | 282.34 | 1187941 | 49.6 | No | McClatchy |
| Richmond Times Dispatch (14) | 186296 | Va. | 106.27 | 996512 | 56.0 | No | Media General |
| Roanoke Times & World News (4) | 91469 | Va. | 240.83 | 235932 | 56.3 | No | Landmark Comm. |
| Washington Post (216) | 724242 | D.C. | 0 | 7608070 | 33.8 | Yes | Washington Post |
| Albuquerque Journal (22) | 107555 | N.M. | 1886.19 | 712738 | 48.9 | Chain | E.W. Scripps Co. (Calif.) |
| Austin American-Statesman (38) | 183952 | Tex. | 1524.58 | 1249763 | 57.9 | Chain | Cox Newspapers |
| Salt Lake City Desert Morning News (50) | 131710 | Utah | 2231.26 | 1333914 | 65.2 | No | Desert Morning News Co. |
| Idaho Falls Post Register (3) | 26542 | Ind. | 2256.63 | 50730 | 77.5 | No | Lee Enter., Iowa |
| Modesto Bee (14) | 83878 | Calif. | 2807.02 | 446997 | 52.4 | No | McClatchy |
| Press Enterprise (Riverside) (12) | 185053 | Calif. | 2639.47 | 255166 | 53.4 | No | Press Enterprise Co. |
| Salt Lake Tribune (7) | 207254 | Utah | 2231.26 | 1333914 | 65.2 | No | Media News Group (CO) |

* In parentheses next to the name of each newspaper is the number of news stories on the president.

94

TABLE 5.2. *Days used in the analysis*

| Date | Day of week | Stories, $n$ | Stories, % |
|------|-------------|--------------|------------|
| January 17 | Monday | 40 | 3.91 |
| February 6 | Wednesday | 47 | 4.6 |
| March 16 | Thursday | 61 | 5.97 |
| April 3 | Monday | 43 | 4.21 |
| April 23 | Sunday | 70 | 6.85 |
| May 12 | Friday | 54 | 5.28 |
| May 29 | Monday | 40 | 3.91 |
| June 1 | Thursday | 52 | 5.09 |
| June 7 | Wednesday | 41 | 4.01 |
| July 7 | Friday | 56 | 5.48 |
| July 31 | Monday | 44 | 4.31 |
| September 5 | Tuesday | 41 | 4.01 |
| October 6 | Friday | 53 | 5.19 |
| October 15 | Sunday | 71 | 6.95 |
| November 11 | Saturday | 82 | 8.02 |
| November 22 | Wednesday | 44 | 4.31 |
| December 6 | Wednesday | 36 | 3.52 |
| December 13 | Wednesday | 47 | 4.6 |
| December 14 | Thursday | 38 | 3.72 |
| December 22 | Friday | 62 | 6.07 |

*Source:* Local Presidential News Database for calendar year 2000. See text for details.

to presidential news, "Over the course of a year or more . . . there is a familiar cyclical quality to it all [the congressional session], one which is shaped by election demands, new Congresses, new Presidential administrations, recesses and district work periods, and end-of-session backlogs. *When* one studies congressional press coverage influences *what* one will find" [italics in original]. Results and interpretations may be distorted depending on the temporal sampling frame employed."

For instance, Cornwell (1959) and Balutis (1976, 1977) sampled the first week of several months per year, but we do not know how representative these days are. Farnsworth and Lichter (2005) code news from only the first year of a new president in their study, but Cohen (2008) finds a surge in presidential news during their first year in office, presumably to satisfy a curious public about a new president.

To avoid the problem of temporal selection bias, I randomly selected twenty days in 2000. Table 5.2 lists the twenty days and several of their characteristics. Eleven of the twelve months of the year are represented, although one month, December, has four dates, the most of any month, including two adjoining days. Each day of the week is also represented, although Tuesday and Saturday appear only once and Wednesday five times, when on average we would expect each day to appear nearly three times.

Finally, deciding on the newspaper content to select for analysis is an important consideration. Not only do we have scarce information about how much news about the president appears in local newspapers, but we also have little knowledge of where presidential news occurs within those newspapers. Nor do we know what kind of news about the president in local newspapers may affect readers' opinions. Readers may rely on editorials and columnists' articles from the op-ed pages if they trust their local newspaper. Or, trusting their local newspaper to be less biased than the national news, they may rely most heavily on straight news reports. Considering our lack of knowledge, rather than preselect a story type or location, I searched for *any* reference to the president anywhere in the newspapers. The specific search attempted to retrieve all articles in each newspaper on each date that included both the words "president" and "Clinton."

## THE APPEARANCE OF THE PRESIDENT IN
## LOCAL NEWSPAPERS

The process described located 825 newspaper items across 480 paper-days. On average, presidents received 1.7 stories per day, receiving multiple stories for 164 paper-days (34.2%). But some newspapers also failed to report on the president on a given day, which occurred 197 times (41.1%), with the president receiving only one story per paper-day 119 (24.8%) times. Not surprising, the *Washington Post* reported the most stories on the president, 216 times, or 26.2% of all stories. Other newspapers covered the president infrequently, such as the *Idaho Falls Post Register* and the *Capital Times* of Madison, Wisconsin, offering their readers only three and four stories across these days, respectively. The president appeared in local newspapers more often than not and often multiple times in the same newspaper on the same day.

There is also variability in news coverage across days, with an average of fifty-one stories per day across all twenty-four newspapers, ranging from thirty-six to eighty-two stories per day with a standard deviation of 12.6. The president received some coverage from at least several newspapers every day, although there are lighter and heavier presidential news days. The president received higher-than-average amounts of coverage on weekends, averaging 74.3 stories.[3] Peake's (2007) decision to only sample weekdays, thus, may miss some of the most important days for presidential news in local newspapers.

Several factors may account for the weekend surge in presidential news coverage. For instance, the Sunday newspaper is much larger than standard weekday issues. Furthermore, weekends tend to produce less news from government than weekdays. Congress rarely holds weekend sessions and much of the bureaucracy work only on weekdays. But the White House is not idle during the weekend. Administration spokespeople regularly appear on the Sunday news talk shows, and presidents since Reagan have generally given a Saturday radio address, both activities that may generate news about the president.

Figure 5.1 presents a histogram of the distribution of the number of presidential stories by newspaper-day. On nearly 41 percent of newspaper-days, the president is absent from a newspaper, and he appears only once for nearly another 25 percent. But the president appears in multiple stories on about one-third of these newspaper-days, receiving a large number of stories, five or more, on forty-five occasions (9%).

The vast bulk of presidential mentions in news items do not appear on the front page – only 118, or about 14 percent, appear on page one. A search for presidential news on only the front page would have overlooked the overwhelming majority of presidential news in local newspapers. Thus, Peake's (2007) study, which restricts itself to front-page stories, may underestimate by a large margin the amount of local news on the president.

---

[3]  A Poisson regression of the number of stories per day on a dummy variable for weekend (Saturday and Sunday = 1, otherwise = 0) is highly statistically significant (coefficient = 0.46, $SE$ = 0.08, $p$ = 0.000).

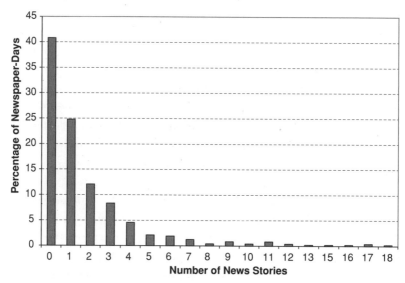

Figure 5.1. Distribution of News Stories on the President by Newspaper-Day, 2000. *Source:* Local Presidential News Database.

Generally, presidents appear in local newspapers in straight news reports. The LexisNexis database usually identifies the type of item (e.g., news, editorials, letters to the editor), doing so for 93 percent of the cases here. Presidents appeared in an item labeled as a news story, local news story, or news brief in 65.5 percent ($n = 540$). But the president was also mentioned in other types of news items with some frequency: editorials, 6.6 percent ($n = 54$); opinion, 10.1 percent ($n = 83$); and analysis, 8.2 percent ($n = 8$). Letters to the editor mentioned the president 2.7 percent ($n = 22$) of the time. The president appears in a variety of places in local newspapers, but primarily in straight news and, to a lesser extent, in opinion pieces, like editorials and columns.

### Summary

How does this data collection compare with the two other major local news data collections, those of Peake (2007) and Eshbaugh-Soha (2008a, 2008b)? Recall that Peake's sample consists of one hundred newspapers on twenty-one weekdays for a five-month period (June through October) 2006, eliciting 841 front-page stories.[4] The major limitations of Peake's design stem from the use of newseum.org for data collection. Newseum.org is a Web site associated with Newseum, a newspaper museum, located in Washington, D.C. Each day newseum.org presents in pdf format the front pages of more than five hundred newspapers worldwide. Although editors may reserve front-page placement for the most important news, the bulk of presidential news in local newspapers appears on other pages. A study of only front pages may give us a skewed picture of presidential news in local newspapers.[5]

Eshbaugh-Soha's (2008a, 2008b) study is more expansive than either this or Peake's study in its temporal scope, sampling from forty-three dates across two years (1995 and 2003), but it used only seven newspapers. The dates he chose were based on a sample of presidential speeches or public statement, with the assumption that presidents must do something publicly for there to be news coverage about him. Although this a reasonable assumption, if we expand our definition of "newspaper coverage" to all items in a newspaper that mention the president, such as editorials, columns, and news analysis, Eshbaugh-Soha's design will miss references to the president on non-event days.

Given that we know so little descriptively about local newspaper coverage of the president, we do not know the implications of Peake's and Eshbaugh-Soha's designs, which restricts the sample to front pages and event-driven days. My sample is more general, collecting any printed mention about the president on any day. Still, my data exist for only

4   Presidents appeared on about 40 percent of front pages in Peake's sample compared to the 24.6% (118/480) in my sample. Differences in sampling design, the newspapers and/or dates chosen may account for the differences. Peake's use of 2006, in which the U. S. was involved in a war, compared to my use of a lame duck presidential year may account for the difference. Until we collect more data, we will be unable to resolve these differences. Still, despite the difference in volume of front-page stories, the factors that produce front-page presidential stories may be the same across our studies. As the findings reported in Chapter 7 indicate, Peake and I find many similar factors associated with the production of front-page news stories on the president.
5   Unfortunately, other than for selected historic days, newseum.org does not maintain an archive. Newspapers front pages appear on the Web site for only one day, the day of publication, thus obviating the possibility of replicating Peake's study.

one calendar year, and thus poses its own issue of generalizability. Thus, in Chapter 6, I present data on local coverage of the president from 1990 through 2006.

## NEWS MANAGEMENT AND THE QUANTITY OF COVERAGE

The theory outlined in Chapter 4 focuses on the effectiveness of presidential news management on local newspaper coverage. As noted earlier, we can only look at the impact of presidential public activities and not at the full scope of a president's news management strategy. Presidential activities may variously affect the production of presidential news through their ability to stimulate public demand for news about the president, to reduce the costs of news collection, and/or to correspond to journalists' professional judgments that a presidential action is newsworthy. The empirical strategy in this chapter asks whether the volume of presidential news varies systematically with the president's public activities, identifying other variables that also may affect local news coverage.

### Public Activities

Factors such as presidential actions, decisions, and pronouncements constitute the raw materials of presidential news: Most news about the president reports on the president doing something (e.g., Eshbaugh-Soha, 2008a, 2008b). Presidents who fail to act, and to communicate publicly that they are acting, may not generate much news. In general, then, indicators of presidential activities should be positively associated with the amount of presidential news. Thus, the "Public Activity Hypothesis": The more public activities in which the president engages, the greater the level of presidential news.

These public activities of the president may stimulate reader demand, reduce the cost of news collection, and correspond to professional norms of journalists about newsworthiness. For instance, presidents who perform numerous public activities may not only convey a sense of action and decisiveness to citizens, but may also suggest that the president is engaged across a host of policies and issues. Citizens may equate such wide presidential activity with the importance of the president. As the public comes to think of the president as increasingly important, they will demand more news about him. Journalists, too, may come to think of the president as important, leading to a convergence in journalist and voter definitions of presidential newsworthiness and importance.

Such presidential activity may reduce the cost of collecting news. Rather than scour numerous agencies of government and committees in Congress for news about governmental activity, newspapers may consolidate and concentrate their news-gathering efforts on the White House. The amount of time and effort, as well as the necessary personnel to collect a wide range of news about government, may be reduced as a result of focusing news collection efforts on the president and his activities. Thus, through presidential activity across many issues, newspapers learn about those issues, but from one government venue, the White House, and possibly from one governmental perspective, the administration's. When other actors, such as members of Congress, bureaucrats, and interest group leaders, are sought out for news, it is as a reactor or commentator on news that was stimulated by a presidential activity.

### Presidential Activity Levels and the Distraction Hypothesis

The Public Activity Hypothesis suggests that greater public activity levels should result in higher amounts of presidential news coverage. But presidents may engage in too many activities, overloading both reporters and citizens with their frenetic level and scope of activity. Overactive presidents may undermine the production of presidential news, but such overactivity may be a conscious strategy designed to distract attention away from controversial presidential decisions and actions.

Assume, for example, that on one day a president makes one major announcement. Journalists will have a relatively easy time translating that announcement into a news story. A single, daily presidential activity focuses attention on that action and signals that the activity, and its subject matter, is important. Next, assume that on the next day the president makes two announcements, but because of the finite size of the news hole and competition from other events, a typical newspaper can file only one story about one of those announcements. Which one should the newspaper go with? In such a case, the president may have muddied the importance signal to journalists. Which of the two activities is more important? Journalists may have to work harder to decide which activity is more important and become the one that should be covered in the news. Perhaps they will seek other sources or will have to do more background work or research on the two activities. The cost of news production, consequently, increases.

As the number of presidential activities per day mounts, the dynamic suggested here should set in. We should not see a linear relationship between presidential public activities and news stories. At some point, adding another activity will not result in an additional news story, and it may detract from the overall production of presidential news as the presidential activities compete with each other for journalists' attention and judgments about relative importance.

If presidents are rational and if their public activities can influence the quantity of presidential news, why would presidents overact, undercutting the amount of their news coverage? I argue that sometimes presidents want to divert attention from controversial decisions and actions. They can do so by increasing the number of events and announcements in any one day or series of days. With a news hole of finite size, after a certain number of events, any attention that journalists pay to one presidential event may lessen the attention that they can pay to another presidential event.

This is a conscious strategy on the president's part, the "Distraction Hypothesis," which predicts a curvilinear relationship between the number of presidential daily activities and news coverage. More presidential activities per day will lead to increased news coverage, but only up to a point, at which time each additional activity will decrease the amount of presidential news coverage. Later chapters present further evidence in support of this distraction strategy.

### Foreign Policy Activity

Some presidential activities may be more newsworthy than others. Scholars often distinguish between the foreign and domestic presidencies, the "Two Presidencies" thesis.[6] It suggests that presidents have greater control and influence in the realm of foreign than in

---

[6]  See Wildavsky (1966), Shull (1991), and Canes-Wrone, Howell, and Lewis (2008).

domestic policy making because the public and the political system hold stronger expectations for presidential leadership in the former than in the latter. Presidential influence derives from this expectation. In part, the public expectation that the president should take the lead in foreign policy making draws on the idea that foreign policy issues may pose a threat to the nation's security and sometimes require swift action. Presidential foreign policy activities may be especially newsworthy because of the inherent threat to national security and the ability of the president to present himself as a decisive and sole actor for the nation. Furthermore, the president possesses advantages in the acquisition and control of information in foreign policy. He may be, at times, the only source of information. The combination of these factors makes him especially newsworthy when engaged in foreign policy–related activities (Bennett, 1990; Entman and Page, 1994; Hallin, 1986; Hallin and Gitlin, 1994; Mermin, 1999; Zaller and Chiu, 2000). In other words, foreign policy activity affects presidential news coverage through both citizen demand and journalist definitions of importance and newsworthiness. Thus, the "Foreign Policy Activity Hypothesis" states that presidential foreign policy activities will lead to higher levels of news coverage.

### Saturday Radio Addresses

The news management perspective also suggests that presidents will take advantage of opportunities offered to them to get their message out to the public through the news media. On some days, presidents have to compete with other events and newsmakers. But not all days are news heavy; competition for news attention will vary across days, and there are some days that are especially known for being light news days. Across the days of the week, there is a cycle to the production of newsworthy events. Most major political institutions are in session only during weekdays. These are among the heaviest news days. The weekends typically produce the least amount of political news because government offices, especially Congress, are not in session.

Presidents understand this cycle and, at least since Ronald Reagan have taken advantage of the dearth of institutional activity on the weekends to gain news attention on these days. Administration spokespeople often will appear as guests on the Sunday news talk shows to tout and publicize the administration's policies, actions, and decisions. One aim is to set the Monday morning news agenda, if not the news agenda for the entire week. But the administration cannot monopolize the Sunday talk shows. Thus, since Reagan, presidents have turned to the Saturday radio address.[7]

The Saturday radio address initially seemed an odd communication venue for presidents. Radio's audience is relatively small, except for talk radio and work commuting hours. The Saturday radio addresses do not attract a large listening audience. Reagan did not employ radio on Saturday to attract a wide mass audience, but instead to set the news agenda on the slowest news day of the week.[8] The topic of the radio address often becomes the subject of the Sunday news talk shows.

It is relatively easy for news organizations to monitor the Saturday radio address and write a story about it the next day. All that is required is an in-house radio and a reporter to listen to the speech. The White House also provides news organizations with the text of the speech to ease news reporting. Saturday radio addresses have become an economical way for newspapers to cover the president, especially for those far from Washington, D.C., and without the resources to cover the president routinely. Thus, we put forth that on Sundays following a Saturday presidential radio address, there will be an increase in the amount of presidential news, the "Saturday Radio Hypothesis."

Research, however, shows that over time, the amount of news coverage of the president's Saturday radio address has declined, presumably because its novelty has worn off (Horvit, Schiffer, and Wright, 2008). Still, the Saturday radio address may be effective in generating news coverage compared with other types of activities and may be especially easy for local newspapers to use in collecting news on the president.

**Press Conferences**

Zaller (1998) argues that journalists want to maintain their independence from politicians while also being active participants in the news

---

[7] George H. W. Bush gave only 20 Saturday radio addresses, but Clinton and George W. Bush maintained Reagan's tradition of a weekly radio address.

[8] There is only a sparse literature on presidential radio addresses, which primarily study their content. See Martin (1984), Rowland and Jones (2002) and Han (2006), whereas Sigelman and Whissell. (2002a, 2002b) look at the image that the president portrays on radio, what they call his "persona."

production process. When political candidates treat them as passive conduits to the mass public, journalists covering the campaign will look elsewhere for news and will be more likely to produce negative and critical news accounts of the candidate. Zaller's "Product Substitution" hypothesis is applicable to the presidential governing context, as well as to the presidential election campaign context for which it was developed.

Among the many methods presidents use to communicate to the public via the news media, the press conference offers perhaps the greatest opportunity for journalist participation in news production. Press conferences typically begin with a prepared statement that the president reads, followed by reporters' questions. By having reporters ask questions and by answering them, presidents allow reporters to become active participants in the news production process. Through these questions, reporters help set the news agenda, bringing up topics and perspectives that the president might not have touched on in his prepared remarks. Also, reporters are highly likely to report on their question-and-answer time in the stories about the press conference. Criticism by journalists that a president has not held a press conference in a long period of time suggests a journalist demand for presidential press conferences.

Press conferences present the risk to the president that reporters' questions will steer the news agenda away from the topic(s) that the president wants to emphasize, that a reporter may ask a question that the president is unprepared to answer, and/or that the president may do a poor job answering the question. Clayman and colleagues (2006, 2007) document the increasing aggressiveness and hostility in reporters' questions to presidents at press conferences during the past forty years.

To some degree, the president may mitigate these risks by limiting the duration of the question-and-answer period, by addressing only questions related to the topic(s) of the press conference, and/or by calling on select reporters who are known to be favorable to the administration, as opposed to more hostile or aggressive reporters. Yet, even when presidents employ these risk minimization techniques, journalists are likely to prefer the press conference format to other presidential communication forms that put them in a more passive role. In addition to the setting of the press conference, in which journalists "interact" with the president personally, making these events newsworthy, presidents hold press conferences only rarely, heightening their newsworthiness.[9]

Press conferences, because of their rarity, signal an important activity. Thus, press conferences may generate presidential news because they stimulate voter demand and because journalists think that press conferences are important. Also, at least for journalists in attendance, the press conference provides a relatively easy way to collect news about the president. Thus, the "Press Conference Hypothesis" argues that press conferences will result in higher levels of news coverage.

### Press Conference–Washington Bureau Interaction Hypothesis

Some news organizations are better situated to take advantage of press conferences than others, in particular those with a reporter at the press conference. News organizations with a Washington bureau are more likely to have a reporter present at a presidential press conference than those without a Washington news bureau because most presidential press conferences are held at the White House. Presidents also hold press conferences with some regularity on their trips to foreign nations. Again, news organizations with Washington bureaus are more likely to have a reporter traveling with the president in his international travels; Washington bureau reporters are the most likely to be assigned by their news organizations and cleared by the White House to accompany the president on overseas travel. Thus, the "Press Conference–Washington Bureau Interaction Hypothesis" suggests an interaction between having a Washington news bureau and a press conference. Only those newspapers with Washington news bureaus will see higher levels of news coverage associated with press conferences.

### Location–Washington Bureau Interaction Hypothesis

For much the same reasoning that underlies the Press Conference–Washington Bureau Interaction Hypothesis, the location of a presidential activity will affect the production of presidential news. When

---

[9] Eshbaugh-Soha (2003) and Kumar (2003) document the rise in press conference frequency in recent years.

presidential communication activities take place in Washington, D.C., news organizations with a Washington news bureau will be better able to cover the event than news organizations without a permanent news bureau in the nation's capital. The same will hold true for presidential events when presidents travel overseas. News organizations with Washington news bureaus will dominate the production of presidential news when presidential events occur in overseas.

Presidents seem well aware of this. As the Washington press corps has become more antagonistic to presidents, presidents have looked to the local news media for more favorable coverage and for coverage that is more likely to follow the president's lead. As long as presidents remain in Washington, the Washington press corps will dominate the production of presidential news.

Presidents can lessen the hold of Washington-based reporters by traveling around the nation. Such travel may not only make the president more available to local news media, but may also reduce the availability of the president to the Washington press. Only some of the Washington press corps will travel with the president around the nation. Also, the topic of the president's domestic trip may not be deemed newsworthy, perhaps being viewed rather as particular to the locality or region of the president's visit. For the Washington-based press, traveling outside Washington not only adds to the cost of news production. These reporters do not think that such trips always address national concerns, so they are less important than activities that take place in Washington. Thus, the "Location–Washington Bureau Interaction Hypothesis," which asserts that there is an interaction between the president's location and the presence of a Washington news bureau and the production of presidential news. When the president is not in Washington and the news organization has a Washington news bureau, we should see a drop in presidential news.[10]

## Other Factors

In addition to these presidential activities, attributes of newspapers may affect the amount of presidential news reported in their pages.

---

[10] Eshbaugh-Soha (2008a, p. 114) finds that there is a greater likelihood of presidential news when he is in Washington.

Some of these factors have been hinted at previously, such as the inter-action of a Washington news bureau with the location of the presiden-tial event. The following suggests that resources, including having a Washington news bureau, plus distance to Washington and a newspa-per's political agenda, may also affect the amount of presidential news in local newspapers.

*Resources.* When comparing news organizations, economies of scale may affect the ability to absorb the cost of presidential news. Assume that for each newspaper, it costs roughly the same amount to produce one presidential news story: There are fixed costs to producing a news story; a reporter, for instance, must be assigned to write the story. The opportunity costs of working on a presidential news story will keep the reporter from simultaneously working on another story.

However, newspapers budgets vary; some newspapers have larger budgets than others. The relative budget that a single presidential news story will assume will be much smaller for newspapers with larger than for those with smaller budgets. A larger budget may translate into a larger staff; for instance, a newspaper may hire two reporters com-pared with another that can only employ one. With two reporters, one can work on a presidential story while the other can work on another news topic, thereby mitigating the opportunity costs for the newspaper. However, the larger newspaper with two reporters may be spending no more on the labor costs of hiring reporters as a percent-age of the total budget than the smaller newspaper that can hire only one.[11] Both Peake (2007) and Eshbaugh-Soha(2008a) find that news-papers with larger circulations, a measure of newspaper resources, tend to print more news about the president than small-circulation newspapers. This leads to the "Resources Hypothesis": Larger, richer newspapers will publish more presidential news than smaller, poorer newspapers.

[11] Smaller newspapers may mitigate these production costs by purchasing news from wire services and news syndicates, which will allow them to publish a presidential news story while its staff reporter works on a non-presidential news story. Large newspapers may also buy some presidential news from these sources, which many do.

***Washington Bureau.*** Despite increased presidential travel around the nation, most presidential news emanates from Washington, D.C. Even when the president is touring the United States or visiting a foreign nation, announcements pertaining to presidential affairs are usually issued in the White House by the press secretary, administration officials, cabinet officers, and the like. Collecting such news directly, in contrast to purchasing it from a wire service, requires having a journalist in Washington. Newspapers may deploy reporting resources to the nation's capital in two ways to collect news about the president directly – either by housing a full-time, permanent bureau or by detailing reporters to Washington on occasion. Newspapers with a Washington bureau or reporter based in Washington have direct access to a greater quantity of news about the president than do newspapers without such reporters. We should expect that the deployment of reporters to Washington, especially on a permanent and institutional basis in a news bureau, will lead to a greater quantity of presidential news in the newspaper's pages.

Six of the newspapers in the sample had Washington bureaus.[12] Two of the smaller newspapers belonged to chains with Washington bureaus,[13] but several major chains lack a Washington bureau (e.g., McClatchy). Having a Washington bureau seems to be related to the amount of presidential news. The five newspapers with Washington bureaus, not counting the *Washington Post*, publish on average 48.6 presidential news stories, compared with 30 for the papers that are members of chains with Washington bureaus, and 19.1 for the sixteen newspapers without any access to Washington bureaus. This leads to the "Washington Bureau Hypothesis": Newspapers with Washington bureaus will feature more presidential news than those without Washington bureaus.

Notably, the newspapers with bureaus are the top six in terms of circulation. Having a Washington bureau may be a function of newspaper resources – richer newspapers (those with larger budgets) can dedicate permanent staff to Washington because they have the resources

[12] *Washington Post, Chicago Sun-Times, Milwaukee Journal Sentinel, St. Louis Post-Dispatch, Boston Herald,* and *New York Daily News.*

[13] *Albuquerque Journal* of Scripps and *Austin American-Statesman* of Cox.

to do so. Yet, it may be the case that having a Washington news bureau results in an amount of presidential news greater than that expected from the general resource level of a newspaper. In other words, a Washington bureau may be a special type of resource that leads to especially high levels of presidential news. Assume two newspapers with equal resources: One has a Washington bureau and the other does not. We might expect the newspaper with the Washington bureau to print more presidential news than the newspaper without one. The multivariate analysis reported in the following will allow us to untangle the effects of overall newspaper resources and having a Washington bureau on the amount of presidential news.

***Distance to Washington, D.C.*** In addition to having a Washington bureau or buying presidential news from a wire service, the only way to collect presidential news directly, if the president is not visiting the locality, is to send a reporter to Washington. The geographic distance of the newspaper from Washington imposes a variable cost on such temporary staff deployment. As the distance from Washington grows, so does the cost of sending a reporter there in both dollars and the amount of time the reporter spends in and en route to Washington. Reporters temporarily deployed to Washington who work for newspapers far from the capital will spend more time away from their desk in the home office than reporters temporarily assigned to Washington whose home newspaper is not located as far away. Thus, a newspaper located relatively near Washington may send a reporter to the nation's capital expecting his or her return shortly. Newspapers farther away will have to do without the services of the reporter at the home office for a longer duration. Furthermore, there are other expenses that distant newspapers may have to pay, such as transportation and hotel costs.

Compare two papers of relatively equal circulation, the *Austin American Statesman* and the *Bergen (NJ) County Record,* the first more than fifteen hundred miles from Washington and the second fewer than two hundred and fifty miles from Washington. Its location in the New York metropolitan area allows the *Bergen Record* reporter to use the Washington, D.C., shuttle, which operates from several airports on an hourly basis and has quite low fares because of the competition among airlines that operate shuttle services to Washington. Furthermore, the flight time from New York to Washington is about one hour. The flight time from Austin to New York is several hours. The data here show that the *Record* has more articles on the president than the Austin paper – fifty-one to thirty-eight. This leads to the "Distance to D.C. Hypothesis": The greater the geographic distance from Washington, D.C., the less news about the president published in the newspaper.

*Newspaper Political Agendas.* As developed earlier, the presence of a political agenda at a newspaper may affect the amount of presidential news. The basic notion underlying this idea is that the content and characteristics of the news reflect the ideological and/or political orientations and preferences of news producers. News producers may use newspapers as a platform to publicize their views and to influence public opinion, political elites, and the course and conduct of public policy.

The link between the political agenda and the tone or "bias" of news stories is relatively clear; a budding literature has begun to explore this connection, but the link between a political agenda and the amount of presidential news is subtler. First, assume that not every newsworthy event can be "spun" easily. Reasonable people will view some events as good news (or bad), and no amount of story bias will be able to alter that perspective. For instance, most people view increases in unemployment and inflation or a military defeat as bad news. Incorporating voices into such stories that argue that such news events should be looked on positively will not be convincing. By contrast, other types of newsworthy events may be somewhat more ambiguous in their interpretation. It is on these types of stories that biased story presentations may have the greatest ability to affect public opinion. When looking for bias in the news, we need to distinguish between those stories that are somehow ambiguous or unclear in meaning or that people need help in interpreting from those that are easy to interpret and for which a consensual understanding exists.

Thus, depending on the nature of the event, news producers opposed to the president may not be able to write a story critical of him that people will take as credible or reasonable. In mirror image, news producers supportive of the president may be more likely to publish stories that cast the president in a positive light and to refrain from publishing stories that can only be interpreted negatively, the "Newspaper Political Agenda Hypothesis." There is some, although far from consistent, support for this hypothesis. Both Peake (2007, 61) and Eshbaugh-Soha (2008a, 114) find that newspapers that endorsed the president were more likely to publish presidential news.[14]


## VARIABLES

The dependent variable for this analysis is the number of presidential news stories per newspaper per day. There is considerable variance in presidential news coverage totals, ranging from zero to eighteen stories per newspaper-day, with an average of 1.7 and a standard deviation of 2.7.

To test the Presidential Public Activity hypothesis, I count the number of presidential "speeches" in the preceding day, using the American Presidency Project Web site of the University of California at Santa Barbara as the data source.[15] Speeches, as used here, consist of all presidential public messages, statements, speeches, and news conference remarks on a given day that are published in the *Public Papers of the President*. In general, I use the American Presidency Project to collect all data on presidential activities, except when noted otherwise. The number of presidential speeches per day averages four, with a range from zero to twelve, and a standard deviation of 3. To test the Distraction Hypothesis, I again use the number of speeches on the previous day, but also a second term, the square of the number of speeches. This hypothesis expects a positive sign for the number of speeches, but a negative sign for the squared term, indicating an increase in presidential news as the number of speeches increases up to a point. At that point, each succeeding speech no longer adds to the amount of news but actually begins to erode it.

---

[14] This assumes that the "wall of separation" between editorial, opinion, and analysis and the news is breached. Kahn and Kenney (2002) find that the tone of news coverage of Senate candidates corresponds with newspapers' endorsement of the Senate candidate.

[15] http://www.presidency.ucsb.edu.

The Foreign Policy Activity Hypothesis is general across presidential foreign policy activities, but here I test only one version, whether or not the president was in a foreign nation on the previous day. Presidential foreign policy activities range from more or less important, but all presidential trips to foreign nations are important. Thus, we can view this as a best-case test of the hypothesis. If we fail to unearth more news coverage on days when the president is outside the United States, then it is unlikely that foreign policy activities, other than the most extreme cases, such as in the aftermath of September 11 or the invasions of Afghanistan or Iraq, will generate a greater amount of news coverage on the president.[16]

The Saturday Radio Address Hypothesis uses a dummy variable for whether the president aired a Saturday radio address to the nation on the previous day, whereas the Press Conference Hypothesis employes a dummy variable for whether the president gave a press conference on the previous day. Because of the disagreement about what constitutes press conferences, I use as a criterion whether the administration labeled the presidential activity as a press conference.

Two hypotheses require interaction terms. To test the Press Conference–Washington Bureau Hypothesis, I create an interaction term by multiplying two dummy variables, whether the newspaper has a Washington bureau or is a member of a chain with a Washington bureau times a dummy for whether there was a presidential press conference on the preceding day. The interaction for the Location–Washington Bureau Interaction Hypothesis multiples the same Washington–bureau or chain member dummy with a dummy for whether the president was in a domestic U.S. location (neither Washington nor a foreign country) on the preceding day.

Newspaper circulation figures, as obtained from the ABC Audit Bureau, measure newspaper resources, a common practice in research (Peake, 2007; Eshbaugh-Soha, 2008a, 2008b). The newspapers in this sample have weekday circulation figures that range from about 18,000 to nearly 725,000, averaging 196,000, with a standard deviation of

---

[16] The data source: State Department, "Presidents and Secretaries of State Foreign Travels" (http://www.state.gov/r/pa/ho/trvl/).

about 189,000. Two dummy variables are used to test the Washington Bureau Hypothesis, one for whether the newspaper has its own Washington news bureau, and the second for whether the newspaper belongs to a chain with a Washington news bureau.

The Distance to D.C. Hypothesis is tested with a variable that measures the number of miles from the newspaper's local market to Washington, D.C. The newspapers differ in their distance from Washington. One newspaper, the *Washington Post*, is located in the nation's capital. Others are more than 2,000 miles from Washington, D.C. The average newspaper is 978 miles away (standard deviation = 891 miles).

The Political Agenda Hypothesis suggests the interaction between several variables. First, I measure general political orientation toward the president with two dummy variables, one each for whether the newspaper endorsed the Democratic or Republican presidential candidate in the 2000 election. It is not clear how endorsements should affect the amount of news directly. Recall that the idea presented earlier suggested that a newspaper's political agenda will affect whether or not stories about the president are published given the ability to interpret events for readers. When events are not easily interpreted for readers, newspapers that support the president (or his party) will go with stories that reflect well on the president, but deciding not to publish stories that reflect poorly on him. The reverse will be the case for newspapers antagonistic toward the president. To capture the tenor of the external environment of events, I use presidential approval, assuming that when approval is high, relevant events will tend to be positive, and when approval is low, such events will tend to be negative.[17] I then multiply these endorsement dummies by presidential approval in the preceding month, using this lagged designation to establish causal direction between approval and news stories. For Republican-endorsing newspapers, I expect a negative sign between this interaction and the amount of presidential news, but a positive sign for Democratic-endorsing newspapers.

[17] Brace and Hinckley (1992) distinguish between positive and negative events, finding an association between event polarity and approval.

## ESTIMATION ISSUES

Several complications and issues arise in analyzing these data. The data consist of a modified, pooled cross-sectional (newspaper) time series (day), and the dependent variable is a count of presidential stories per newspaper-day. Because ordinary least squares (OLS) estimation is thus inappropriate for these data, I use a negative binomial count model.[18] However, the possibility exists that newspapers follow each other in deciding what news to publish on a given day. They may do this to avoid being "scooped," to monitor reporters in the field, and to make sure that their definition of news corresponds to the consensus of other news producers. Thus, news on a particular day about the president across newspapers may not be independent. To account for this possibility, the analysis clusters on day.[19]

Finally, I add a dummy variable for the *Washington Post*. The *Post* is not only located in Washington and generates the largest amount of presidential news, but it also may be thought of more as a national than local newspaper, at least with regard to presidential news. Of course, those who reside in the metropolitan Washington, D.C., area and subscribe to the *Post* daily view it as their local newspaper.

## RESULTS

Table 5.3 presents the results of the analysis. As hypothesized, several presidential activities affect the amount of presidential news, as do some characteristics of newspapers. Newspaper political agendas, by contrast, do not appear to affect the amount of news about the president in local newspapers.

First, and far from surprising, the *Washington Post* dummy indicates that on average, the *Post* produces nearly one more newspaper story

[18] Time series cross sections require that the time units be equally spaced, not the case here. A negative binomial distribution corrects for over-dispersion in the dependent variable, that is, when the standard deviation is larger than the mean. The alpha coefficient measures overdispersion, here alpha equals 0.36, which is larger than 0, with a chi-square of 45.79, $p = 0.000$.

[19] With panel designs, another option instead of random effects is fixed effects, but when doing so, all the variables measured at the day-level, that is all the presidential activity variables, drop out of the estimation.

TABLE 5.3. *Negative binomial estimation of presidential activities and newspaper characteristics on the amount of presidential news*

| | Coef. | Robust Std. Err. | Z | Significance* |
|---|---|---|---|---|
| Washington Post | 0.92 | 0.13 | 6.99 | 0.00 |
| Presidential Activities | | | | |
| N of Speeches | 0.18 | 0.03 | 6.13 | 0.00 |
| N of Speeches-squared | −0.013 | 0.002 | −5.85 | 0.00 |
| Foreign Location | −0.01 | 0.11 | −0.09 | 0.47 |
| Radio Address | 0.69 | 0.06 | 11.40 | 0.00 |
| News Conference | 0.04 | 0.10 | 0.42 | 0.34 |
| News Conf. × Wash. Bureau | −0.02 | 0.08 | −0.29 | 0.39 |
| Dom. Location × Wash. Bureau | −0.12 | 0.09 | −1.32 | 0.09 |
| Newspaper Characteristics | | | | |
| Circulation (000s) | 1.86E-03 | 3.30E-04 | 5.64 | 0.00 |
| Washington Bureau | 0.38 | 0.13 | 3.08 | 0.001 |
| Distance to D.C. | −0.0001 | 0.00006 | −2.03 | 0.02 |
| Newspaper Political Agenda | | | | |
| Dem. Endorsement | −1.25 | 1.96 | −0.64 | 0.26 |
| Rep. Endorsement | −0.004 | 2.64 | 0.00 | 0.50 |
| Dem. Endorsement × Approval | 0.02 | 0.03 | 0.59 | 0.28 |
| Rep. Endorsement × Approval | −0.0008 | 0.04 | −0.02 | 0.50 |
| Pres. Approval | −0.01 | 0.03 | −0.40 | 0.35 |
| Constant | 0.08 | 1.79 | 0.04 | 0.48 |
| /lnalpha | −1.02 | 0.31 | | |
| Alpha | 0.36 | 0.11 | | |

* One-tailed test, all variables predict direction.
*Source:* Local Presidential News Database, see text for details.

on the president than the other newspapers. This effect is highly significant ($t = 6.99$, $p = 0.000$), although the magnitude of the effect is somewhat smaller than one would expect by looking at the average level of presidential news across the newspapers. The *Washington Post* averages 10.8 stories per day; the other newspapers average only 1.3.

With regard to presidential activities, the greater the volume of presidential activities, measured here as speeches, the more presidential news there will be. The coefficient suggests that each additional speech is associated with 0.18 more news stories per day. The number of presidential speeches ranges from zero to twelve, with an average of four and a standard deviation of 3.0. Each standard deviation increase in presidential speech activity will result in 0.54 more stories per day,

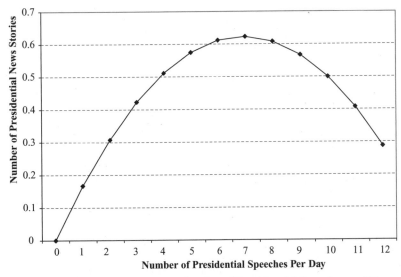

Figure 5.2. Relationship Between Number of Presidential Speeches and Number of News Stories.

a considerable increment given that there are on average 1.7 stories per day. That the coefficient here is less than 1.0 reinforces Barrett's (2007) point that only a small percentage of presidential public activities receives news coverage.

Consistent with the distraction hypothesis, the square of the number of speeches shows a negative sign, indicating that at a certain point, any additional speech reduces the amount of presidential news coverage. The coefficient for this variable is −0.013. At one speech per day, the impact here is slight, −0.013. At the average number of speeches, four, the effect grows to −0.05 and at the maximum number of speeches per day, twelve, the impact is −0.16. Figure 5.2 displays graphically the impact of the number of speeches per day, showing clearly the curvilinear relationship. Presidents receive their highest news coverage totals at about seven or eight public speeches. Thereafter, each additional speech begins to slowly erode the amount of presidential news coverage. At the maximum number of speeches, twelve, a president can expect only 0.29 news stories, or about the same number that he would have received had he made three public speeches.

I also experimented with another nonlinear relationship between presidential public activity and news based on a diminishing returns hypothesis, which argues that each successive presidential public activity will produce a smaller increment of additional news. Unlike the curvilinear model, diminishing returns does not predict a decrease in news production after reaching a certain number of presidential activities, but rather a flattening after reaching a certain number of activities.

To test the diminishing returns model, I logged 1 plus the number of presidential activities [log(1 + number of activities)]. We must add 1 here because on some of the days in the sample the president did not engage in any public activities, and we cannot take the log of zero. I also created a second variable, the square root of the number of presidential activities ($\sqrt{\ }$ Number of presidential activities). In two estimations, I added either of these news variables to the ones already used in the analysis from Table 5.3. For neither of these estimations did the logged or square root variable attain statistical significance, but the variables measuring the curvilinear relationship (number of presidential activities and the square presidential activities) remained significant. According to these data, it appears that the president's public activities has a curvilinear impact on presidential news coverage.

There are costs to high levels of public activity with regard to news coverage. Presidents may increase their public activity level not only to increase news coverage, but also to divert attention from some presidential actions. Overloading the news media with presidential activities may be a conscious presidential strategy to limit news and public attention on particular, perhaps unpopular or controversial actions. Presidents may manage their news coverage totals through deft regulation of their public activities.

The way and timing that presidents seek news coverage is also important. The radio address hypothesis suggests that presidents since Ronald Reagan have turned to this oft-neglected medium, not to attract a wide listening audience, but to take advantage of the low activity level of other news-making institutions of government on the weekend to set the news agenda during slow news days. It appears to pay off. The Saturday radio address produces about 0.7 news stories, a healthy amount given the small average of news stories on the president per day.

None of the other presidential activity variables, including visiting a foreign nation, holding a news conference, the interactions between a newspaper having a Washington bureau and the president being located outside Washington (but within the United States), nor the president holding a news conference attain statistical significance.

All three characteristics of newspapers consistently affect the amount of presidential news – circulation, access to a Washington news bureau, and distance from Washington. In each case, the sign is as expected – higher circulation and access to a Washington news bureau lead to more presidential news stories, whereas greater distance from Washington lowers presidential news totals. Specifically, each additional hundred thousand newspaper readers leads to approximately another 0.2 newspaper articles, a seemingly small amount. However, recall that the most presidential articles per day totals only eighteen, averaging only 1.7. The 0.2 increment amounts to more than 10 percent of the average number of presidential articles per day. Comparing the *Post*, with more than 700,000 readers, with the smallest newspapers, with fewer than 20,000 readers, we can conclude that the *Post*-sized newspaper offers its readers approximately 1.4 more articles on the president on an average day.

Access to a Washington news bureau adds an additional 0.4 newspaper articles per day, about a quarter of the average daily number of presidential newspaper articles. Finally, being distant from Washington decreases the amount of presidential news. Like circulation totals, the effect may appear substantively small – 0.012 fewer stories per 100 miles, or 0.12 per 1,000 miles. For newspapers on the West Coast, which are from 2,000 to 3,000 miles from Washington, the effect ranges from 0.24 to 0.36. Again, these values may appear modest unless one takes into account the small number of presidential news stories for the average newspaper on an average day.

Finally none of the variables testing the newspaper political agenda hypothesis affects presidential news totals. This differs from the conclusions reached by Peake (2007) and Eshbaugh-Soha (2008a,

2008b), who find that newspapers that endorse the president also print more news about the executive, although they do not consistently show such an endorsement effect.

## CONCLUSION

The thesis of this study is that local newspapers have become important elements of presidential communications to the mass public in the post-broadcast age. To play an important role in presidential communications efforts, local newspapers must print a sufficient quantity of news about the president, and presidents must be able to affect characteristics of that news. This study, thus, joins two literatures – that on presidential news management and that on local news coverage of the president. This chapter provides empirical evidence on the quantity of presidential news and the ability of presidents to manage that quantity.

Using a random sample of newspapers across a random sample of days in 2000, we find that, on average, newspapers publish 1.7 news items on the president per day, but that the number of news items varies systematically across newspapers and days. As expected, characteristics of local newspapers, in particular their resource levels, strongly influence the quantity of news published on the president. Newspapers with larger circulation, those with access to a Washington news bureau, and those located closer to Washington, D.C., will publish more news on the president. In contrast, there is little evidence that a newspaper's political agenda affects news quantity, although a political agenda may affect other attributes of presidential news, such as tone (see Chapter 7).

Critically, this analysis finds that presidents can affect the volume of their news coverage through their public activities (Althaus, 2001). If these public activities reflect the president's news management strategy, then we have evidence of the effectiveness of some types of presidential activities on the volume of news coverage. In particular, the amount of news on the president increases when he makes a Saturday radio broadcast and with the number of speeches he makes. But presidents need to be careful not to speak too much. After seven or eight public comments, any additional speech will begin to erode news coverage.

A standard assumption in the literature is that more news is better for the president, the "monopolization" effect (Miroff, 1982). The primary advantage of monopolizing the news space is to push other political leaders out of the news, which is assumed will reduce the perceived importance of these other leaders and increase the perceived importance of the president in the eyes of citizens. If presidents were rational, we would find them speaking at optimal levels, but these data indicate that at times presidents speak too much and thus are not behaving rationally.

An alternative perspective is that presidents may increase their activity level to divert or dilute attention to some actions he takes, actions that must be made public but that might be controversial or unpopular. The "monopolization" perspective assumes that all news must be good for the president, but this alternative perspective suggests otherwise, that presidents are sometimes required to speak publicly about issues, policies, and actions that are controversial and/or politically costly. By speaking too much, presidents undercut the amount of news attention such actions receive, a way of mitigating their harm to the president. This perspective provides a more nuanced understanding of presidential news management than is evident in the existing literature on the public presidency and press–presidential relationships.

Still, the data used here were collected only for 2000, a lame duck presidential year. Can we generalize these findings? To do so requires data from other time points. The next chapter uses a time series of local news from 1990 through 2006, the era in which local newspapers have become important to the president.

# CHAPTER 6

# Trends in Local Newspaper Coverage
## of the Presidency, 1990–2007

Severe party polarization and a fragmented media in the post-broadcast age have led presidents to update their going public leadership style. Presidents now go local much more and go national much less. Although going local entails visiting localities, news coverage provides a more systematic and sustainable method of presidential communications aimed at local public opinion, as long as presidents can influence their local news coverage and such coverage, in turn, affects local public opinion. Chapter 5 demonstrated that presidential public activities and characteristics of newspapers systematically affected news coverage levels of the president in local newspapers. If presidential public activities reflect their news management strategy, the findings from Chapter 5 provide some support for the idea that presidents can affect their local news coverage. However, there are several problems with that analysis.

First, it is based on data for 2000. One may question how typical 2000 is compared with other years. For instance, 2000 was a lame duck year. During lame duck years, public and media attention begin to turn toward the selection of a new president. Based on data collected for this chapter and described more fully in the following, in 2000 the *Washington Post* published an average of 360.3 stories per month on President Clinton, compared with a monthly average of 463.1 for all other months from 1990 through 2007. A similar difference is found for a sample of fifty-six local newspapers across the same years. In 2000, those local newspapers averaged 76.1 stories per month on Clinton but 112.7 stories per month on the president for all other months from 1990 through 2007.[1] Although the volume of news coverage in 2000 may be less than for other years, the processes that lead to presidential news coverage may remain the same once we have taken into account the president's lame duck status in 2000.

Second, Chapter 5 also failed to consider the possible impact of national news outlets on the local production of presidential news, the consonance hypothesis (Comstock and Scharrer, 2005, 178–182). The consonance hypothesis argues that different news outlets will produce roughly the same news for a host of reasons. Intermedia agenda setting, in which major national news outlets set the agenda for other news producers, is one such mechanism. This chapter considers whether local newspapers follow an important national newspaper, the *Washington Post*, in their coverage of the president.

To assess the generalizability of the results from Chapter 5 and to test for intermedia agenda setting effects, for this chapter I collected data on the amount of news on the president in the *Washington Post* and fifty-six local newspapers monthly from 1990 through 2007. This chapter begins with a discussion of the consonance hypothesis and intermedia agenda setting, followed by a discussion of the time series data and the analysis of those data. The variables used in the analysis in Chapter 5 are also used as much as possible in this chapter. To foreshadow the results, although several particulars of the analysis and findings differ from those of Chapter 5, again we find that presidential public activities directly affect the local production of presidential news. But local newspapers to some degree follow the lead of the *Washington Post* in their coverage of the president, providing evidence for intermedia agenda setting.

## NEWS MEDIA CONSONANCE, INTERMEDIA AGENDA SETTING, AND PRESIDENTIAL NEWS

Newspapers differ in many fundamental ways; these differences should affect the mix of news they publish. For instance, they have different

---

[1]  For both the *Post* and the sample of local newspapers, the difference between coverage in 2000 and the other years that Clinton served in offices is statistically significant.

readerships, serve different localities, and encounter different events. Yet, the research on news production suggests otherwise, that there is general consistency or convergence in news coverage across newspapers and other news media; this is the consonance hypothesis (Comstack and Scharrer, 2005). Local television stations uniformly seem to emphasize crime in their newscasts (Dowler, 2006), whereas urban newspapers give special attention to urban development issues, often supporting those efforts (Kaniss, 1991).

Several factors may give rise to consonance in news across outlets. News organizations will produce similar news because they "use similar means to collect the news, which result in similar judgments about what is newsworthy, and they compete with one another so one medium seldom ignores what other outlets are carrying" (Comstock and Scharrer, 2005, 180).[2] For national and international news, there should be even higher levels of consonance because of intermedia agenda setting effects, in which local news outlets emulate the elite newspapers, like the *New York Times* and the *Washington Post*, for several reasons. First, local news personnel respect the elite press and may aspire to employment at such outlets for the prestige, compensation, and influence that may come with working for an elite press outlet. Career aspirations may lead local journalists to emulate the practices and news product of the national, elite press. Second, the elite press defines standards of journalistic excellence, at least among news personnel and professionals.

Third, the local news media generally lack the resources to cover national, international, and presidential news in the depth and scope of the elite press. The results in Chapter 5, as well as those of Peake (2007) and Eshbaugh-Soha (2008a), show that newspaper resources affect coverage of the president. Without sufficient resources to cover "non-local" news as thoroughly as the elite press or the expertise to wade through the many national, international, and presidential events to rate their relative importance, resource-limited local newspapers may reduce their news decision costs by running stories that the elite press deems important. Thus, the elite press serves as a filter

[2]   On the shared news standards of editors, see Gladney, 1996.

for the local news media in deciding which national, international, and presidential events are newsworthy. From this subset of "important" stories, local newspapers will pick and chose which ones to run, basing this "second-stage" decision on factors such as local taste and interest, whether there may be a local angle to the story, and the skills and expertise of local reporters and editors.

Considerable research finds support for intermedia agenda setting (Comstock and Scharrer, 2005, 178–182; Golan, 2006). Protess and McCombs (1991) in particular find that the elite newspaper coverage affects the news coverage of local newspapers and television. In presidential election campaign reporting, Shaw and Sparrow (1999) find that although local newspapers do not entirely mimic the campaign reporting of the national press, the national press has some influence on local reporting of the campaign.

These hypothesized intermedia agenda setting effects may limit the ability of presidents to affect their local news coverage. Presidential public activities may only affect local news coverage insofar as the national news media report on them. Presidents, in other words, will have only an indirect impact on local news coverage. To directly affect local newspaper coverage, presidents may have to target local newspapers and localities more precisely – for instance, by visiting the locality or allowing local journalists to interview them. Given the number and variety of local outlets, such precise targeting surely raises the costs of local news management for the president and may reduce the attractiveness of such a leadership and news management strategy. If, however, presidential public activities have a direct effect on local news coverage, then presidents can more efficiently manage their local news.

This chapter estimates intermedia effects with regard to presidential news and whether presidential public activities affect local news coverage of the president, controlling for those intermedia effects. To that end, I collected a monthly time series from 1990 through 2007 of presidential news coverage in the *Washington Post*, a major national newspaper, and a sample of fifty-six local newspapers. The large number of local newspapers, plus the long temporal span, should provide us with a greater ability to generalize than the data in Chapter 5, which used only data for 2000.

## COLLECTING DATA ON LOCAL NEWS COVERAGE
## OF THE PRESIDENT OVER TIME

The sheer volume of news, the multitude of news outlets, and, until recently, reliance on human coders has hampered collecting data on trends in local newspaper coverage of the president. Electronically accessible archives of large numbers of news outlets help overcome these data collection barriers to some degree, although data collection on certain types of content in news stories may still require human coding. Thus, the next several chapters, which look at the tone of presidential news and other characteristics in the sample of news stories introduced in the last chapter, rely on human coding. Perhaps in the future, "smarter" automated content analysis systems will allow more nuanced collection of news content. At this time, however, the most reliable automated techniques to collect such data count words (e.g., Hart, 1987, 2002).

Word counting may be an appropriate technique for collecting data on the quantity of news, if not on other aspects or attributes of news content. For example, in the previous chapter, a computer-based search of a sample of newspapers in the LexisNexis database began by locating all news stories that mentioned the president, using the search terms "president" and "Clinton." Cohen (2008) used a similar technique to count all news on the front page of the *New York Times* that mentioned the president from the mid-1800s to the late 1990s.

Here I use a similar technique. The LexisNexis database, used to collect the sample of presidential news in 2000, contained only a limited number of local newspapers until recent years.[3] Thus, to create a time series of local news on the president that covers both a wide range of newspapers across a reasonably long period of time, I turned to another online news archive, Newslibrary (www.newslilbrary.com). Newslibrary is a subscription service with more than two thousand participating news outlets. However, retrieving the full text of each news article from Newslibrary is costly and, thus, impractical for in-depth

[3] A search on Lexis-Nexis for "president" and "Bush" for January 1, 1990, through January 5, 1990, recovered news stories for only the *New York Times, Washington Times, Washington Post, St. Petersburg Times, Boston Globe,* and *USA Today,* not exactly a random sample or a very heterogeneous group.

content analysis. Newslibrary does provide the text of the headline and lead paragraph free of charge and allows one to search its entire database of newspapers and other news media for the occurrence of words within the text.

Despite the vast number of news outlets that are now members of Newslibrary, again, only a small number have submitted their news content to the database for a relatively long period of time. In particular, only fifty-six local newspapers, including the *Washington Post*, have been continuous members since the beginning of 1990. Thus, I performed two searches on the Newslibrary Web site, one for all articles in the *Washington Post* that mentioned the words "president" and the president's last name, that is, "President Bush" or "President Clinton," depending on who was in office at the time, that appeared anywhere in the text of the story for each month from 1990 through 2007. The second search asked for the same information for all fifty-six local newspapers collectively.

The decision to aggregate across the fifty-six local newspapers requires justification. I could have, for instance, sampled from the fifty-six newspapers and collected information on each separately. However, fifty-six is a small base to use for sampling, and it is unclear how many newspapers would be required for the final sample. Without a better idea of the relevant population characteristics of newspapers, we will be uncertain as to the representativeness of the drawn sample, a criticism that also applies to the fifty-six newspapers selected here. Large samples are not necessarily free from bias.

Second, I aggregated the fifty-six newspapers because I am less interested in the behavior of a specific newspaper than with local newspapers in general. The fifty-six newspapers vary considerably – they come from twenty-eight states and from all four regions, including large newspapers like the *San Francisco Chronicle* and smaller ones like the *Watertown (New York) Daily Times*. Table 6.1 lists the fifty-six newspapers.

Aggregating the fifty-six local newspapers will help smooth or cancel out any newspaper idiosyncrasies, and insofar as the fifty-six are somewhat representative of all local news coverage on the president, we get a sense of presidential news coverage in the average or typical local newspaper. The time frame of 1990 to 2007 provides us with a long enough period to look at factors that might affect the amount

TABLE 6.1. *Local newspapers used in the analysis for chapter 6*

| Source | State | Source | State |
|---|---|---|---|
| *Anchorage Daily News* | Alaska | *Twin Cities Star Tribune* | Minnesota |
| *Los Angeles Daily News* | California | *St. Louis Post-Dispatch* | Missouri |
| *San Diego Union-Tribune* | California | *New Hampshire Union Leader* | New Hampshire |
| *Fresno Bee* | California | *Hackensack Record* | New Jersey |
| *Modesto Bee* | California | *Press of Atlantic City* | New Jersey |
| *Orange County Register* | California | *Albany Times-Union* | New York |
| *Sacramento Bee* | California | *Buffalo News* | New York |
| *San Francisco Chronicle* | California | *Syracuse Post-Standard* | New York |
| *San Jose Mercury News* | California | *Watertown Daily Times* | New York |
| *Torrance Daily Breeze* | California | *Charlotte Observer* | North Carolina |
| *Colorado Springs Gazette* | Colorado | *Fayetteville Observer* | North Carolina |
| *Denver Post* | Colorado | *Grand Forks Herald* | North Dakota |
| *El Nuevo Herald* | Florida | *Akron Beacon Journal* | Ohio |
| *Miami Herald* | Florida | *Oklahoma City Oklahoman* | Oklahoma |
| *Palm Beach Post* | Florida | *Tulsa World* | Oklahoma |
| *St. Petersburg Times* | Florida | *Portland Oregonian* | Oregon |
| *Atlanta Journal-Constitution* | Georgia | *Harrisburg Patriot-News* | Pennsylvania |
| *Bloomington Pantograph* | Illinois | *Philadelphia Daily News* | Pennsylvania |
| *Springfield State Journal-Register* | Illinois | *Philadelphia Inquirer* | Pennsylvania |
| *Wichita Eagle* | Kansas | *Columbia State* | South Carolina |
| *Lexington Herald-Leader* | Kentucky | *Austin American-Statesman* | Texas |
| *Baton Rouge Advocate* | Louisiana | *Dallas Morning News* | Texas |
| *Times-Picayune* | Louisiana | *Houston Chronicle* | Texas |
| *Boston Globe* | Massachusetts | *Salt Lake City Desert News* | Utah |
| *Springfield Republican* | Massachusetts | *Richmond Times-Dispatch* | Virginia |
| *Worcester Telegram & Gazette* | Massachusetts | *Seattle Post-Intelligencer* | Washington |
| *Detroit Free Press* | Michigan | *Seattle Times* | Washington |
| *St. Paul Pioneer Press* | Minnesota | *Madison Capital Times* | Wisconsin |

of presidential news, and the two series allow us to compare "overall" local coverage of the president with coverage in a major national news outlet. Moreover, the 1990 to 2007 time frame is the period in which local newspapers have become especially important to presidential leadership efforts. For our purposes, it is useful to have data that cover as much of this period as possible.

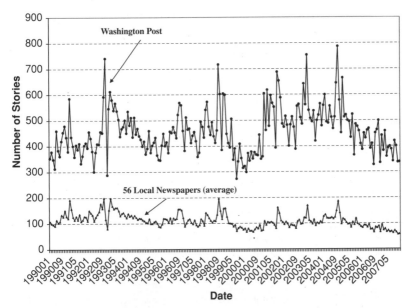

Figure 6.1. Trends in Presidential News Coverage, 1990–2007.
*Source:* www.Newslibrary.com.

## COMPARING PRESIDENTIAL NEWS IN LOCAL AND
## NATIONAL NEWSPAPERS, 1990 to 2007

Based on this retrieval, the *Washington Post* published 98,799, and the local newspapers 1,338,519 stories mentioning the president from 1990 through 2007. The "average" local newspaper published 23,902 presidential news stories. Per month, the *Washington Post* published 457.4 presidential news stories compared with 110.7 per month for the "average" newspaper, or about fifteen stories per day in the *Post* and about three and a half for the average local newspaper. Although the *Post* clearly publishes more news on the president than local newspapers, local newspapers still publish a considerable quantity of presidential news, as also found in Chapter 5.

Figure 6.1 plots the trend in presidential news in the *Post* and the average of the fifty-six local newspapers by month from 1990 through 2007, 216 months. In every month, the *Post* reports more news on the president than local newspapers. The number of stories in the *Washington Post* ranges from 273 to 787, with a standard deviation of

90, whereas the local newspapers set ranges from 56 to 199, with a standard deviation of 28. Also, both series seem to track each other. Often when the *Post*'s coverage peaks, local newspapers' do as well, and the two series correlate at 0.63 ($p = 0.000$).

Occasionally the two series diverge, with a slight upward trend for the *Post* and a downward trend for the local newspapers.[4] Cohen (2008) and Patterson (2000) find declines in presidential news during the past thirty years for the *New York Times* and the three broadcast networks. Thus, it is somewhat odd to find an upward trend for the *Post* series here, but the time periods for Cohen's and Patterson's studies differ from that used here, which may account for this difference. Plus, during most of George W. Bush's administration the nation was at war, which may have led to increased news levels, a hypothesis tested in the following.

## ACCOUNTING FOR TRENDS IN PRESIDENTIAL NEWS IN LOCAL AND NATIONAL NEWSPAPERS

The chapter picks up on the themes from Chapter 5, the impact of presidential public activities, while also adding the intermedia agenda setting perspective to account for presidential news coverage. Because this analysis averages the fifty-six local newspapers, we will not be able to look at the impact of local newspaper characteristics on presidential coverage, often important predictors of presidential coverage in local newspapers (Peake, 2007; Eshbaugh-Soha, 2008a). Finally, this analysis controls for presidential cycles and other important events, such as war and scandal (Cohen, 2008).

### Presidential News Management
Like Chapter 5, this chapter considers whether presidential public activities affect trends in presidential news in the *Washington Post* and the fifty-six local newspapers, including several presidential activity variables used before, in particular the number of presidential

---

4   For the *Post*, the correlation with time is 0.16, $p = 0.03$, and for the local newspapers, $r = -0.49$, $p = 0.000$. A regression of both series on a time counter indicates a monthly increase of 0.22 stories for the *Post* and a monthly decrease of $-0.22$ for the local newspapers.

speeches per month, the number of days per month that the president visited a foreign nation, and the number of press conferences held per month.[5] However, I am unable to include information on the Saturday radio address, as I did in Chapter 5. Across these data, Presidents Bill Clinton and George W. Bush gave radio addresses virtually every Saturday, whereas George H. W. Bush did so less frequently and systematically. Thus, for the Clinton and Bush II presidencies, this variable is a constant, but for Bush I, a radio address variable is nearly perfectly colinear, with a dummy variable for President (George H. W. Bush = 1, Clinton and Bush II = 0). Because we cannot distinguish radio broadcast effects from presidential effects, the radio variable is not used here.

I am, however, able to incorporate a presidential activity that could not be used in Chapter 5, the number of major presidential addresses given per month,[6] defined as in Ragsdale (1998, 149–150): prime-time address aired on at least one of the three major broadcast networks, including State of the Union and Inaugural addresses. On average, presidents made 0.26 major speeches per month, ranging from 0 to 2, with a standard deviation of 0.5. Major speeches are rare events.

We expect major speeches to generate a lot of coverage in both the national and local news media. Almost by definition, these speeches are important. Local journalists do not have to do much work to determine their importance or newsworthiness, and the White House engages in considerable prespeech publicity, notifying the news media of the timing and content of the upcoming speech. These services help journalists prepare to cover the speech. Texts of the speech are often provided to journalists as well, and local reporters can watch the speech in their locality without having to travel to Washington, permitting low cost coverage.

---

[5] For the speeches and press conference variables, I again used the American Presidency Project Web site (http://www.presidency.ucsb.edu/ws/) and the U.S. State Department Web site (http://www.state.gov/r/pa/ho/trvl/) for information on presidential travel. Presidents average 103 monthly speeches (range = 40 to 208; standard deviation = 27.9), 2.1 days of travel outside the United States per month (range = 0 to 13; standard deviation = 2.9), and 2.2 press conferences per month (range = 0 to 9; standard deviation = 1.7).

[6] In Chapter 5, no major address was delivered for the days sampled.

### Long-term Trends, Presidential Term Cycles, and Important Events

In addition to these presidential activities, long-term trends, presidential cycles, and major events may affect the amount of presidential news. Including these factors insures against spurious results and provides a more complete understanding of trends in presidential news, which is important given the dearth of studies on these trends, especially those that test rival hypotheses (Cohen, 2008) and/or look at local coverage patterns (Peake, 2007; Eshbaugh-Soha, 2008a).

*Long-term Trends.* Several studies have documented a decline in hard and presidential news and a rise in soft news during the past quarter century or so (Cohen, 2008; Patterson, 2000). Factors such as the rise of cable television and the Internet (Cohen, 2008), increased competition among news outlets (Hamilton, 2003), shifting public attitudes toward the news media, and changing journalistic styles (Clayman et al., 2006; Patterson, 2000), have been implicated in these trends. The data in Figure 6.1 suggest a modest declining trend for local newspapers, whereas the *Post* seems to be moving in the opposite direction. I included a monthly time counter to pick up any long-term trend.

*Presidential Cycles.* The rhythm of the presidential term may affect the amount of presidential news. A brief surge in presidential news occurs when a new president takes office, as public curiosity about their new leader peaks (Cohen, 2008, 62–63, 81–85). Drawing out the implications of this surge with regard to new presidents, the longer the president is in office, the more likely it is that this novelty and curiously will wear off. And as the next presidential election approaches, without the sitting president as a candidate, public interest will shift to the candidates for the presidency and away from the lame duck president. To measure this, I counted the number of months that the president has been in office.

The reelection campaign of a sitting president may revive interest in the incumbent, if only for the duration of the campaign. Elections mobilize the public, generating interest in the campaign. Presidential elections seem especially effective in this regard compared with other elections. Journalists also consider presidential elections to be highly important and newsworthy. Thus, we are likely to see a surge in news coverage of an incumbent president running for reelection during the campaign season, defined as September and October of presidential elections years, which are coded 1 and 0 for all other months (e.g., September 1992 = 1).

Finally, there is an annual cycle to the presidency that revolves around the State of the Union address. The State of the Union address has evolved into the primary occasion in which the president presents to the public and Congress his legislative agenda for the upcoming year (Cohen, 1997; Light, 1999; Hoffman and Howard, 2006). There is great anticipation of what the president will mention and propose in his address, and a flurry of activity attends the address as the administration prepares its proposals for submission for Congress and builds public support behind those efforts.

Rather than thinking of the State of the Union address as a speech broadcast to the nation on one night early in the calendar year, we should view it as part of a process or campaign lasting several weeks or more. In the weeks prior to the address, administration officials debate the content, wording, and priorities of legislative proposals to be contained in it. Trial balloons may be floated to get a sense of public and congressional reaction, and the administration also begins its pre-address publicity phase to drum up interest and focus attention on the president. After the broadcast, the president follows up with additional speeches, announcements, and meetings, providing details for proposals mentioned in the address, riding the heightened interest and attention that the address generated. To capture this effect, I used a dummy variable, coded January and February = 1, 0 otherwise.[7]

***Other Events: Wars and Scandals.***  Finally, other major events may either increase news coverage about the president because of their association with him or push the president from the news pages. From 1990 through 2007, there were several major events of substantial duration and relevance to the president.

First, the nation fought several major wars. During wartime, presidents assume their commander-in-chief role overtly and explicitly, and wars increase feelings of threat in the public, who turns to the

---

[7]  I use January and February because the State of the Union address is usually delivered in late January or early February, complicating our ability to measure this effect precisely using monthly data.

president for reassurance and leadership. Wars are among the most
momentous of decisions: Few events can rival wars in newsworthiness.
Thus, we should expect an increase in news coverage during wartime,
but Cohen (2008) finds little support for the hypothesis that wars
stimulate presidential news coverage (81–85), arguing that battlefield
commanders may attract more news attention than presidents.

To capture the hypothesized impact of war on news coverage, I
used a dummy variable for the first Gulf War (August 1990 through
February 1991 = 1, 0 otherwise), a dummy variable and counter for
the Iraq War (March 2003 and thereafter = 1, 0 otherwise; March
2003 = 1, April 2003 = 2; December 2007 = 58, 0 otherwise). The
Iraq War counter measures whether interest in the war decreases over
time because of its long duration, a form of war fatigue. Similarly, I
used a dummy variable for September and October 2001 to measure
the effects of the September 11, 2001, terrorist attacks.

During this time period, one major scandal rocked the presidency –
the Monica Lewinsky scandal and impeachment of President Clinton.
We expect a surge in news during the scandal period because of
heightened public interest and journalistic values, which made this
an important story. Cohen (2008) found increased news coverage of
the president during this scandal period in his study of the *New York
Times*. I measured this with a dummy variable, coded 1 for the months
from the opening of the scandal to the impeachment vote (January
1998 through February 1999, 0 otherwise).

## RESULTS

The analysis proceeds as follows[8]: First I estimated a model to account
for temporal variation in the *Washington Post* series. Then I turned to

[8] Several technical estimations issues must be addressed. First, how should we treat
the count of news stories? Count models, like Poisson, are most appropriate for
relatively rare events. When an event, like the publication of a presidential news
story, becomes frequent, the Poisson converges to a normal distribution, which
allows us to use regression models. Both of our dependent variables occur quite
frequently, on average 457 per month for the *Post* and 110 for the local papers. Thus,
I used regression instead of count statistical modeling. Also, analyses using a count
specification (arpois command in Stata), which allows modeling of autoregressive
processes on count data, closely correspond to the regression results presented. The

the local newspaper series. The *Post* series is entered as a variable in the local news series and served as our indicator of intermedia effects. If *Post* coverage of the president affects local news coverage, then we can say that intermedia agenda setting effects exist.

Both models also included a lagged dependent variable, which assumes that news organizations use news-gathering routines, such that past practices and definitions of newsworthiness carry over from the recent past to the future. Events may disrupt those routines in the short term to produce either higher or lower levels of certain types of news coverage. In some instances, these events may be incorporated into news production routines and definitions of newsworthiness, producing a lasting effect on news coverage. The lagged dependent variable captures this effect.[9]

### Presidential News Trends in the *Washington Post*

Table 6.2 reports results for the *Washington Post*. Almost all of the control variables affect *Post* presidential news coverage, as hypothesized. Last month's amount of news strongly affects the current month's news coverage of the president, indicating the strong pull of organizational routines on presidential news coverage. Based on the regression

second major issue concerns the temporal dynamics of the series, whether they are stationary or not. Dickey-Fuller unit root test indicates that the series are stationary. The critical value at 0.001 for the Dickey-Fuller test is −3.47. The test statistics for the *Post* is −8.51 and for the local newspapers is −5.70, indicating stationarity for both. Other diagnostics revealed disturbances in the residuals, indicating complex moving average processes; MA(1) MA(3) for the *Post* and MA(1) MA(2) for the local newspapers. Controversy exists with regard to applying corrections for such complex temporal processes when employing a lagged dependent variable, as I do here. Whether I correct for the moving average processes in the residuals or use ordinary least squares (OLS) without any correction for disturbances in the residuals it has no effect on the independent variables other than trivial shifts in the size of the coefficients.

9   Debate exists regarding the use of lagged dependent variables in estimations. Achen (2000) opposes the practice, arguing that lagged dependent variables will suppress the effects of independent variables, but Keele and Kelly (2006) suggest that they can be used effectively in certain circumstances. Here the lagged dependent variable has a theoretical rationale and is not employed to adjust for autocorrelation, a common procedure. Moreover, in the estimations presented below, not only are most of the other independent variables statistically significant, but including or excluding the lagged dependent variable has little effect on those variables.

TABLE 6.2. *Impact of presidential public activities and intermedia agenda setting effects on news coverage of the president, 1990–2007*

| Variable | Washington Post | | Local Newspapers | |
|---|---|---|---|---|
| | Coef. | SE | Coef. | SE |
| *Washington Post* | — | | 0.16$^{\ddagger}$ | 0.01 |
| *Washington Post*-Lag | 0.42$^{\ddagger}$ | 0.09 | — | |
| Local Newspapers-Lag | — | | 0.07 | 0.05 |
| Trend | 0.40$^{\ddagger}$ | 0.12 | −0.30$^{\ddagger}$ | 0.04 |
| Time in Office Counter | −1.00$^{\ddagger}$ | 0.24 | −0.05 | 0.06 |
| Reelection Dummy | 133.11$^{\ddagger}$ | 24.08 | 19.93$^{\ddagger}$ | 5.60 |
| January-February Dummy | 24.57$^{*}$ | 11.70 | 2.97 | 2.38 |
| September 11 Dummy | 116.13$^{\dagger}$ | 37.97 | 21.92$^{\dagger}$ | 8.76 |
| Lewinsky Scandal Dummy | 55.96$^{\ddagger}$ | 17.45 | 18.42$^{\ddagger}$ | 5.07 |
| First Gulf War Dummy | 16.92 | 21.61 | 8.10 | 6.21 |
| Iraq War Dummy | 38.47$^{*}$ | 18.26 | 19.77$^{\ddagger}$ | 5.62 |
| Iraq War Counter | −1.21$^{\dagger}$ | 0.51 | −0.010 | 0.15 |
| Log of Speeches | 52.97$^{\dagger}$ | 17.46 | 8.26$^{\dagger}$ | 3.46 |
| Press Conferences | 0.46 | 3.10 | 0.74 | 0.54 |
| Days Outside of US | −0.25 | 1.73 | −0.21 | 0.28 |
| Major Speeches | 29.98$^{\ddagger}$ | 9.28 | 4.99$^{\dagger}$ | 1.68 |
| Constant | 0.34 | 91.49 | 16.96 | 17.77 |
| MA(1) | −0.34$^{\ddagger}$ | 0.10 | 0.36$^{\ddagger}$ | 0.09 |
| MA(3) / MA(2) | 0.17$^{\dagger}$ | 0.07 | 0.22$^{\dagger}$ | 0.08 |
| $R^2$ / Adj. $R^2$ | 0.56 | 0.53 | 0.87 | 0.86 |
| Breusch-Godfrey LM Test: | | | | |
| lag 1 ($p$) | 0.99 | 1.49 | −1.08 | 1.20 |
| lag 2 ($p$) | 0.43 | 0.51 | −0.49 | 1.42 |
| lag 3 ($p$) | −0.16 | 0.67 | 0.01 | 0.22 |
| lag 4 ($p$) | −0.10 | 0.25 | −0.03 | 0.16 |

N = 215.   $^{*}p < 0.05.$   $^{\dagger}p < 0.01.$   $^{\ddagger}p < .0001.$
*Source:* See text for details.

coefficient, each past month's news story leads to 0.4 news stories on the president in the current month.[10]

Results also show an upward trend in presidential news coverage. Each successive month leads to an increase of approximately 0.4 news

---

[10] We can assess how long past news coverage persists with the formula $T = 1/(1 −b(\text{lag}))$. Substituting the b of 0.4 for b(lag) produces $T = 1.67$ months: Past news coverage continues to affect news coverage levels of the president for the next 1.67 months. Although past news coverage is a statistically significant influence on current and future news coverage, the speed with which past news coverage levels dissipate indicates the responsiveness of the *Washington Post* to changes in the presidential news environment.

stories, with 184 more news stories in the last compared with the first month of the series, approximately 18 percent of the average number of news stories across the series ($84/457.4 = 18.4$). The *Washington Post* seems to have been bucking the trend of declining hard and presidential news (Cohen, 2008; Patterson, 2000). It is unclear what is driving this rising trend. Perhaps the global war on terror and the Iraq War, among other factors, refocused attention on government and politics compared with the 1980s and 1990s.

Consistent with expectations, the longer a president serves in office, the less news the *Post* reports. Each additional month in office leads to a 1.00 reduction in the number of presidential news stories. At the end of one full term, a president will see forty-eight fewer monthly articles than during his first month in office. At the end of a full second term, the loss totals ninety-six stories. But during election campaigns when the incumbent is running, the president can expect an additional 133 news stories during the campaign season. The cycle associated with the State of the Union address also boosts the level of presidential news by about twenty-five stories.

Other events, like wars and scandals, also affect *Post* coverage of the president. Of the two major wars, the first Gulf War did not significantly affect the amount of presidential news. By contrast, the invasion of Iraq led to an increase in presidential news, but as that war lingered, news coverage of the president declined. The war in Iraq led to an increase of 38.5 stories on the president, which was offset by a decline of 1.2 stories each month that the war persisted. At the end of two full years of war, in February 2005, the net effect of the Iraq war is still positive, with about ten news stories per month. After thirty-two months, slightly fewer than three years, the net effect reduces to zero. By the end of the series, with the war having lasted fifty-eight months, we see a loss of nearly thirty-one monthly news stories.

During the critical months of September and October 2001, in the wake of the terror attacks on the United States, President Bush received 116 more news stories than he would have received otherwise. This is a massive impact on his news coverage and underscores the effect of the terrorist attacks on the national mood and perhaps the nation's desire for presidential leadership and assurance. Increased news attention on the president may explain the revival

of Bush's public standing and his continual use of the war on terror theme throughout his presidency. Finally, the Lewinsky scandal–
impeachment period also led to increased news coverage. During
these months, the *Post* gave the president an additional fifty-six news
stories.

Our primary interest rests with the impact of presidential public
activities and intermedia effects. With regard to major presidential
speeches, each major, prime-time address is associated with an additional thirty news stories per month. As this variable ranges from zero
to two major speeches per month, in a month when the president
addresses the nation twice, he can expect about sixty additional news
stories in the *Post*. Notably, the impact of major speeches controls for
the effects of the State of the Union address. By addressing the nation
on prime time, presidents can expect approximately one additional
news story per day during the month of the address. But presidents
can use prime-time addresses only infrequently. Frequent resort to
prime-time address would undermine their importance to voters.

Thus, presidents rely heavily on other methods of attracting public
and news attention. Daily presidential activities provide the primary
raw material for news about the chief executive. The last chapter found
a curvilinear effect, in which each additional presidential activity or
speech per day resulted in additional news coverage, but only up to a
point, at which further presidential activity begins to detract from the
amount of news on the president. I attempted to replicate the curvilinear model in this analysis but was unsuccessful because of the high
correlation between the number and square of the number of presidential speeches needed to model the curvilinear function ($r = 0.98$).
With both added in the estimation, neither proved statistically significant. When entered alone, the monthly count of presidential speeches
has a positive and statistically significant effect on news coverage.

The aggregation of presidential activities and news coverage into
monthly units, compared with the daily data in the previous chapter,
accounts for the failure to find support for the curvilinear model. The
monthly aggregation of presidential activities truncates the lower and
upper tails on the daily distribution of presidential activities. Recall
that in the previous chapter, daily presidential activity ranged from

zero to twelve, with an average of four. For these monthly data, presidential activity or speeches range from 40 to 208, with an average of about 103. Assuming thirty days per month, we can convert these monthly data in daily counts, which results in daily ranges from 1.3 to 6.9, a much truncated range compared to the daily data. However, the average, 3.4, is quite similar.

Keeping this aggregation property in mind, I experimented with a logged version of the presidential speech variable, as I did in Chapter 5, to test the diminishing returns model, that each additional presidential activity produces a smaller added increment of news coverage. There is some suggestion in these data that the diminishing returns model performs somewhat better than the linear one. The $t$ values and significance levels for the log version are slightly better than for the linear count, whereas the standardized regression coefficients are nearly identical.[11] In an estimation that uses both, neither reaches statistical significance, again because of their high intercorrelation ($r = 0.98$). Table 6.2 presents the results of the logged version, but the substantive findings would be nearly identical if we used the number of presidential speeches instead. Given the slightly better fit, I have decided to go with the logged results. At average levels of monthly activity (4.6 log units), presidents can expect about 243 news stories. This compares with 196 at minimum activity levels (3.7 log units) and 281 for maximum activity levels (5.3 log units). A one standard deviation (0.27) increase in presidential activity generates 14.3 additional stories per month.

The substantive point to draw from these data is that some types of presidential activities affect the amount of news coverage that the president receives in an elite, national media outlet. Insofar as presidents regulate their public activity levels, they can affect how much news they receive. For instance, during periods of "bad" news, presidents may want to minimize their news coverage. They might be able to accomplish this by restricting their public activity level or, alternatively, by jacking up their activity level with "positive" events in the hope of reducing coverage given to the "bad" events.

---

[11] For the count of speeches variable, b = 0.51, SE = 0.19, $t$ = 2.70 and $p$ = 0.007, whereas for the logged version, b = 49.84, SE = 17.76, $t$ = 2.81, and $p$ = 0.005.

**Trends in "Typical" Local Newspapers**

Do these presidential public activities directly affect news coverage in local newspapers, or, as the intermedia agenda setting hypothesis predicts, do local newspapers merely follow the lead of the *Post* in covering the president? If intermedia agenda setting determines local news coverage of the president, then we should see coverage of the president in the *Post* affecting local newspaper coverage, without presidential activities registering as significant predictors of local news coverage.

The estimation for local newspapers differs from that for the *Post* in two ways. First, I replaced the lag of the *Post* variable with the lag for local newspapers to assess the impact of local newspaper routines on news. Second, I added the contemporaneous number of *Post* stories to test the intermedia agenda setting hypothesis. Table 6.2 presents the results.

First, the number of news stories in the *Washington Post* has a strong positive effect on local newspaper coverage of the president. Each additional news story in the *Post* leads to 0.16 news stories in local newspapers. Although this may seem like a modest impact, recall that local newspapers report less news on the president than the *Post*. At average reporting levels in the *Post* (457.4), local newspapers will offer readers 73.2 news stories. Intermedia effects appear to strongly affect local news reporting of the president. But a considerable amount of local news reporting on the president still derives from other sources. For instance, the $R^2$ is 0.86 with the *Washington Post* variable included, but it drops to 0.74 when it is excluded. Based on such a calculation, intermedia effects account for about 12 percent of the variance in local news reporting, a substantively significant but not dominant amount.

Past news coverage in local newspapers does not affect current news coverage. It appears that local newspapers have not established an internal organizational routine with regard to covering the president, other than relying on national news coverage as a cue. Local news coverage of the president is a function of intermedia effects and short-term reaction to relevant presidential events, such as presidential activities.

Some presidential public activities directly affect local news reporting of the president, controlling for these intermedia effects: Intermedia effects tell part of, but not the whole story of local presidential news coverage, echoing Shaw and Sparrow's work (1999). Consistent with these results, neither press conferences nor travel outside the United States affects news reporting totals, but major speeches and the log of monthly presidential speeches do. Each major presidential speech results in an additional five news stories per month for a maximum effect of ten stories when the president makes two such broadcasts in a month.

For presidential speeches, average logged activity levels (4.6) will lead to about thirty-eight monthly news stories on the president (4.6 times 8.3). This compares with about thirty-one and forty-four stories, respectively, for presidential activity at its minimum (3.7) and maximum levels (5.3). A one standard deviation shift in such presidential activity (0.27) leads to only about a 2.2 shift in news coverage, which, like the results for the *Post*, appears small, but there is little variation in public presidential activity on a monthly basis.

It is important to note that presidential activities have a significant effect on local presidential news coverage *independent of intermedia effects*. Although presidential activities do not seem to produce as much local news as the intermedia effects, at times presidential activities can produce a substantial amount of local news coverage. Daily presidential activities, the primary raw materials for presidential news, lead to an average of about one story per day in local newspapers. Such activities keep the president in local newspapers on a daily basis at higher levels than they would be if local newspapers only followed the lead of national news outlets. Some local news reporting on the president, thus, is independent of national news coverage.

Many of the other control variables also affected local news coverage of the president above and beyond the effects of the *Post*. Local newspapers exhibit a declining trend in presidential news coverage, which runs counter to the upward trend of the *Post*. Each successive month decreases presidential news in local newspapers by about 0.30 stories. From the first to last month in the series, presidents can expect about sixty-five fewer stories (0.30 times 215 months). This downward shift is somewhat offset by the growth trend in the *Post* through the intermedia effects of the *Post* on local coverage.

Only one presidency cycle variable affected local news coverage of the president, the reelection season. During election months with an incumbent president, local newspapers will add 19.9 presidential stories. But neither the January/February period associated with the State of the Union address nor the counter of how long a president has served in office affects local news totals directly. Any effects of these cyclical variables are seen in *Post* coverage of the president. That presidential reelections garner especially greater coverage in local newspapers, even after controlling for their strong effects on the *Post*, suggests that either local journalists view reelections as especially newsworthy or that local newspaper readers demand high levels of such news.

Several of the major event variables also affect local presidential news coverage, but neither the first Gulf War dummy nor the Iraq War counter produced statistically significant effects. The remaining variables each had similarly sized effects. The two months associated with the September 11 terrorist attacks led to nearly twenty-two more local news stories during those months, and local newspapers reported about eighteen more news stories on the president during the Lewinsky scandal period. The Iraq War lead to an increase of about twenty stories per month.

**CONCLUSIONS**

The analysis in this chapter supplements that of Chapter 5. Using a sample of days and newspapers for 2000, Chapter 5 found that presidential public activities, in particular the number of daily speeches and the Saturday radio broadcast, resulted in local news coverage of the president. There are two important limitations to the analysis of Chapter 5: the restriction to 2000, a lame duck presidential year, and the inability to control for intermedia agenda setting effects. The first limitation is important for assessing the generalizability of the findings. The second limitation is important for assessing whether presidential activities designed with news coverage as a goal can directly affect local news coverage or whether local news coverage of the president is filtered by national news coverage. If the national media entirely determine local news coverage of the president, then presidents cannot effectively use a local support-building strategy that relies heavily on garnering local newspaper coverage.

With these limitations in mind, I collected time series data on local and national news coverage of the president from 1990 through 2007, the period for which we should find presidents using a local support-building strategy. The analysis in this chapter finds that although national presidential news strongly influences local news coverage of the president, national coverage does not fully determine local presidential news coverage. Presidential public activities, which in part are designed to produce news coverage, directly affect local newspaper coverage of the president independent of national news coverage.

Still, there are important limitations to the analyses presented in both of these chapters. They tell us only about the quantity of presidential news, not its content. In a comparison of the quantity of local and national news on the president, the possibility exists that, despite the similarities in quantity, the mix of news stories, their content and emphasis, and other attributes might vary. The next chapter addresses these concerns by asking what affects the tone of local news coverage of the president in local news.

# CHAPTER 7

# On the Tone of Local Presidential News

The rise of party polarization, the increasing negativity of the national news media to the president (Clayman et al., 2006, 2007; Cohen, 2008), and the fragmentation of the news media in the post-broadcast age, among other factors, have led presidents to revise their leadership and support-building strategies. Presidents of the past two to three decades no longer rely so heavily on a leadership strategy that tries to mobilize broad-based national support (i.e., going national). Instead, presidents increasingly turn to narrower constituencies for support (Cohen, 2008), such as localities.

For a going local strategy to be successful in building support for the president, the local news media must cover the president in sufficient quantity, and presidential leadership efforts must affect local news coverage of the president. The previous two chapters provided evidence for both of these points using two sets of data, one from a random sample of days and local newspapers in 2000 and the second from a time series of local newspaper coverage from 1990 through 2007.

Yet, it is not enough for presidents to be covered in local newspapers and for presidential actions to affect the amount of local coverage. Local newspapers must cover the topics that presidents want covered; that is, the local news agenda must, to some degree, follow the president's agenda. Moreover, presidents want their news coverage to be positive and supportive. Presidents, among others, believe that negative and critical news coverage will undermine their leadership efforts (Brody, 1991).[1]

---

[1] Brody's (1991) seminal study shows that positive news coverage is associated with higher approval and negative news coverage with lower approval. However, at least

**145**

Arguably, presidents have turned their leadership efforts increasingly to local news media because they think the local media will be less harsh in its coverage of them and/or that they will have greater success in affecting the tone of local news than they will with the national news media. Graber (2001, 232) and Cohen and Powell (2005) suggest that local news coverage of the president will be more positive than national news coverage, although neither study provides systematic, direct evidence. Recent studies of local news coverage of the president (Eshbaugh-Soha and Peake, 2006; Barrett and Peake, 2007; Peake, 2007; Eshabaug Soha, 2008b) find variability in how local newspapers cover the president. The question raised in this chapter asks whether presidential actions can affect the tone of local newspaper coverage of the president.

The most important factor under presidential control that affects the tone of news coverage is whether the news directly quotes or heavily paraphrases the president and/or administration spokespeople. Presidents are more likely to receive positive news coverage if they are directly quoted than not quoted. Moreover, the results presented demonstrate that presidents are quoted in the news frequently and that often, *only the president or administration spokesperson is quoted.* These findings somewhat counter conventional wisdom, which predicts that presidents will not be quoted much and that the dictates to write a balanced news story should result in negative and critical comments from other political leaders, especially when the administration is quoted. Thus, this chapter not only analyzes the factors that affect the tonality of presidential news in local newspapers, but it also assesses the factors associated with the decision to quote the president.

## RESEARCH ON THE TONE OF PRESIDENTIAL NEWS

Studies of the tone or valence of presidential news are rare, and those that look at the tone of local news coverage of the president are

for the past quarter century, Cohen (2008) fails to detect a connection between the tone of national news coverage and presidential approval. Even if the tone of national news coverage no longer affects presidential approval, the tone of local news coverage may have such approval implications, for instance, because of the higher credibility and relatively large audiences of local newspapers.

even rarer. The sheer volume of news about the president makes it costly, time-consuming, and difficult to collect data on the tone of presidential news. The number and variety of local news outlets compound the cost of collecting presidential news.

Assessing the quantity of news entails an electronic search of newspaper archives that can efficiently gather news reports that contain word combinations accurately. In contrast, determining the tone of a news story requires appraising meaning. The presence of words may elicit the tone of a news story, but in the case of presidential news stories, we need to determine if the relevant words pertain to the president, for instance, whether the president is being supported or criticized. Intelligent automated programs that can reliably assess this and other types of meaning in news stories and other texts are still in their infancy. Consequently, most studies of tonality in presidential news rely on human coding, an extremely costly data collection method with its own issues of reliability, validity, and measurement error.

As a consequence of these barriers to data collection, there are few studies of the tone of presidential news, the bulk of which only look at national news,[2] and only a handful of studies that look at the tone of local news. For example, Eshbaugh-Soha and Peake (2006) and Barrett and Peake (2007) consider only coverage of presidential trips to localities, whereas Peake (2007) and Eshbaugh-Soha (2008b) study broader samples of presidential news.

Several of the studies on news tone merely present descriptive statistics on the tone of presidential news (e.g., Grossman and Kumar, 1981; Farnsworth and Lichter, 2005) or the impact of the tone of news on presidential approval (Brody, 1991; Erikson, MacKuen, and Stimson, 2002). Others grapple with the factors that affect the tonality of presidential news, providing some insights and hypotheses for this analysis. None, however, tests for whether the president can affect the tone of his news coverage, other than the few studies that look at presidential travel to localities, which *do not* find that local travel uniformly results

[2]  E.g., Grossman and Kumar, 1981; Brody, 1991; Groeling and Kernell, 1998; Erikson, MacKuen, and Stimson, 2002; Farnsworth and Lichter, 2005; Cohen, 2008; Groeling, forthcoming.

in positive coverage (Eshbaugh Soha and Peake, 2006; Barrett and Peake, 2007).

According to that research, the local political context and characteristics of newspapers seem to affect the tonality of presidential news. Using an economic model, Eshbaugh-Soha (2008b) found that corporate-owned and larger newspapers have higher levels of negative news, presumably because negative news attracts readers. Similarly, he found a positive association between community political leanings and tonality, with newspapers seeking to avoid alienating readers and their political sentiments. It is important to note that, Eshbaugh-Soha found that unfavorable sources led to negative news. Peake (2007) also found that the local political context affects tone, and in some specifications, corporate ownership leads to negative news, but unlike Eshbaugh-Soha (2008b), he found that endorsements affect tone. In their study of President George W. Bush's domestic trips in 2001, Barrett and Peake (2007) again found that local political context affects tone, as do the availability of adversary sources and whether the item is analytic or not, but that the partisan tilt of a newspaper has little impact.

Across these studies, findings are often mixed and contradictory, probably a function of different sampling frames, measurement, and model estimations. But all seem to agree that local political context affects the tonality of presidential news in local newspapers. None, however, looked at the ability of the president to affect the tone of his local news coverage, the primary question of this research. Barrett and Peake's (2007) study of Bush's domestic travel, which matches newspaper coverage to the locality the president visited, suggests that this type of presidential activity, which may be designed explicitly to produce positive news, is ineffective (also see Eshbaugh-Soha and Peake, 2006, who make a similar point). Extrapolating from this finding, one might expect only limited ability of presidents to affect their local news coverage.

## MEASURING THE TONE OF PRESIDENTIAL NEWS

The studies reviewed code the tonality of presidential news in a variety of ways. Although the assumption underlying this literature is that the tone of presidential news can be measured, no consensus has emerged on the procedures for doing so. Some studies code at the statement level (Farnsworth and Lichter, 2005); others code the general impression of the entire story (Patterson, 2000). Still others use sentences, which they then aggregate to the story level (Peake, 2007; Eshbaugh-Soha, 2008b). Until we have a better understanding of reader psychology, debate will continue on the proper units to code (e.g., statement, sentence, paragraph, or story) and what constitutes a negative or positive story.

With this in mind, the coding procedure used here aims to maximize intercoder reliability to minimize the number of choices that coders have to make. Tonality was coded only for stories that mention the president. A controversial assumption underlies this coding rule if we aim to understand the impact of news on presidential approval, one important reason for wanting to know something about the tone of news and the topic of Chapter 8 (Brody, 1991; Cohen, 2008; Groeling, forthcoming). This coding rule assumes that only news that explicitly mentions the president will enter into the public's evaluations of the president. Yet, presidents may be held accountable for news (events and conditions) in which they do not appear, such as the state of the economy (e.g., the monthly report on changes in unemployment and/or inflation). However, the immediate aim of this research is to understand the factors that affect the tonality of presidential news, with an eye on whether presidents can affect the tone of their news coverage.

Coders were asked to read through each story that mentioned the president and code the first sentence that made a positive or supportive comment about him as well as the first sentence that made a negative or critical comment. This creates two dummy variables, one for whether a positive/supportive comment was made (coded 1, 0 signifying no positive/supportive comment in the story) and another for whether a negative/critical comment was made (coded 1, 0 signifying no negative/critical comment in the story).

To determine whether a positive/supportive or negative/critical comment was made, coders were instructed to "consider the story from the president's viewpoint: If you were president, would you feel that the story hurts or helps you? If you think that the story will hurt, then code it as negative; if it helps, then code it as positive. Positive or negative comments can be found in quotes of someone being interviewed in the story, the description by the journalist, or even a personal comment by the journalist. More specifically, negative news stories will have someone in the story, including the journalist, who will "criticize the president and/or the president's policy, action, nomination, etc., or oppose the president, or point out a failure for the president (e.g., loss in a vote in Congress)." By contrast, a positive news story will have someone in the story, including the journalists, who "praise or laud the president and/or the president's policy, action, nomination, etc., or demonstrate support for the president, willingness to follow the president, or point to a success."

Some stories may include both positive and negative comments and/or sentences. Other stories may be purely descriptive, offering no position for or against the president or any judgment about the president as a leader, his policies, or actions. Through this coding scheme, stories will fall into one of four categories: They will have either a positive but no negative comment (*Positive*), have a negative but no positive comment (*Negative*), have both a positive and a negative comment (*Balanced*), or have neither a positive nor a negative comment (*Descriptive*).

Measuring the tone of presidential news using these coding rules makes several underlying assumptions about reader psychology. First, newspaper readers do not interpret a news story as positive or negative toward the president unless there is an overt comment in the story. Second, newspaper readers will see a story as either "positive" or "negative" toward the president when it contains either positive or negative comments. Readers will, by contrast, classify stories that contain some combination of positive and negative comments as mixed or balanced.

Recall that the coding scheme only asked coders to score the first positive and first negative comment, not the total number of positive and/or negative comments. At this point, we do not know how readers process tonal or directional statements in news stories. Do they tally up all positive and negative comments, registering a story as positive if it contains more positive than negative comments? Do they count each tonal comment equally in classifying a story as positive or negative? Do they count early comments more heavily than later ones, or does the first directional comment determine the reader's assessment of the

TABLE 7.1. *Distribution of positive and negative comments in presidential news stories*\*

| | Negative comment | |
|---|---|---|
| Positive comment | No | Yes |
| No | 354 (42.9) | 216 (26.2) |
| Yes | 155 (18.8) | 100 (12.1) |

\* Cell entries are n's and percentage of total in parentheses.
N = 825.

*Source:* Presidential Local News Database, Calendar Year 2000.

story's tone? Do some comments count more heavily among readers because of the commenter, as Groeling (forthcoming) suggests? Do different readers assess comments differently? For instance, do more educated and politically informed readers take into account more information than less educated and politically informed readers, and do the more educated and politically informed make more refined judgments?

At this point, we do not know the answers to these questions and, thus, cannot settle on the best method for collecting meaningful data on the tonality of presidential news. The categorization scheme used here does not make refined coding decisions because of the lack of a strong theory of reader psychology to guide coding.

A research assistant and this author coded each story at least twice. Coding of positive and negative comments appears quire reliable. There is 95.5 percent agreement for coding positive comments and 96.6 percent agreement for negative comments. Intercoder reliability statistics, which provide more formal tests, are also quite impressive. For Cronbach's alpha, the reliability coefficient should exceed 0.8, which it does in both cases, with 0.96 for negative codes and 0.95 for positive codes. Cohen's kappa should exceed 0.7, which is also the case for both the negative codes at 0.93 and the positive codes at 0.90. These are quite high intercoder reliability scores for data such as these.

The modal category stories contain neither a positive nor a negative comment; that is, they are purely descriptive (42.9%; see Table 7.1), repeating Grossman and Kumar's (1981) finding for an earlier time period. A substantial percentage of stories (12%) are "balanced," containing both positive and negative comments. But purely negative stories are more common than purely positive ones by 7.4 percent. Negative or positive stories occur quite frequently, with about one-quarter of stories being negative (26.2%), compared with one-sixth (18.8%) being positive. Despite claims of massively negative presidential news, we found that the largest category contains no directional comments, and whereas purely negative stories occur more frequently than positive ones, they do not do so by a startling or overwhelming amount. The dependent variable used in the following combines the positive/negative dummy variables, producing a three-category variable: negative is scored $-1$ (26.2%), neutral/balanced is scored 0 (55.0%), and positive is scored 1 (18.8%).

## PRESIDENTIAL NEWS MANAGEMENT AND THE TONE OF LOCAL PRESIDENTIAL NEWS

The theory presented in Chapter 4 argues that presidential news management affects news production indirectly, either through subsidizing news production costs, stimulating demand, and/or by influencing journalists' perceptions of story importance. Analyses in Chapters 5 and 6 provide evidence that presidential public activities, indicators of presidential news management strategies, affect the quantity of presidential news. News coverage must reach a minimum quantity before it will be useful for the president's leadership aims. But presidents also care about the way in which a story is written as well as its content. Coverage by a newspaper will do little good for the president if the story focuses on topics that differ from those of concern to him; that is, if the news agenda on the president differs from the president's agenda. Similarly, presidents prefer that stories support rather than criticize him and his actions.

Can presidential news management activities affect the tone of news coverage, as we have found it seems to affect the quantity of presidential news? It may be harder to affect tone than quantity. The presidential desire for positive news runs counter to journalistic norms for balanced, objective reporting, in which two sides of an issue are presented, the president's and a critic of the president. The presidential desire for positive news might also run counter to the economics of news production, according to which there seems to be a belief that negative news is of more interest to readers than positive news.

Moreover, Zaller's (1998) product substitution hypothesis suggests that the more presidents control and restrict reporter access to information and limit journalists as active participants in the news production process, the more negative the news will be. Restricted access in the White House not only will lead journalists to write critical stories, but will also compel them to find alternative news sources. For most policy areas, save perhaps foreign policy, there are many sources of information besides the president and the administration, such as members of Congress and representatives of interest groups, to whom journalists can turn, many of whom may be administration critics. Thus, presidents may not be as able to influence the tone as prior the quantity of their news coverage.

## Location

The rising aggressiveness of the Washington press corps (Clayman et al., 2006, 2007) motivated presidents to finds way to reduce the hold of Washington-based reporters on the production of presidential news. Richard Nixon established the Office of Communication to diversify administration outreach efforts (Maltese, 1992), and presidents increased their local travel (Powell, 1999; Cohen and Powell, 2005; Graber, 2001), assuming that the local media would offer the president a gentler hand with regard to news coverage (but see Barrett and Peake, 2007; Eshbaugh-Soha and Peake, 2006). Presidential location may hypothetically affect the tone of news, with stories emanating from Washington being more negative than either domestic or foreign stories because of the concentration of Washington-based reporters at presidential events in the nation's capital.

## Foreign Policy Topics

Presidents arguable possess greater resource advantages in foreign than in other policy areas.[3] Unlike domestic policy, where many news

---

[3]  See the vast literature on the "two presidencies" thesis. Shull (1991) brings together most of the major works. Also see Canes-Wrone et al. (2008) for a recent test.

sources exist and are willing to speak to the press to publicize their viewpoints, a greater proportion of foreign policy news emanates only from the executive. To some degree, the president is a monopoly provider of information on foreign policy topics, especially in the early stages of international crises and other major events that involve the United States. Journalists may have no one else to turn to, in effect becoming "government's little helper" (Zaller and Chiu, 2000) by providing primarily supportive news. If journalists "index" debate on foreign policy issues but the president is usually the only authoritative source, presidents should receive more positive news coverage on foreign policy and international relations issues than on domestic ones.[4] To test this hypothesis, each presidential news story was coded for whether a foreign policy issue was the primary topic of the story.

### Radio Addresses

The previous results suggest the agenda-setting power of the Saturday radio address (also Horvit, Schiffer, and Wright, 2008) but no one to date has assessed whether the radio address stimulates supportive news coverage. Presidents give Saturday radio addresses to fill a slow news period, the weekend, when Congress is out of session, which suggests the decreased availability of administration critics. Because it may be harder for journalists to find sources to comment on the president's address on Saturday, we should expect the radio address to stimulate not only news coverage, but also positive news coverage compared with other days of the week.

### Press Conferences

Press conferences may provide journalists with an important forum to co-produce the news by asking presidents pointed questions. Clayman et al. (2006, 2007) find that over time, journalists have become more aggressive in their questioning of presidents at press conferences. Perhaps because of this aggressiveness, among other factors, presidential press conferences decreased in frequency until the late

---

4  Bennett (1990) provides the seminal statement of the indexing hypothesis, which has spawned a large literature that mostly presents supportive evidence (e.g. Entman and Page, 1994; Hallin 1986; Hallin and Gitlin, 1994; Mermin, 1999; Zaller and Chiu, 2000).

1980s (Hager and Sullivan, 1994), when an uptick in press conferences began (Eshbaugh-Soha, 2003; Kumar, 2003, 2007). Aware of
the potential risk of press conferences, presidents can reduce the risk
by not taking questions from reporters, clearing questions prior to
the press conference, allowing questions only on particular topics,
selecting only friendly reporters to ask questions, and/or punishing
reporters who ask "the wrong" questions after the press conference
is over.[5] Although these devices may reduce the risk potential of a
press conference, they probably will not eliminate the risk. Thus, we
hypothesize that news following the day when the president gives a
press conference will have a higher probably of being negative than
news on days that do not follow presidential press conferences.

### Presidential Activities and the "Distraction" Hypothesis

Chapter 5 presented evidence of a curvilinear relationship between
the quantity of presidential public activities (speeches) and the
amount of news coverage. I argued that presidents increase the number of activities to very high levels to distract press coverage from
controversial actions and decisions, the distraction hypothesis. This
hypothesis should also apply to the tone of presidential news. Following a coalition of minorities process (Mueller, 1970), we should expect
that presidential announcements, decisions, actions, appointments,
and the like often will meet with opposition and criticism. Presidential decisions, in other words, benefit some citizens but not others.[6]
As the number of presidential decisions increases, the number of citizens or groups that dislike a presidential decision should increase. This
should lead to an increased likelihood of negative news as journalists

---

[5]  For instance, after directly challenging Richard Nixon at a 1974 press conference
before the National Association of Broadcasters, then–CBS White House correspon-
dent Dan Rather was removed from the White House press corps and moved to CBS's
*60 Minutes* (Paletz and Vinegar, 1977–1978).

[6]  Canes-Wrone (2001a) argues that when there is a wide distance between the public's
and president's preferences and the status quo is closer to the president's preference
than the public's, the president should not go public, but stay private. From her
perspective, we should not observe presidents taking unpopular stands in public.
The difference here is that Canes-Wrone's theory applies to the production of public
policy. My analysis applies to a broader set of circumstances, some of which require
presidential action, and thereby force a public announcement, such as appointing
someone to office.

seek out opposition sources to comment on (criticize) the president. Yet, following from the distraction hypothesis, after a certain number of presidential actions on a given day, the news media will be overwhelmed with topics on which to report, and reporting costs increase as journalists must determine which topics are the most important. In efforts to cover fully the president's decisions, even the major decision of the day may receive less news attention to make room for the other presidential activities of that day. Through these distraction processes, once a certain amount of activities has been reached, further activities by the president will no long lead to more negative news, but actually will reduce the amount of negative news. As we saw with regard to the quantity of presidential news, we should see a curvilinear relationship between the daily amount of presidential activity and the tone of presidential news. As in Chapter 5, I test this hypothesis with the number and the square of the number of presidential speeches.

## Quoting the President

Presidents may find it advantageous for their news coverage if they can persuade the news media to directly quote them (or an administration spokesperson). First, quoting the president may reduce the amount of news space afforded to administration critics, as news space is finite and limited. Second, journalists may be more likely to quote presidential statements that support the president's position and goals than more neutral, descriptive information that the president also might supply. Such supportive or "spin" comments from presidents and administration spokespeople provide frames that journalists can use to write their stories. This leads to a third benefit to the president of being directly quoted: The president gets to set the terms of debate, that is, frame an issue or controversy. A fourth benefit is that a quote allows the president to counter a critic directly. This may blunt the effect of the criticism.[7]

---

7  An important research question asks who wins with the public when a critic challenges the president and the president responds. For those without strong priors or predispositions, the institutional prestige and position of the president should give him some advantages. As anecdotal evidence, in the budgetary debates between President Clinton and the Republican Congress in 1995, Clinton emerged as the winner in the public eye, despite his recent defeat on his health care reforms. In fact, Republicans in part may have challenged the president because that defeat

From another perspective, being quoted may not provide the president with any advantages. Journalists may quote presidents in stories only for controversial subjects, which may bring greater attention to the controversy than the president would prefer. Also, by framing the issue, presidents may ease the job of journalists in tracking down a source to interview, someone who may criticize and counter the president. Furthermore, presidents may be quoted only when they make comments in response to critics; that is, quotes may merely present a defensive reaction from the president, rather than allow the president to frame the terms of debate.

Ideally, a president prefers that he alone is quoted and that no opponent is also quoted in the story. The norms to produce objective news, that is, balanced stories in which both sides of a debate are allowed to present their case, may mean that presidents rarely appear as the lone voice in a news report. In fact, when they engage in activities that lend themselves to quotes, these actions may serve as lightening rods for journalists to find alternative and critical sources.

Another possibility exists: that presidents are rarely directly quoted or even heavily paraphrased in news stories. The sound bite literature on presidential campaigns suggests that the amount of space on broadcasts in which candidates are allowed to speak for themselves has diminished. Journalists instead act as news event mediators, replacing candidates as speakers in news stories (Adatto, 1990; Barnhurst and Steele, 1997; Bucy and Grabe, 2007; Hallin, 1992; Lowry and Shidler, 1995, 1998; Russomanno and Everett, 1995). Although the sound bite literature focuses on campaigns and broadcasting, the same general patterns may apply to local newspaper coverage of presidents in office. From another perspective, Barrett (2007) finds that presidential announcements about their legislative positions often fail to receive any news coverage.

Presidents may use several rhetorical or other devices to increase the likelihood of being quoted. First, pithy or catchy phrasing and easily conveyed arguments may lead journalists to quote the president (or his

seemed to weaken his public standing and lead to the strong Republican showing in the midterm elections. Thus, even when the president seems weak, he may still be a potent rival. More systematic research on this point, however, needs to be done.

spokesperson) directly or to heavily paraphrase him. Journalists also may be more apt to quote the president if, instead of merely providing journalists with a handout on the president's decision or action, he actually makes a public statement, preferably one that can be filmed for television. Taking the time to make such a statement, even if no questions from reporters will be allowed, signals the importance of the president's announcement.

At this point, we know little about how often the president is quoted, the conditions under which he is quoted, and the implications of being quoted. With that in mind, each story is coded for whether the president and/or a top administration spokesperson was directly quoted or heavily paraphrased. The president is quoted in about 7.5 percent of stories (62 of 825). Invariably, when quoted, the president/spokesperson had something positive to say. Journalists, it seems, like to quote valence statements, at least when they come from the president.

To the president's advantage, when he is quoted, only occasionally are opposition voices or critical comments also in the news story. Only slightly more than half of the time when the president is quoted is a critic also quoted (53.2%). The president is allowed to speak uncontested 46.8 percent of the time that he is quoted. Thus, quoting the president leads to either a positive or a balanced story, based on the coding scheme here, and uncontested presidential quotes account for a significant minority of all positive news about the president (18.7%).

According to these data, it appears that a strong association exists between being quoted and positive news. Providing material to quote does not always or routinely lead journalists to seek out critics of the president. It may be the case that the decision to publish a positive story affects whether the president will be quoted, in effect reversing the causality between quoting and the final tone of a story. Before making such a claim, we need to determine if quoting, when controlling for the other variables in the analysis, has any impact on story tone. The analysis presented in the following finds such an effect. Consequently, the last section of this chapter raises the question of what factors determine whether a president is quoted, to shed some light on this issue.

## NEWSPAPER CHARACTERISTICS AND THE TONALITY
## OF PRESIDENTIAL NEWS

Most of the existing research on the tone of local presidential news focuses on newspaper characteristics, especially from an economics of news production perspective (Barrett and Peake, 2007; Peake, 2007; Eshbaugh-Soha, 2008b). These studies generally find that corporate-owned newspapers produce negative news at higher rates than independent newspapers and that the local political context, an indicator of the news preferences of readers, also affects the tone of presidential reporting.

This analysis controls for the following attributes of newspapers and the local environments in which they operate. As in past research, I used a dummy variable for whether a corporation owns the newspaper.[8] Because corporations keep a close eye on the bottom line and assume that negative or critical news is more likely to generate reader interest, corporate newspapers are hypothesized to produce more negative news on the president than are independent newspapers.

Also included is a variable for circulation size, often used as a measure of resources (Eshbaugh-Soha, 2008b). More resourceful newspapers, according to this argument, need to rely less on White House and official sources in producing news stories. Being more independent, resourceful newspapers may be more likely to take a critical stand. Thus, we expect higher circulations to be associated with a greater incidence of negative news.

I also coded each newspaper for whether it had access to a Washington news bureau, with the hypothesis that such newspapers will be more likely to produce negative news. Reporters with a Washington news beat, as is the case for those who work from these news bureaus, are more likely to hold the assumed antagonistic or confrontational news-gathering style and orientation (Clayman et al., 2006, 2007) and, thus, write negative news stories more frequently than reporters not working in the nation's capital.

---

[8]  The following newspapers in these data are coded as independent: Madison, Wisc., *Capital Times*; *Milwaukee Journal Sentinel*; *South Bend Tribune*; *Providence Journal-Bulletin*; Bergen County, N.J., *Record*; *Augusta Chronicle*; Annapolis, Md., *Capital*; Charleston (S.C.) *Gazette*; *Salt Lake City Desert Morning News*; and the *Press Enterprise* (Riverside).

Also, in accordance with existing research (Peake, 2007; Eshbaugh-Soha, 2008b), I measured the political leanings of the local environment with the Gore percentage of the two-party 2000 presidential election vote in the region that the newspaper considers its primary distribution area. Newspapers will reflect reader preferences so as not to alienate them and also to develop a reputation as part of the local community (McManus, 1994; Underwood, 1998; Hamilton, 2003; Cohen, 2008).

Finally, I coded for the national political context, with the president's approval level in the most recent Gallup reading prior to the date of publication, according to the hypothesis that when presidents are less popular, there is more material or reason to criticize them. When presidents are highly popular, less material exists that can be used for criticizing them. Also, in the spirit of the local political context argument, newspapers may be reticent to criticize a president when he is popular, again to avoid alienating readers.[9]

### Political Agenda of Newspapers and Tone

The connection between a newspaper's political agenda and the tone of presidential news is clear-cut – news producers will use their newspaper as a forum to publicize their political views, perhaps to persuade its readers or to influence policy debate (Bovitz, Druckman, and Lupia, 2002). This idea closely resembles the debate on bias in the news. Anecdotally, for instance, some claim that news executives, such as Rupert Murdoch, use their control over news organizations, *New York Post* and Fox Cable News, to further their political agendas. Critics from both the right and left, such as conservatives Ann Coulter and Bernard Goldberg and liberal Eric Alterman, charge that the media, especially the national news media, are politically biased. The literature on local newspapers and the presidency finds mixed results here: Peake (2007) shows endorsement effects on tone, but Eshbaugh-Soha (2008b) does not.

---

[9] As far as I can tell, this hypothesis has never been tested, much less considered. The literature on tone and popularity (e.g., Brody, 1991) views news as exogenous to approval. My hypothesis opens up the possibility of a more complex relationship between tone and approval, with approval being able to affect subsequent tone.

TABLE 7.2. *Relationship between newspaper endorsement behavior in 2000 and news tone*

|  | Newspaper endorsement in 2000* | | |
|---|---|---|---|
|  | Republican (n = 253) | No endorsement (n = 158) | Democrat (n = 414) |
| Negative | 29.3 | 26.0 | 24.4 |
| NeutralBalanced | 54.6 | 61.4 | 52.9 |
| Positive | 16.2 | 12.7 | 22.7 |

* Cell entries are column percents. Chi-square = 10.4 ($p$ = 0.035), Kendall's Tau$_b$ = 0.07 (Asymptotic Standard Error = 0.03), Pearson's $r$ = 0.08 ($p$ = 0.02).

Following past practices (Peake, 2007; Eshbaugh-Soha, 2008b), I used the newspaper's presidential endorsement behavior in 2000 to determine the political tendencies of the newspaper producing the endorsement hypothesis. Newspapers that endorsed Bush in 2000 are coded −1, those that endorsed Gore +1, and newspapers that did not endorse a presidential contender are coded 0.

At the zero-order level, there appears to be some difference in the slant of presidential news consistent with this hypothesis. Table 7.2 shows that Democratic newspapers are more likely to report positive (22.7%) news than newspapers that made no endorsement in 2000 (12.7%) and newspapers that endorsed Bush (16.2%). Democratic-endorsing newspapers also printed less negative news than either of the other types of newspapers (Democrat endorsement = 24.4%, no endorsement = 26.0%, Republican endorsement = 29.3%). Although there appears to be slight differences, these are statistically significant.

These data also show two other important attributes of news tone across these types of newspapers. A majority of news for each type of newspaper is balanced or neutral, with nonendorsing newspapers leading here. Second, negative news outweighed positive news for each type, with both Republican-endorsing and nonendorsing newspapers publishing about 13 percent more negative than positive news, but a much narrower difference for Democratic-endorsing newspapers at 1.7 percent. These data are consistent with the notion that news on the president has tended on balance to be more negative than positive, especially in recent decades (Cohen, 2008).

## Type of News Item

Whereas past research on local presidential news has collected only data on straight-news reports, I collected data on any type of news item that referred to the president. This decision was guided by a lack of knowledge about "news coverage" on a larger scale about the president as well as about how readers process such information. From a descriptive standpoint, it is informative to learn something about mentions of the president across different types of news items, from straight news to analytic pieces, to editorials and columnists, and even to letters to the editor, and whether any association exists between type of news item and tonality. For example, the "wall of separation" model between editorials and news predicts that straight news should be composed mostly of balanced or neutral stories and that positive- and negative-toned stories will be more common in analytic pieces, editorials, and letters. Kahn and Kenny (2002), however, in their study of local coverage of Senate elections find that newspapers seem to breach this wall, with endorsements correlating with the tone of coverage of candidates in straight-news stories.

Furthermore, we know little about how average citizens process different types of news items when evaluating the president. On the one hand, readers may view all "news items" as authoritative by the mere fact of being published. On the other hand, readers may discriminate across type of news items. The small literature on endorsements suggests that such editorial decisions affect voting decisions and election outcomes (Erikson, 1976; Hollander, 1979; Coombs, 1981; Hurd and Singletary, 1984; Kahn and Kenney, 2002; Druckman and Parkin, 2005), which suggests the potential for editorial and other types of publication effects on public evaluations of the president.

I classified news items into five categories based on how the newspaper identified the story: straight news (59.6%); op-ed pieces, which combine editorials and columnists (16.6%); analysis (8.2%); letters to the editor (2.7%); and a residual category of various other news items that appear infrequently or stories that the newspaper failed to supply with an identification (12.8%). Most of the news items published on the president are straight news reports. If the wall of separation between "opinion" and "news" exists, then this category should have

TABLE 7.3. *Type of news item and tone*

| Tone | Straight news | Op-ed | Analysis | Letter to the editor | Other |
|---|---|---|---|---|---|
| Negative | 20.5 | 43.1 | 32.3 | 50.0 | 21.7 |
| Neutral or Balanced | 60.4 | 36.5 | 50.0 | 45.5 | 59.4 |
| Positive | 19.1 | 20.4 | 17.7 | 4.5 | 18.9 |
| Net Negative* | 1.4 | 22.7 | 14.6 | 45.5 | 2.8 |
| N | 492 | 137 | 68 | 22 | 106 |

* Positive percentage minus negative percentage.
*Source:* Local Presidential News Database, 2000.

fewer positive- or negative-toned stories, which may account for why the majority of news items here are neutral or balanced.

Table 7.3 presents a cross tabulation of the tonality of each type of news item. As the table indicates, straight news presents the highest total of neutral or balanced stories, at 60.4 percent. Not unexpectedly, the op-ed category has the lowest percentage of neutral or balanced mentions, at 36.5 percent. Moreover, straight news seems to be evenly balanced between negative and positive news stories, with only 1.4 percent more negative than positive stories. In contrast, the other three categories, op-ed, analysis, and letters to the editor, lean decidedly in the negative direction. One-half of all letters are critical of the president, as are 43.1 percent of editorials. The following analysis presents results using the op-ed and letters-to-the-editor variables. In various experiments, neither straight news nor news analyses reached statistical significance.

## ANALYSIS ISSUES

This analysis of news tone employs the data from the Local Presidential Database used in Chapter 5, but unlike that chapter, which aggregated by day to obtain a count of the number of presidential news stories per newspaper-day, this analysis uses these data at the story level. The unit of analysis here is story-newspaper-day, 825 observations.[10] Using

[10] Peake (2007) aggregated news stories to obtain a score for each newspaper. Doing so, however, restricts his ability to test for story-specific factors that might affect tone.

the individual news story as the unit of analysis raises several analytic issues.

First, because the dependent variable is coded −1 for a negative story, 0 for a neutral or balanced story, and +1 for a positive story, I used ordered probit. Second, on many occasions, newspapers reported multiple news items on the president. The same presidential event may inspire several items in a newspaper. The tone of such related stories may not be independent of each other. Furthermore, even if each news item reported or referenced different presidential events, how one event is reported may affect the tone of how a second story is reported. One presidential event may color how editors and news production personnel view other presidential events on the same day. To take into account these possibilities – that several reports on the president on the same day may not be independent – I clustered the analysis on day.

Third, on nearly two hundred newspaper-days, a newspaper failed to report a story about the president. Insofar as factors that affect the production of presidential news also affect the tone of that news, our sample of 825 might be biased. Newspapers that are antagonistic to the president, for instance, might not report a story supportive or positive toward the president. In statistical terms, our sample is censored on the days that newspapers failed to report a story on the president.

To take into account bias, I employed a Heckman selection model. The Heckman selection model proceeds in two steps. The first step estimates whether a newspaper ran a story on the president, coded 1 if there is a story, 0 if there is no story. I use variables from the earlier analysis that were found to predict the quantity of presidential news as predictor variables for this first stage.[11] Then these selection

---

[11] Because the dependent variable is dichotomous, the first stage estimates use probit, with the following independent variables: newspaper circulation, distance of the newspaper from Washington, D.C.; newspaper access to a Washington, D.C., news bureau; the number of presidential speeches and the number of speeches-squared; and whether the president gave a radio address on the previous day. All but the Washington bureau variable were statistically significant. More detailed results can be obtained from the author.

A major complication arises in this procedure in STATA 9.0, the analysis package that I used. It does not have a Heckman selection routine for the case of the second stage as an order probit and the selection stage as probit. The dependent variable in this analysis is ordered probit. Thus, I ran the estimation in two stages, first the probit

estimates are entered into the tonality equation. The Mills Inverse
Ratio, essentially a variable produced from the estimates of the first
stage, is entered into the second stage equation as a variable. In all
cases, the Mills Ratio failed to reach statistical significance. Comparison of second stage estimations with and without the Mills Ratio shows
identical results, with only minor differences in the size of coefficients.
Thus, I presented results without using the Heckman Selection estimations.

**RESULTS**

Table 7.4 presents the ordered probit results of two estimations,
one that includes all of the variables discussed earlier and a second,
reduced form that includes only statistically significant variables. The
reduced form estimation is useful because it reveals that one variable,
newspaper endorsement patterns, which did not appear to be significant in the full estimation, is now significant. First, note the variables
that failed to reach statistical significance. These included several presidential activity variables – giving a news conference, a news story on
a foreign policy topic, and locating the presidential event in Washington, D.C. None of these affected the quantity of presidential news,
either.

Perhaps more important, none of the newspaper characteristics
variables was found to be significant. These variables included corporate ownership, circulation, whether the newspaper had access to a
Washington bureau, and local political sentiment. The results here

---

selection model. From that I computed the Mills Inverse Ratio from the predicted
values of the probit selection model. The Mills Inverse Ratio is then entered into an
ordered probit estimation of the dependent variable, tone, as a variable. One may
recover the Mills Inverse Ratio (MIR) by running the Heckman routine in STATA. By
specifying the "Mills" option, STATA will create a new variable for the Mills Inverse
Ratio.

I also ran a standard Heckman selection model, which uses regression for the
second stage and probit for the selection stage. The results of this analysis parallel
the ordered probit results presented in the following. Furthermore, the lambda
coefficient, which tests for the effects of selection on the second stage results, is not
statistically significant, reinforcing the interpretation that selection does not affect
the tone of presidential news.

TABLE 7.4. *Impact of presidential activities, newspaper characteristics, newspaper political agenda, and type of news item on tone of presidential news*

| Variable | Full-form estimation | | | | Reduced-form estimation | | | |
|---|---|---|---|---|---|---|---|---|
| | Coef. | SE | Z | P | Coef. | SE | Z | p |
| *Presidential Activities* | | | | | | | | |
| N of Speeches | -0.06 | 0.03 | -2.04 | 0.02 | -0.05 | 0.03 | -1.87 | 0.03 |
| N of Speeches-squared | 0.006 | 0.002 | 2.80 | 0.002 | 0.005 | 0.002 | 2.63 | 0.004 |
| President Quoted | 1.04 | 0.15 | 6.93 | 0.000 | 1.00 | 0.14 | 7.26 | 0.000 |
| Radio Address | -0.10 | 0.05 | -2.02 | 0.04* | -0.12 | 0.05 | -2.36 | 0.02* |
| News Conference | 0.11 | 0.10 | 1.10 | 0.27 | | | | |
| In Washington, D.C. | -0.03 | 0.11 | -0.30 | 0.76 | | | | |
| Foreign Policy Topic | -0.14 | 0.09 | -1.63 | 0.10 | | | | |
| Presidential Approval | 0.03 | 0.01 | 2.18 | 0.02 | 0.03 | 0.01 | 1.90 | 0.03 |
| *Newspaper Characteristics* | | | | | | | | |
| Corporate Ownership | -0.08 | 0.09 | -0.91 | 0.36* | | | | |
| Circulation (1,000) | -0.000 | 0.00 | -0.29 | 0.77* | | | | |
| D.C. Bureau Access | -0.003 | 0.13 | -0.03 | 0.49 | | | | |
| Local Gore Vote in 2000 | 0.01 | 0.01 | 0.92 | 0.18 | | | | |
| *Newspaper Political Agenda* | | | | | | | | |
| Endorsement in 2000 | 0.06 | 0.04 | 1.37 | 0.09 | 0.07 | 0.04 | 1.84 | 0.03 |
| *Type of Item* | | | | | | | | |
| Op-ed | -0.30 | 0.13 | -2.28 | 0.01 | -0.29 | 0.13 | -2.21 | 0.02 |
| Letter to Editor | -0.77 | 0.26 | -2.95 | 0.002 | -0.73 | 0.27 | -2.72 | 0.003 |
| Cut 1 | 1.17 | 0.67 | | | 0.95 | 0.88 | | |
| Cut 2 | 2.78 | 0.69 | | | 2.55 | 0.90 | | |
| N | 825 | | | | 825 | | | |
| Wald chi-square | 338.11 | | | 0.000 | 240.76 | | | 0.000 |
| Log pseudo-likelihood | -782.8 | | | | -785.1 | | | |
| Pseudo $R^2$ | 0.05 | | | | 0.04 | | | |

* Two-tailed test, either because direction is not predicted or results contrary to prediction. All other $p$ values are based on one-tailed tests.

Order-probit results, clustered on day.

TABLE 7.5. *News tone probabilities*

| | Tone | | |
|---|---|---|---|
| Variable | Negative | Neutral or balanced | Positive |
| Approval* | −0.10 | 0.02 | 0.10 |
| Endorsement[†] | −0.04 | 0.008 | 0.04 |
| Op-ed[+] | 0.10 | −0.03 | −0.07 |
| Letter to Editor[+] | 0.27 | −0.14 | −0.13 |
| Number of Speeches[‡] | 0.02 | −0.003 | −0.01 |
| Number of Speeches-squared[‡] | −0.002 | 0.0003 | 0.0014 |
| President Quoted[+] | −0.22 | −0.12 | 0.34 |
| Radio Address[+] | 0.04 | −0.01 | −0.03 |

\* Based on a 10 percent change in approval.
[†] Shift from Republican to Democratic endorsement.
[‡] Based on increase of one speech.
[+] Dummy variables.
*Source:* Based on results of analysis from Table 7.4.

differ from past research. Eshbaugh-Soha (2008b) finds that corporate ownership, large newspapers, and local political sentiment affect tone. Peake (2007) finds similar results for corporate ownership and local political sentiment; the latter is also important in the work of Barrett and Peake (2007). Differences in sampling and measurement strategies may account for the divergence between their findings and mine. Also, none of the other studies looks at the impact of presidential activities, another factor that might account for the divergence in findings.

**Newspaper Political Agendas and Tone**
Turning to specific coefficients, consider first newspaper endorsement effects and type of news item. Results indicate that Democratic-endorsing newspapers are more likely to publish positive news than Republican-endorsing newspapers, consistent with the party of the president at the time. Because the magnitude of ordered probit coefficients is not intuitive, in Table 7.5 I presented probabilities, which offer a more intuitive grasp of the magnitude of effects. According to that analysis, a Democratic president has a 0.04 greater probability of positive news from a Democratic-endorsing than a Republican-endorsing newspaper, and a similar 0.04 greater probability of seeing negative

news from a Republican-endorsing than a Democratic-endorsing newspaper.

Although these probabilities appear small, they are based on statistically significant effects controlling for a host of other variables. Also, the bulk of presidential news, based on the data used here, is either neutral or balanced. The measurement of tone here is quite crude, and even the endorsement variable may not capture fully a newspaper's partisan proclivity or attitude toward Bill Clinton. Some newspapers could have been positively disposed toward Al Gore, endorsing him, but may have still disliked Bill Clinton. The endorsement measure will not pick this up. Given these limitations, it may be a wonder that we found any significant effect from the endorsement variable.

**Political Context and Tone**
Unlike Peake (2007) and Eshbaugh-Soha (2008b), who find that local political preferences affect the tone of presidential news, this analysis did not detect such an effect, but instead found that national approval of Bill Clinton did affect tone. The probabilities, too, are quite strong. A 10 percent rise in presidential approval will reduce by 10 percent the probability of a negative news story and increase by the same amount the probability of a positive news story. That presidential approval in 2000 only varied by 10 percent, from a low of 57 percent to a high of 66 percent, suggests sensitivity to presidential approval on the tone of presidential news stories.

Two processes may be at work, as noted earlier. When presidents are popular, there may not be much negative news to report and vice versa when presidents are unpopular. Or newspapers may self-censor their reports on the president to correspond to the approval climate so as not to alienate readers or appear out of step with prevailing political sentiments. Because Clinton was popular during the entire period studied here, the second process may be driving the relationship between approval and the tone of presidential news. More data with greater variance in the approval variable and controls for events will be necessary to sort out these differing causal linkages.

This result also suggests that we need to turn our attention to the possibility that news is not entirely exogenous on presidential approval, but that approval conditions news reporting on the president.

Presidential activities that lift approval may result in more positive news, which may result in higher approval. Chapter 8 tests another part of this linkage, that newspaper tone affects approval.

### Story Type and Tone

Results also indicate a relationship between type of story and tone. Like the zero-order correlations discussed earlier, op-ed pieces and letters to the editor are more likely to be negative than other types of news items. The probabilities indicate that an op-ed piece has a 10 percent greater probability of being negative and a 7 percent lower probability of being positive. Letters to the editors suggest even stronger effects. A letter has a 27 percent greater chance of being negative than other news items and a 13 percent lower chance of being positive. But letters that mention the president are rare, composing less than 3 percent of the total number of news items on the president. A question for future research is whether the negativity of letters derives from the greater likelihood of those displeased with the president to write a letter or if editors are more likely to publish critical letters.

### Tone and Presidential Activities

The results in Table 7.4 tell us that a variety of presidential public activities affect the tone of presidential news reports. Contrary to expectations, radio addresses lead to negative, not positive news. The probabilities in Table 7.5 indicate that on the day after a Saturday radio address, the probability of a negative news story increases by 0.04, whereas the probability of a positive news story declines by 0.03.

It remains unclear why radio addresses stimulate more negative news. One possibility may have to do with the timing of the radio broadcasts, which are usually early on Saturday afternoon. Newspapers, for instance, have several hours to find a source to interview about the president's radio address. Moreover, radio addresses have become a routine fixture of the presidency. The administration provides advance notice of the address to maximize news coverage. Advance notice allows critics to prepare comments to counter the president and to seek out reporters. More research will be needed to test this possibility, but from these results, it appears that in broadcasting radio

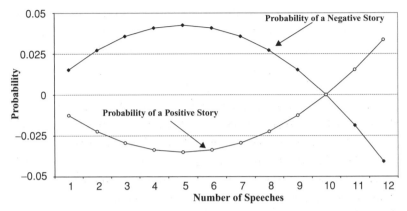

Figure 7.1. Probability of a Positive or Negative Story by Presidential Speech Activity. *Source:* Based on Results from Table 7.4.

addresses on Saturday, presidents face a trade-off between increased news coverage and a higher chance of negative news.

Presidential speeches have a curvilinear effect on news tone, further evidence supporting the distraction hypothesis. First, following from a coalitions of minorities perspective (Mueller, 1970), each additional speech increases the probability of a negative news story, but once the president gives a certain number of speeches, the probability of negative news declines. Table 7.5 presents the probability results. Given the calculations associated with the curvilinear model, Figure 7.1 plots the respective probabilities of a positive and negative news story by the number of presidential speeches across the entire range of such daily activity (0–12). These calculations take into account both the linear and quadratic components of the curvilinear model.

The figure clearly shows the curvilinear effect. For instance, with one speech, presidents can expected an increased probability of 0.015 of a negative news story and a decreased probability of 0.013 of a positive news story. At four speeches per day, on average, the probability of negative news increases by 0.04 and positive news decreases by 0.03. The same basic pattern holds through six speeches per day, but beginning with the seventh speech, the probably of negative news begins to decline and that of positive news to rise. Once the president has made ten such speeches, the probability of both positive and negative news hits zero, after which presidents are more likely to see positive news than negative. On hitting the maximum here, twelve, the probability of negative news declines by 0.04 and rises for a positive news story by 3 percent. Again, we note that these probability effects appear small, but recall the earlier discussion on measurement, especially in the dependent variable, that may make it hard to detect any results.

From a substantive perspective, this result reinforces the finding of curvilinear effects in Chapter 5 on the quantity of presidential news. The distraction hypothesis suggests that presidents will increase the number of daily activities to divert attention from potentially controversial announcements, actions, or decisions. Another benefit attends from hyperactivity – the president can reduce the probability of negative news. Presidents seem to be purposive, thoughtful, and strategic in modulating their daily activity. These two findings of curvilinear effects present us with strong evidence of presidential news management effects on news coverage.

Finally, being quoted has pronounced effects on the tone of presidential news. When a news story quotes the president, the probability of negative news recedes and positive news grows. Whereas many of the previous findings demonstrated modest probability effects, the probabilities here are impressive: Being quoted reduces the probability of negative news reporting by 22 percent and raises that of positive news by 34 percent.

Obviously, this result raises the question of the causal connection between positive news and being quoted. Do reporters search for a quote from the president because they intend to write a positive story? Or do quotes result from presidential activities, from the president providing something quotable? The next section addresses this question.

## WHY PRESIDENTS ARE QUOTED IN THE NEWS

What leads to presidents being quoted in news stories? Two sets of factors come to mind. Most presidential quotes present him saying something positive about an action or decision. Reporters do not quote the president merely to convey objective or descriptive information. Perhaps reporters quote the president because they have already decided to publish a positive story and search for appropriate presidential statements. On the other hand, quotes may derive from the actions of presidents and their spokespeople. Quality of language, provision of a pithy or colorful comment, may lead to its being quoted. Making an oral announcement, rather than merely providing reporters with text, may increase the odds of being quoted. The president may also manipulate the timing, location, and subject matter of his announcement, which may increase the probability that he will be quoted. With these data, I attempted to sort through some of these possibilities.

The dependent variable for this analysis is the dummy variable of whether the news directly quotes or heavily paraphrases the president and/or official spokesperson, coded 1, otherwise 0. As this variable is binary, probit estimation is used. Again, I began with a Heckman selection framework, because this dependent variable may be censored – presidents can only be quoted if the newspaper publishes a story on the president. The decision to publish a story on a president may in part depend on whether the president provided quotable material. Finally, the analysis clusters by day because multiple stories in the same newspaper on the same day may reference the same event, and/or the tone of one story may affect the tone of another story. In other words, news mentioning the president on a particular day may not be independent observations. Clustering by day helps account for this possibility.

Unlike the prior analysis, here the Heckman results affect model estimation (see Table 7.6). The selection model includes the following variables, all of which proved to be statistically significant: newspaper circulation, distance to Washington, access to a Washington news bureau, corporate ownership, and the radio address dummy. In the Heckman selection stage, radio addresses do not have a direct effect on whether a story quotes the president, although it affects whether a newspaper publishes a story on the president. But in a probit analysis, radio addresses directly affect the presidential quote variable, which would be mistaken given the Heckman selection results.

Table 7.6 reports the results of a reduced form model that only includes statistically significant variables. Several variables from the full estimation did not reach statistical significance: presidential approval,

TABLE 7.6. *Heckman selection model of factors influencing newspaper quoting of presidents*

| Variable | Coef. | SE | $t$ | $p$ | Impact |
|---|---|---|---|---|---|
| Circulation (per 1,000) | 1.26e3 | 6.3e4 | 2.02 | 0.02 | 2.18e4 |
| Gore Vote in 2000 | −0.05 | 0.01 | −3.94 | 0.000 | −0.008 |
| Endorsed a Candidate in 2000 | 0.73 | 0.20 | 3.63 | 0.000 | 0.10 |
| Op-ed Piece | −0.51 | 0.27 | −1.91 | 0.03 | −0.09 |
| Foreign Policy Topic | 0.43 | 0.15 | 2.87 | 0.002 | 0.07 |
| Constant | 0.32 | 0.42 | 0.78 | 0.44 | |
| Selection Model | | | | | |
| Circulation (per 1,000) | 3.35e3 | 2.87e4 | 11.69 | 0.000 | |
| Distance to D.C. | −0.0001 | 0.00004 | −2.75 | 0.000 | |
| Washington Bureau | 0.66 | 0.09 | 7.44 | 0.000 | |
| Corporate Ownership | −0.87 | 0.13 | −6.94 | 0.000 | |
| Radio Address | 0.71 | 0.32 | 2.26 | 0.01 | |
| Constant | 0.35 | 0.17 | 2.09 | 0.04 | |
| Athrho | −0.90 | 0.26 | −3.40 | 0.001 | |
| Rho | −0.71 | 0.13 | | | |

Wald test of indep. eqns. (rho = 0): chi$^2$(1) = 11.55 Prob > chi$^2$ = 0.0007 n = 1022, censored = 197, uncensored = 825 clustered on day, 20 clusters Wald chi$^2$(5) = 62.51, Prob > chi$^2$ = 0.0000, Log pseudolikelihood = −554.0589.
*Source:* Local Presidential News Database, 2000.

access to a Washington news bureau, whether the president was located in Washington, the number of speeches and the number of speeches-squared, and the radio address dummy.[12] Finally, because both Democratic- and Republican-endorsing newspapers demonstrated significant effects on quoting the president, I combined them into one variable, whether the newspaper endorsed a candidate for president in 2000.

Results indicate that a combination of newspaper characteristics and presidential activities affect the probability that a story will quote the president. First, larger newspapers are more likely to quote the president, although the effects appear modest in magnitude. As probit coefficients are not intuitively interpretable, I converted them to probabilities, which are reported in the Impact column in the table. Each additional thousand subscribers increases the probability of quoting

[12] Two variables could not be entered into the estimation, news conferences and letters to the editor. Letters never quote the president, and there was not enough variance on the news conference variable to be entered into the estimation.

the president by 0.000287. In this sample, newspapers range in circulation from about 18,000 to 724,000, averaging 330,000. An average newspaper will have a nearly 9 percent higher probability of quoting the president, whereas the largest newspaper will have approximately an 11 percent higher probability of quoting the president than an average-sized newspaper and nearly a 20 percent higher probability than the smallest newspaper. From this, we can infer that newspaper resources, measured here as circulation, lead newspapers to quote the president more frequently, perhaps because greater resources allow them to write more detailed stories and to do more research.

Similarly, newspapers that endorse presidential candidates are also more likely to quote the president. Endorsing newspapers have a 7 percent greater probability of quoting the president than nonendorsing newspapers. That both Democratic- and Republican-endorsing newspapers quote the president implies that endorsing newspapers take their political role more seriously than nonendorsing newspapers. Endorsements might reflect the political agenda of newspapers, but they may also reflect the importance that a newspaper ascribes to political reporting in other ways, which may be distinct from promoting the newspaper's agenda. If endorsement only indicated a newspaper's propensity of promoting its political agenda, we would not see Republican newspapers quoting Clinton often, as doing so would lead to positive news coverage.

Oddly, the Gore vote in 2000, an indicator of local political preferences, is negatively associated with quoting the president. A 10 percent shift in these preferences, which is nearly one standard deviation (11.5), decreases the probability of the president being quoted by 8 percent. Comparing communities least supportive of Gore with those most supportive (22.5 vs. 66.9) produces a 35 percent decrease in the probability of quoting the president. Because quoting a president reduces the amount of negative news coverage, it is not clear why newspapers would seem to run counter to local political preferences. Perhaps they do so to appear more "evenhanded" or independent than if they "pandered" to local political tastes.

Not surprising, op-ed pieces, editorials, and columns were less likely to quote presidents than other type of news items. Such pieces are not about reporting the news but taking stands on issues and evaluating presidential actions. Op-ed pieces are 7 percent less likely to quote presidents than other newspaper items.

Each of these variables is a characteristic of the newspaper, its context, political behavior, and/or type of news item and not something about which presidents can do a great deal. Of activities open to presidential control, what we can think of as aspects of his news management strategy, only one affected the probability of being quoted – whether foreign policy was the topic of the story. Presidents have a 7 percent greater probability of being quoted in a story about a foreign policy than on other topics.

Why are presidents more likely to be quoted in a foreign policy story than on other topics, such as domestic policy? Earlier, I suggested that how a president rhetorically packages and frames his public speeches and announcements may affect whether journalists directly quote the president in their news stories. Although this might be the case for stories about foreign policy, presidential control of information may also play a role. For many foreign policy issues, the administration is the only source of information. This information control gives the president a leadership advantage in foreign policy over domestic issues, where many alternative information sources exist and are easily accessed by journalists. Especially when the foreign policy issue poses some threat to the nation, journalists may feel somewhat compelled to quote the president. Quoting from such an authoritative source might lend greater credence to the story, and a disquieted (or potentially disquieted) public may desire clear evidence on presidential actions and decisions. Admittedly, this is speculative, but it raises another question for future research, and this account seems consistent with the large amount of literature on news coverage of foreign policy.

Whether we take these results as a sign that presidents can manage their news depends on the degree of discretion afforded to presidents to talk about foreign policy instead of other topics. To some degree, presidents have discretion in deciding to work on foreign policy rather than domestic issues. And with regard to public pronouncements on any given day, presidents generally possess a large number of foreign policy items to speak about, and by doing so, displace domestic issues.

However, presidents do not have complete discretion. The actions of other nations may force the president's hand, requiring that he deal with other nations' actions and publicize his response to the nation. Moreover, actions in Congress and reports in the media about foreign policy issues may also impel a presidential response, as research on presidential foreign policy agenda setting suggests (Wood and Peake, 1998; Edwards and Wood, 1999; Peake, 2001). Although presidents may possess some discretion with regard to how much attention they pay to foreign policy, they do not hold complete discretion.

## WASHINGTON POST EFFECTS

Some may criticize the inclusion of the *Washington Post* in the previous analyses of tone and quoting the president. Commonly, the *Post* is regarded as a national newspaper, but this research is concerned with local newspaper coverage of the president. Furthermore, a large percentage of the stories on the president in this sample, about 26 percent, come from the *Post*. Are we mixing apples and oranges, national and local newspapers here, and is the *Post* driving the results? That the time series analysis of Chapter 5 indicates the agenda setting impact of *Post* reporting on local newspapers suggests just such a possibility. But recall, too, that for the vast bulk of *Washington Post* readers, the *Post* serves as their local newspaper, and many "local" newspapers retain Washington news bureaus and, thus, to some degree may mimic the news-gathering routines and behavior of the *Post*. We cannot firmly or clearly draw a line distinguishing local and national newspapers. Many "local" newspapers possess some national newspaper characteristics, and the two newspapers commonly considered to be paradigmatic examples of national newspapers, the *Washington Post* and *New York Times*, possess local newspaper characteristics as well.

To check for *Washington Post* effects in the previous analysis, I re-estimated the analyses for both tone and quoting the president but deleted the *Washington Post* from the set of cases analyzed. Results with and without the *Post* are remarkably similar.[13] For the analysis of news tone, one formerly significant variable, the endorsement variable, fails to reach statistical significance when excluding the *Post* cases. All variables retain their significance and tell essentially the same substantive

[13] The analysis is not presented here, but I will supply details to interested readers.

story. The analysis of quoting the president without the *Post* cases is quite similar to the results with the *Post* cases included. One formerly significant variable, the op-ed, drops out. All others remain significant, providing us with the same substantive story as before. Most important for this analysis, the presidential activity variables show similar effects in either specification. Other than a single variable, *Washington Post* news reporting is not driving the results on the tone of presidential news or the probability that a president is quoted in a news story.

**CONCLUSION**

This chapter provides additional evidence that presidential news management strategies can affect the tone of presidential news coverage, as the previous two chapters found that such activities can affect the quantity of presidential news. Specifically, presidents can modulate their quantity of daily speeches to mitigate negative news. From a coalition of minorities perspective (Mueller, 1970), insofar as presidential decisions and actions create winners and losers, the losers would object to the president's decision. In some, perhaps many, instances, the press would use losers as sources in news stories to criticize the president, leading to negative news coverage. However, by increasing his daily activity, presidents can reduce the attention given to any such controversial decision. Thus, we find a curvilinear effect of presidential daily activity on news tone. As presidential activity increases, so does the probability of negative news, but only up to a point. On reaching and surpassing that point, the probability of negative news then begins to recede, paralleling the finding of activity on news quantity. Very high levels of daily activity not only reduce the probability of negative news, but also reduce the overall level of news coverage. It appears from this effect that presidents are rational in regulating their daily activity levels.

When the news media quote the president, the probability of negative news also decreases. Such quotes often convey the president's point of view – in modern political parlance, his "spin." Quoting the president allows him to counter criticism and other negative remarks found in a news story. More important perhaps is that often when reporters quote the president in a story, he stands alone, uncontested by critics, which leads to positive news coverage. That presidents so often appear alone in news stories may bolster their leadership image. Without critics providing a voice in a news story, it may appear to readers that the president not only has taken the lead, but that other political leaders tacitly approve of his action.

The analysis also found that local newspapers are more likely to quote the president when he speaks on foreign policy than on other topics. Speaking about foreign policy may indirectly affect the tone of news coverage through its impact on the president being quoted. This process may in part account for presidential leadership advantages in foreign policy compared with other issues areas. When dealing with foreign policy, the president is more likely to be quoted, and often his is the only voice in the story, which leads to positive news coverage. The president may stand alone in foreign policy news because of his control over information about such issues. For domestic issues, by contrast, there are many alternate sources of information that journalists can use as sources.

Presidential impacts on news tone do not stop with the direct effect of public activities. We also found that news tone follows presidential approval – presidents will see more favorable news coverage when they are popular than when they are unpopular. Although events such as the state of the economy strongly drive approval trends, some research suggests that presidential activities, such as speeches and dramatic events (MacKuen, 1983; Ragsdale, 1984, 1987) and rhetorical optimism (Wood, 2007), may also influence approval levels. Insofar as presidents can boost their standing with the public, they may see more favorable news coverage, and as I will show in Chapter 8, the tone of news coverage may, in turn, affect public approval of the president.

The analysis also found that newspaper endorsements affect the tone of presidential news, which raises the thorny issue of media bias.[14] It is impossible to tell from such data if Republican-endorsing

---

[14] The literature on media bias has grown in recent years. Most of it pertains to election coverage because of the ability to compare the coverage of competing candidates. Extensive reviews can be found in D'Alessio and Allen (2000) and Cohen (forthcoming), the latter reviewing the implications of media bias on the president in particular.

newspapers are being biased *against* the president or if Democratic-endorsing newspapers are being biased in *favor* of the president. All that we can say is that the tone of presidential news in Democratic- and Republican-endorsing newspapers systematically differ and that the "wall of separation" between editorial and news functions may have been breached (Kahn and Kenney, 2002; Peake, 2007).

Furthermore, the finding here may be particular to the time period and president. Bill Clinton inspired intense partisan loyalty and opposition, as seems to be the case for his successor, George W. Bush (Jacobson, 2007). Peake's (2007) study, like this one, focused on Bush and found endorsement effects. Eshbaugh-Soha's (2008b) included the first Bush and Clinton in his analysis, but did not find endorsement effects on news tone. More research on more presidents will be necessary to sort out these conflicting findings. Moreover, the fact that newspapers are now less likely to endorse candidates for office than in the past raises the issue of the relevance or importance of this finding (Ansolabehere, Lessem, and Snyder, 2006). In Chapter 8, using endorsements as an indicator of overall news tone, I showed the effect of endorsements on voters' assessments of the president, suggesting that even if fewer newspapers now endorse or otherwise are associated closely with one partisan viewpoint or the other, endorsements still may be politically consequential.

Returning to our larger story, presidents found that because of the rise of party polarization and the fragmentation of the news media, their going national leadership strategy of the 1960s through the 1980s became less effective. During the past two decades, presidents have updated their public leadership strategy, targeting narrower groups, such as their party base, select interest groups, and some localities. Presidents have two major options when going local: they can visit localities or they can try to influence their coverage in local newspapers. Visiting may have payoffs for the president in the particular locality visited, but it is a very costly approach to building local support for the president in numerous localities. Local news coverage offers the president a less costly way of reaching local mass publics. However, relying on local news to build local support for the president hinges on his ability to affect that news coverage and for that coverage to affect local public opinion. The empirical analysis of the past several chapters indicates that local newspapers publish a considerable amount of news on the president and that presidential activities can affect the quantity and tone of that news coverage. This leads to the last stage in the going local leadership strategy. Does local news coverage of the president affect local opinion? This is the topic of the next chapter.

# CHAPTER 8

# Local Presidential News Coverage and Public Attitudes toward the President

Because of the rise of party polarization and an increasingly fragmented news media, key characteristics of the post-broadcast age, presidents no longer find a national leadership strategy to be as effective as it once was. In place of going national, presidents now place heavy emphasis on targeting segments of the mass public, in particular their party base, interest groups, and localities, for their leadership efforts. As argued in this book, localities are especially important targets for the president because of the potential influence of local public opinion on members of Congress. If presidents can mobilize local public opinion, then perhaps members of Congress, fearing or wanting to be responsive to their constituents, will also support the president.

Presidents have several ways of reaching local public opinion, including visiting localities and influencing their coverage in local newspapers. Visiting localities may enhance support within the visited locality, but mobilizing support in many localities requires numerous and frequent presidential visits, a costly method. Influencing local news coverage may be less costly and more efficient to presidents, but it is not without pitfalls.

To reach local publics, presidents rely heavily on the local news media, especially local newspapers. Local newspapers still possess relatively large readerships, still command respect from their readership, and they report measurable amounts of news about the president. The analysis of the past several chapters demonstrates that presidents, through their public activities, can influence the quantity and tone of their news coverage in local newspapers, establishing support for the first link in the causal chain. This chapter tests the second link in the causal chain – whether local news coverage of the president affects public evaluations of the president.

In the following I use a data set well suited for this purpose, the 2000 Annenberg National Election Study (ANES). The 2000 ANES specifically asks respondents which newspaper they read. This allows one to match an indicator of the tone of newspaper reporting on the president, as well as other characteristics, in particular access to a Washington bureau, to individual respondents.

Before turning to the analysis, the chapter opens with a discussion of the literature on news effects on presidential evaluations and issues in studying those news effects. Then I offer a theory of how news may affect public evaluations of the president, followed by a discussion of the study design and then the analysis. Controlling for many factors that affect public evaluations of the president, the tone of local news affects how people evaluate the president. Those effects increase for individuals who read local newspapers but do not possess strong political predispositions, and local newspapers that emphasize national news coverage more strongly influence thinking about the president than newspapers lacking such a national orientation to news reporting. This brings us full circle, providing evidence for each link in the causal chain proposed here.

## EVENTS VERSUS NEWS REPORTING ON EVENTS AND PUBLIC ATTITUDES TOWARD THE PRESIDENT

Numerous studies have found that news affects public evaluations of the president. When the news is good or favorable to the president, public approval rises; when the news is bad, approval drops.[1] It is not clear from this research, however, what it is about the news that affects presidential evaluations. Is it the events on which news reports or is it the way that journalists report on those events that affects public opinion toward the president?

---

[1] See Iyengar and Kinder, 1987; Brody, 1991; West, 1991; Mutz, 1992, 1994; Blood and Phillips, 1995; Pan and Kosicki, 1997; Nadeau et al., 1999; Shah and Watts, 1999; Erikson, MacKuen, and Stimson, 2002, ch. 2; Shah et al., 2002; Burden and Mughan, 2003; Gronke and Newman, 2003; Althaus and Kim, 2006.

Whether it is the events or the way that journalists report on them that affects the public tells us much about the role of the news media in democracy, as well as about presidential leadership of public opinion. If it is events, and not the reporting of events, that mainly affect the public, then the news media play a passive role, merely conveying information to the public. Similarly, we should expect minimal impacts on public opinion from presidential attempts to lead, especially when those presidential actions aim at steering news coverage of the president. But if the way the news media report on events can affect public opinion, then the news media will play an active role in shaping public opinion. And presidential success in shaping their news coverage may, in turn, influence public opinion about the president.

Few subscribe to the idea that the news media merely passively convey information to the mass public (Shoemaker and Reese, 1996). News organization routines, the economics of news production, the professional definitions of what is newsworthy, the political agendas of news organizations, and other factors such as presidential activities may affect how news organizations report on events. Insofar as these factors systematically vary across news organizations, we may observe systematic differences in the way news organizations report on the same event.

Yet, in some instances or for some events, reporting differences might not affect public opinion. Some events may be so conventionally understood that no difference in news reporting will affect public judgments. For example, voters tend to view a story that unemployment has risen as bad news no matter how that news is reported.[2] For some events, the way a news organization reports on it may not affect how people interpret or understand it.

To settle the question of the impact of events versus reporting styles of those events requires distinguishing between the *impact of events* and the *impact of reporting of those events* on the public. Past researchers have had difficulty in distinguishing news reporting from event effects. Dalton, Beck, and Huckfeldt (1998, 124) conclude in their study of

---

[2]  A news organization may report that an unemployment increase is good news, perhaps because unemployment increases will dampen inflation or because the administration has emphasized the positive implications of unemployment increases.

mass media effects on voting in 1992 presidential election, "[W]e find evidence of information effects, but it is not clear whether this is the media's independent influence or the effect of the campaign as transmitted by the press."

Recently, Druckman and Parkin (2005) designed a clever field experiment that isolates reporting from event effects. They compared the impact of endorsements on voting in a U.S. Senate election by two newspapers in the Minneapolis-St. Paul metropolitan area. They held the event, the election campaign, constant with the two newspapers endorsing competing candidates. Druckman and Parkin found that the newspapers' endorsements affected the voting behavior of readers of the particular paper (also Kahn and Kenney, 2002).[3]

Druckman and Parkin present tantalizing findings that differences in reporting styles (endorsements) may affect mass behavior, but theirs is essentially a case study of one Senate election in a community with two major competing newspapers.[4] Most communities, even large urban areas, are now served by only one newspaper. This raises a series of questions: Do endorsement effects hold when only one newspaper serves a community, or do voters discount endorsements coming from monopoly newspapers? Are reporting effects limited to endorsements of candidates in elections, or can other aspects of reporting style affect other types of public opinion and behavior? Can reporting differences affect attitudes about the president?

The particular question raised here asks whether the tone of local news can affect public evaluations of the president. If tone affects public opinion toward the president, and presidents, in turn, can affect the tone of their news coverage, as shown earlier, then presidents might be able, through this indirect route, to affect how the public

---

[3]  A small body of research has found that newspaper endorsements seem to affect presidential and Senate voting outcomes. See Erikson, 1976; Hollander, 1979; Coombs, 1981; Hurd and Singletary, 1984; Kahn and Kenney, 2002; Druckman and Parkin, 2005.

[4]  Kahn and Kenney (2002) find that endorsements correlate with newspaper coverage of candidates in the senatorial campaign, which, in turn, affects voting for senator. Newspapers seem to give better news treatment to the endorsed than to the nonendorsed candidate. Thus, endorsement effects on voting may actually be news coverage effects that are due to the relationship between news coverage of candidates and endorsements.

regards them. The key insight of the Druckman-Parkin design is to hold events constant but allow news coverage to vary. This enables them to distinguish the effects of events from news reporting on mass behavior and opinion. The 2000 National Annenberg Election Study's (NAES) rolling cross section, by asking respondents to name the newspaper they read, provides us with some leverage to distinguish events from news reporting of events. Before turning to the study design, the next section presents a theory for understanding the impact of local news on public evaluations of the president.

## A THEORY OF NEWS TONE EFFECTS ON PUBLIC EVALUATIONS OF THE PRESIDENT

The specific question motivating this analysis asks whether the tone of local news about the president, independent of the event reported on, affect readers' evaluations of the president. This question grows from the larger concern of whether presidents can influence public opinion by influencing how local newspapers cover them. We need to distinguish events from reporting effects to determine anything about the type of presidential leadership effects of interest here. As argued earlier, presidential public activities aim to influence characteristics of presidential news coverage and the style of reporting on the president. Presidential public activities, in this sense, may affect public opinion by affecting news coverage, a type of reporting, as opposed to event effect.

Several assumptions about newspaper readers and the mass public provide the foundation for building some theoretical expectations and hypotheses. First, readers use some subset of the news stories about the president to update and (possibly) revise their estimates of his leadership. Events and news stories will vary in their impact on public evaluations of the president. Some events and news stories will weigh more heavily in evaluating the president than others. Edwards, Mitchell, and Welch (1995), for example, show that only salient issues affect presidential approval, implying that salient events and news stories about salient events will have greater impact on public assessments of the president.

Second, events and news can be good, bad, or neutral with regard to presidential leadership. If people view an event and/or a story as good news, support for the president should rise; whereas if they view the event or story as bad, support for the president should be dampened.[5] The tone of an event and news reporting on that event may differ. That is, an event may be "bad news," although newspapers may report it as "good news." Various factors associated with news production processes, including the president's news management strategy, may lead to this difference between an event and how it is reported. We do not know how often the tone of an event and news reporting on that event differ.

Third, we can distinguish between events that readers have a relatively easy time interpreting from those that readers have a hard time interpreting. Readers must interpret the event to apply it to their evaluation of the president. If an event is easy for a reader to interpret, the reader will not need help in making sense of the story and using it to evaluate the president. Under this circumstance, interpretation of the event offered in a news story about the event will have little effect on the reader's interpretation and, thus, little impact of the reader's evaluation of the president. However, if an event is hard for a reader to interpret, the reader may seek guidance or help in interpreting the event, that is, in deciding whether the news is good or bad news for the president.[6] In some instances, when interpreting the event is hard for the reader, the reader may rely on the interpretation found in the news story. Under this circumstance, news reporting may influence readers' interpretation of events, and through that interpretation, their evaluation of the president. Insofar as presidents affect news reporting of

---

5   Neutral stories should have no impact on presidential evaluations. Furthermore, changes in presidential evaluations are only likely when the news story runs counter to a person's presidential evaluation. Bad news will affect evaluations of those who think well of the president, but only reinforce evaluations of those who already think poorly of the president. On persuasion effects, see Page, Shapiro, and Dempsey, 1987. At the aggregate level, one cannot improve levels of presidential support when it nears 100 percent or depress it when it bottoms near zero. See Shah and Watts (1999) and Baum (2002) as two examples of aggregate studies of presidential approval that take into account ceiling and floor effects.
6   It may also be the case that if a story is hard to interpret, the reader will not use it in evaluating the president.

the event, presidents, through the news, may influence how the public assesses their leadership. News reporting effects, and presidential news management effects, will exist for a subset of readers on a subset of events, salient events that are hard to interpret. We should not expect news reporting, and presidential news management effects, to be general across readers and events.

Also, when readers look for help in interpreting an event, newspapers (and the news media in general) provide only one source to which they can turn. They can, for instance, turn to people with whom they interact. But when turning to news outlets for interpretive help, people may not rely equally on all news outlets. People are more likely to rely on news outlets that they view as credible sources of news (and interpretation) about the president.

**Newspaper Credibility**

News outlets seen as credible sources for news (and interpretation) about the president will have greater impact than those seen as not credible. To be viewed as a credible news source about the president, a newspaper must present a sufficient quantity of news about the president and develop a reputation for sustained news coverage of the president. Newspapers vary in their amount of news on the president. As shown earlier, the major national and large metropolitan daily newspapers offer higher quantities of news about the president than do the smaller regional and local newspapers. Major papers often possess a Washington news bureau and may deploy reporters dedicated to the White House beat. Smaller papers, unable to compete with the majors in covering Washington, devote their news reporting efforts to local affairs. When they report presidential news, smaller newspapers often rely on wire service and syndicate reports. As a result, they will not be looked on as credible of a news source on the president as the majors, which routinely cover the president.

**Differences in People's Ability to Understand Events and News**

Just as events differ in their ease of interpretability, people differ in their ability to interpret events. Zaller's (1992) Receive-Accept-Sample (RAS) model provides us with some leverage for understanding which types of people may require assistance in interpreting events. First, voters must learn about the event. Most people do not learn about politically relevant events directly, but indirectly, either from individuals with whom they interact or through reports in the news media (Brody, 1991).

Not everyone learns about events. They may not discuss politics and political affairs with other people and may not read (or watch) stories about those events in newspapers (or on television). These people are unexposed to the event/news story. In RAS terminology, they have not been exposed to the message, and, thus, the event/news story cannot influence them. Neither the event, nor the news story about the event, will enter into their evaluation of the president.

Those who learn of the event will either be able to interpret it on their own ("independent interpreters") or will need help in interpreting the event ("assisted interpreters"). Independent interpreters may resist or reject the interpretation offered in a news story, especially if the news interpretation differs from their own. If the news offers the same interpretation as the individual's, the news may merely reinforce the individual's interpretation. Those needing assistance in interpreting an event will be more likely to accept the interpretation found in news reports.

Zaller's (1992) RAS model generally looks to political predispositions, like partisanship, to differentiate those who will reject or accept the message embedded in communications about events, what I have been calling here the interpretation of the event. This discussion broadens the RAS model from political predispositions as a moderator of communications to include a person's preexisting ability to understand or interpret politically relevant events. Such interpretive ability comes about through several mechanisms, including the individual's store of knowledge about the political world and his or her habits in collecting information about politics and public affairs. There are many ways of operationalizing interpretative ability. I focus on how much people follow public affairs for reasons detailed in the following.

Finally, the primary aspect of news coverage that aids in interpreting an event is not the recitation of facts about the event, but whether the article portrays the event as good or bad for the president, that is, its tone. The previous discussion leads us to several hypotheses:

**General Effects, H1:** The tone of news should strongly affect evaluations of the president in general.

**Newspaper Credibility Effects, H2:** News tone effects on presidential evaluations will be stronger for major than for minor newspapers. We are not likely to find tone effects on presidential evaluations for minor newspapers.

**Reader Type Effects, H3:** News tone effects will be greater for those who read newspapers than for those who do not. Among newspaper readers, news tone effects will be stronger for those who need help in interpreting events than for those who do not need such help.

## DATA AND DESIGN

To estimate the effects of news reporting on opinion and behavior, we must distinguish between the effects of the events themselves from the way that the news reports on those events. Druckman and Parkin (2005) devised a clever experiment to disentangle these effects by holding events constant (the campaign) while allowing news reporting to vary (endorsements). Such a design is practical if there are only a small number of news outlets, but nationally, thousands of outlets offer news about the president. The approach that I take here is to allow both events and news reporting to vary.

The 2000 National Annenberg Election Study (NAES) rolling cross section presents us with an opportunity to distinguish the effects of events and news reporting, in this case news tone, on presidential evaluations.[7] From November 14, 1999, to January 20, 2001, more than 58,000 respondents were asked to use a feeling thermometer scale to rate the president, the dependent variable for this study. During the fourteen-month period, a myriad of events occurred with varying implications for presidential thermometer ratings. By using the full extent of the rolling cross section, we, in effect, randomize the

---

7  Details on the NAES are reported in Romer et al. (2004) and Johnston, Hagen, and Hall Jamieson (2004).

impact of events on presidential evaluations. Furthermore, because the NAES asked respondents to name the newspaper they read, something rarely done in public opinion surveys, we can (theoretically) match the tone of the news about the president published in the respondent's named newspaper. The randomization of events holds the effect of events constant, allowing us to isolate the impact of news tone on presidential evaluations across many types of events.

**Measuring Tone**

Ideally, to measure newspaper tone, one would want to collect large samples of news stories on the president across the newspapers that people read. Such an undertaking is not only impractical, but impossible, given the large number of newspapers (1,400-plus) and the relatively long period during which NAES interviewed respondents.[8] Given these constraints, can we construct a valid and discriminating measure of presidential news tone?

Noting the impracticality of large-scale content analyses of news tone across a relatively long period of time and a large number of newspapers, I used the newspapers' presidential endorsement in the 2000 election campaign as a proxy measure of presidential news tone.[9] Newspapers that endorse Bush are coded "−1", Gore endorsements "1," and no endorsement "0."[10] Here I assume that newspapers that endorse a party's presidential candidate are likely to exhibit similar partisan slant tendencies in their news pages. In other words, newspapers that endorse Al Gore are likely to publish news that tends to be more favorable toward Bill Clinton than newspapers that endorse George W. Bush, and vice versa. Newspapers that did not endorse a presidential candidate in 2000 should fall somewhere in-between.

---

[8] The Newspaper Association of American estimates that in 2000, there were 1,483 daily newspapers. See its Web site, http://www.naa.org/info/factsoo/11.html.

[9] Another complication is matching the content analysis of the particular newspaper the respondent reads with the time period in which the respondent was surveyed. *Editor and Publisher* has been collecting endorsements for several decades (cf. Stanley and Niemi, 1998, 188–190). The George Washington University Web site, Democracy in Action, has reproduced the *Editor and Publisher* survey for 2000 at http://www2.gwu.edu/~action/natendorse5.html. The 2004 endorsements can be located on various Web sites, including http://en.wikipedia.org/wiki/Newspaper_endorsements_in_the_U.S._presidential_election,_2004.

[10] In 2000, 175 newspapers endorsed Bush and 119 Gore.

Is this a reasonable measure of presidential news tone? First, several studies find a connection between endorsement patterns and the tone of news coverage. Kahn and Kenney (2002) show that editorial page endorsements of Senate candidates correlate with the tone of candidate news coverage. Barrett and Barrington (2005) find that subsequent endorsements correlate with the favorability of photographs published in newspapers for local and state-wide candidates in the 1998 and 2002 elections. Peake (2007) finds that endorsement patterns affect the tone of newspaper coverage of George W. Bush in 2006.[11] Chapter 7 showed a correlation between the 2000 endorsement pattern of newspapers in the local news database and the tone of their news on the president, as well as whether the newspaper quotes the president, an important predictor of tone. These results are maintained with controls in multivariate analyses. Thus, we have some reason to believe that endorsements might be a reasonable proxy for the tone of presidential news.

### NAES and Respondent Newspaper Use

For each respondent in the 2000 NAES, I matched the 2000 endorsement with the newspaper that the respondent claimed to have read. Doing so proved laborious and was not always straightforward. The NAES coded the respondent's newspaper into one of two variables. First, variable $ce14$ coded whether a person read one of thirty-one largest newspapers in terms of circulation. These newspapers also have Washington, D.C. news bureaus. Slightly more than 12,000 respondents (20.6%) reported reading one of these newspapers. Another 31,574 respondents were given a verbatim code if they read another paper (the NAES variable is $\_ce14$). For the verbatim coding, NAES listed the name of the newspaper that the respondent offered, but

---

[11] Neither Barrett and Peake (2007) nor Eshbaugh-Soha (2008b) find that endorsements affect tone controlling for other variables. At the zero-order level, there may still be a correlation between endorsements and tone. In a personal communication, Eshbaugh-Soha (June 30, 2008) does not find a correlation between endorsements and tone. But Eshbaugh-Soha's study employed only seven newspapers; only one, the *Pittsburgh Post-Gazette*, endorsed the Democratic presidential candidate in 1992 and 2000. Of the remaining six, four endorsed the Republican in 1992 and five in 2000. There may not be enough variance in Eshbaugh-Soha's endorsement variable to pick up any effects on the tone of news coverage, in part a function of the small number of newspapers.

did not process the variable more than to record verbatim the respondent's answer to the question. Finally, 14,791 (25.3%) did not read any newspaper or were coded as missing data on these two variables (ce14 and _ce14).

Matching the endorsement code to each newspaper named in the verbatim newspaper variable was complicated by the sheer volume of verbatim codes. I identified several thousand individual and unique codes on this variable. It was not always readily apparent which newspaper the respondent claimed to have read because the verbatim newspaper code included a variety of (mis)spellings of newspaper names, often for the same newspaper. This variation may have been a function of respondents having problems recalling the exact name of the newspaper, or of the coder or interviewer having difficulty understanding the name of the newspaper that the respondent gave, among other factors.

Given these issues, from the verbatim code, I matched an endorsement code only if I could unambiguously identify a newspaper from the verbatim newspaper record. Otherwise the endorsement variable was coded "0" (no endorsement). Ambiguity in ascertaining the exact newspaper could occur when the verbatim code did not provide enough information to determine the newspaper's name. This occurred, for instance, when a respondent answered that he or she read the "morning" or "evening" paper, the "local" paper, the "city name" paper (but when there could be several possible papers). In other instances, respondents named a newspaper, but without a reference to the city, and that name could apply to several papers. These problems introduce some measurement error into our variable of interest.[12] Based on this coding procedure, 38.5 percent of respondents were coded as reading a newspaper that made an endorsement, 36.2 percent read a newspaper that either did not make an endorsement or for which I could not match the respondent unambiguously

---

[12] We can assume that the error in measurement, that is, classifying a person as having read a "no endorsement" paper when he or she might have read a paper that endorsed one of the candidates, will be random and, thus, should not affect our ability to detect the true underlying relationship between slant and presidential evaluations unless, however, there is so much measurement error that the resulting variable become useless. As I detect systematic and expected impacts of slant on evaluations, my assumption of random measurement error here seems reasonable.

to a newspaper, and the remaining 25.3 percent did not read a newspaper.

### Presidential Feeling Thermometer as a Dependent Variable

The NAES contains only one question asking respondents about their attitudes toward the president, Bill Clinton, a feeling thermometer. Respondents were asked to rate how coolly or warmly they felt towards Bill Clinton, with 0 being cold, 100 being warm, and 50 being the neutral point. Few analyses of the presidential feeling thermometer currently exist. It is less focused than the job approval question and, thus, allows the respondent to bring all types of evaluations into answering this question. The feeling thermometer, however, correlates strongly with the job approval items in the American National Election Studies. (ANES) Using the ANES pooled data set (1948–2000), the correlation between the presidential thermometer rating and the dichotomous approve/disapprove question is 0.69 ($p = 0.000$, $n = 25,705$), and the correlation with strength of approval is 0.78 ($p = 0.000$, $n = 19,319$). Thus, we can use the feeling thermometer as a general indicator of respondent evaluations of the president.

Clinton's thermometer ratings range at the individual level from 0 to 100, averaging 47.5, with a standard deviation of 36.0. Figure 8.1 presents the time trend for the feeling thermometer using a six-day moving average, weighted by the number of respondents per day. The thermometer rating exhibits considerable short-term variation, as well as the upward trend in the second half of the series. From December 1999 until mid-September 2000, Clinton's thermometer rating oscillated in the 45 to 52 range, resembling a steady-state pattern. Thereafter, until he left office in January 2001, his feeling thermometer steadily rose to 55 degrees by his last day in office. This temporal path looks quite similar to Clinton's approval patterns during the same time period, using such indicators as job approval from the Gallup poll.

### Market Forces

Drawing from the work of Druckman and Parkin (2005; also Hamilton, 2004; Gentzkow and Shapiro, 2006a, 2006b) newspaper tone may be a response to market forces in which newspapers adopt the political

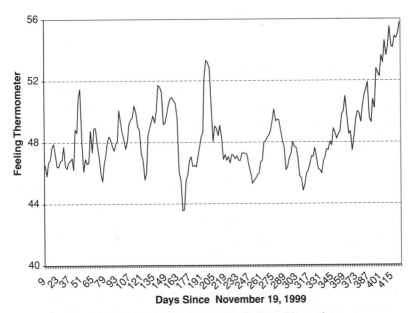

Figure 8.1. Clinton Feeling Thermometer Rating, November 19, 1999–January 20, 2001, Six-Day Moving Average, 2000 National Annenberg Election Study.

(and other) positions and preferences of its readers, not the newspaper's political agenda. Newspapers may decide to reflect community norms so as not to alienate readers, to keep readers from dropping their subscriptions, and to develop a reputation as being representative of local community norms and opinions. If newspapers respond to local forces in this way, then any tone effects that we find might not be due to newspaper effects on the public, but rather to newspaper responsiveness to the local political climate. Thus, it is important to control for market-local forces on newspaper slant.

Measuring these market forces is far from straightforward. No natural geographic unit exists that identifies a newspaper's market. Because of well-developed distribution systems, large urban dailies often penetrate well into outlying areas, in effect becoming regional newspapers. Others, although based in one urban center, attract a national readership. For instance, based on the readership patterns of the respondents in the 2000 NAES, only about 60 percent of the readers of the *New York Times* come from New York, New Jersey, or Connecticut; nearly

17 percent of the *Times* readership lives in California. The Internet has further broken down geographic barriers for newspapers.

Recognizing the problems in identifying a newspaper's market boundaries and collecting relevant data on the more than one thousand newspapers that respondents say they read, I used data on both the county and congressional district in which the respondent lives to measure market forces/political tendencies. Specifically, I used the Democratic percentage of the two-party presidential vote in 1996 and 2000 at the county level where the respondent resides. At the respondent level, these correlate at 0.95[13] Not only does this variable help control for newspaper responsiveness to the local community, but it also controls for local community effects on an individual's ratings of the president.

### Other Control Variables

Finally, controls for other factors that may affect a person's evaluation of the president are entered into the estimated model. Past research on the individual level determinants of presidential approval and availability of such items in the NAES guided the selection of these control variables.[14] The control variables included measures of other political orientations and predispositions, demographics, attitudes on issues, and exposure to other news media (Appendix 8.1 lists the variables and their definitions).

First, partisanship and ideological identification should affect the presidential feeling thermometer, with Democrats and liberals feeling more warmly to Clinton than Republicans and conservatives.

---

[13] I thank Peter Nardulli for sharing the 1996 county vote data with me. I also constructed another local variable, this time using the Democratic percentage of the two-party presidential vote in 1996 and 2000 at the congressional district level. Estimations that used both the county and congressional district variables found only the county variable to be statistically significant. Estimations that use either the county or the congressional district variable find that the county variable performs somewhat more strongly, although either performs well.

[14] A substantial literature exists. See Gilens, 1988; Goidel, Shields, and Peffley, 1997; Greene, 2001; Gronke and Newman, 2003; Krosnick and Brannon, 1993a, 1993b; Krosnick and Kinder, 1990; Miller and Krosnick, 2000; Mutz, 1992, 1994; Newman, 2003; Nicholson, Segura, and Woods, 2002; Tedin, 1986; Valentino, 1999; Waterman and Jenkins-Smith, 1999; and West, 1991.

I also control for demographics, hypothesizing that older, female, minority, and less educated respondents will feel more warmly toward Clinton.

Issue positions may also affect attitudes toward Clinton. The NAES provides us with a long list of issues. I selected those issues that were asked about across all or almost all of the cross sections to minimize loss of cases.[15] Twelve items met this criterion: attitudes on health care spending, school vouchers, abortion, gun regulations, crime, party campaign finance regulations, general campaign finance regulations, perceptions of job discrimination against gays and Blacks, poverty, taxes, and spending on Social Security. For all but campaign finance and regulation, I hypothesize that those who take the more liberal position will feel more warmly toward Clinton than those who take the more conservative position.

It is unclear how campaign finance attitudes will affect evaluations of Clinton. On the one hand, critics charged Clinton with campaign violations in 1996. These charges may have led some voters to not only dislike Clinton but also to support greater campaign regulation and reform. Yet conservatives, who presumably like Clinton less than liberals, may oppose campaign regulations, viewing such regulations as increases in government size and power, which they oppose. Thus, uncertainty exists regarding the direction of campaign finance attitudes on presidential attitudes.

Inclusion of the attitudinal variables puts news tone effects to a hard test. News tone could affect a respondent's attitudes on issues, which might then affect the respondent's attitudes towards Clinton, in effect wiping out or depressing the *direct* effect of tone on presidential attitudes.

I also included controls for exposure to other media to isolate the effects of newspaper tone from exposure to other media. These controls included the number of days in the past week that the respondent

---

[15] NAES did not ask respondents to place Clinton on these issues; thus, we cannot build a distance measure. But respondents may project Clinton's issue position, enlarging or narrowing how far away they think Clinton is, based on whether or not they like Clinton. Using only respondent issue positions eliminates this projection problem. See Green et al. (2002, 207–218) on this point.

watched national network news, local television news, and cable television news and listened to talk radio programs, plus the number of days that a person claimed to have read a newspaper.

Not much guidance exists to predict the direction of impact of these media variables. From the findings of West (1991), who argues that television tends to portray presidents negatively, we can hypothesize that exposure to network news should undercut support for Clinton. By contrast, research suggests that local television news is less critical of presidents than national news (cf. Just, Alger, and Kern, 1996). This leads us to hypothesize that exposure to local television news will increase presidential support. Most talk radio programs take a conservative political slant. Research has found that exposure to talk radio affects listeners, pushing them in a conservative direction regardless of the listeners' preexisting political orientation (see Barker, 1999, 2002; Barker and Knight, 2000). This leads to the hypothesis that exposure to talk radio will undercut support for Clinton.

Finally, I also entered a control for the month when the respondent was interviewed. There are fourteen months from December 1999 through January 2001, for thirteen monthly estimators, with one deleted as the criterion case. These monthly dummy variables help to control for events specific to each month that might move presidential evaluations, thus acting as a further check or control on the news tone variable. The final estimation contains forty controls variables, including the thirteen monthly dummies.

Missing from this model are controls for economic attitudes. The NAES did not ask a full complement of retrospective and prospective personal and sociotropic questions. Only retrospective personal and sociotropic economic questions were asked, and they were asked for only a subset of cross sections. Including these items results in a loss of about ten thousand cases. Analyses with these variables included in the estimations find that personal economics did not affect attitudes toward Clinton. Perceived national economic conditions do show an effect, but the impact is modest and does not affect the other variables in the model, especially our variable of interest, news tone. The results presented in the following do not include the economic perceptions variables.

## ANALYSIS

Table 8.1, Model 1, presents results of regressing news tone on the Clinton thermometer ratings, controlling for local market forces, political attitudes, demographics, media exposure, and the monthly dummies. (The effects for the monthly dummies are not presented.) Results indicate that news tone significantly affects thermometer ratings – those who read newspapers that endorsed the Republican are one degree cooler to Clinton than those who read Democratic-endorsing newspapers. (Recall the independent variable, news tone is a two-step variable, from $-1$ (Republican) to $1$ (Democrat), with nonendorsing newspapers coded "0". Each step increase moves the thermometer rating 0.5 degrees.)

Although the effect of new tone is significant in statistical terms ($p < 0.01$, $t = 2.44$), with 41,145 cases, variables of marginal substantive import may still be statistically significant even when stringent tests of statistical significance are applied. Thus, it is not clear that we should make much of this one-degree effect. But given the crudeness of the measure of news tone and the large number of controls, we might take this as a substantively important finding. In any event, our primary hypothesis did not expect large effects of news tone across the entire sample and for all types of newspapers. Rather, we should observe stronger effects for major (credible) newspapers and for subsets of voters. Before turning to those conditional hypotheses, the discussion turns to the impact of the control variables.

### Impact of Control Variables

Many of the controls perform as hypothesized. First, the political configuration of the community in which a respondent lives affects warmth toward Clinton. Each percentage point increase in voting support for Clinton in the surrounding community leads to a 0.18-degree increase in warmth to the president. All else being equal, we can expect a person living in the most supportive (71) compared to the least supportive local community (15), a 56 percent difference, to be about 10 degrees warmer to Clinton.

TABLE 8.1. *Impact of news tone on presidential feeling thermometer, 2000 National Annenberg Election Study*

| Variable | Model 1* | | | | Model 2† | | | |
|---|---|---|---|---|---|---|---|---|
| | B | SE | T | $p^\ddagger$ | B | SE | t | $p^\ddagger$ |
| News Tone | 0.52 | 0.21 | 2.44 | 0.001 | Xxxx | | | |
| Tone-Major | xxxxx | | | | 1.90 | 0.32 | 5.95 | 0.000 |
| Tone-Minor | xxxxx | | | | -0.61 | 0.29 | -2.12 | 0.034 |
| County Vote | 0.18 | 0.01 | 14.12 | 0.000 | 0.17 | 0.01 | 13.53 | 0.000 |
| Party ID | 6.88 | 0.08 | 85.84 | 0.000 | 6.87 | 0.08 | 85.63 | 0.000 |
| Ideological ID | 1.93 | 0.17 | 11.37 | 0.000 | 1.95 | 0.17 | 11.48 | 0.000 |
| Sex | -4.09 | 0.29 | -14.17 | 0.000 | -4.01 | 0.29 | -13.86 | 0.000 |
| Age | -0.06 | 0.01 | -6.47 | 0.000 | -0.06 | 0.01 | -6.50 | 0.000 |
| Black | 19.82 | 0.76 | 26.01 | 0.000 | 19.77 | 0.76 | 25.96 | 0.000 |
| Asian | 10.08 | 1.29 | 7.79 | 0.000 | 10.00 | 1.29 | 7.74 | 0.000 |
| Hispanic | 15.73 | 0.80 | 19.71 | 0.000 | 15.81 | 0.80 | 19.82 | 0.000 |
| White | 2.10 | 0.66 | 3.20 | 0.001 | 2.05 | 0.66 | 3.13 | 0.001 |
| Education | -0.41 | 0.06 | -6.43 | 0.000 | -0.43 | 0.06 | -6.74 | 0.000 |
| Health Spending | -1.55 | 0.22 | -7.17 | 0.000 | -1.56 | 0.22 | -7.2 | 0.000 |
| Voucher | 0.45 | 0.28 | 1.58 | 0.055 | 0.48 | 0.28 | 1.70 | 0.044 |
| Abortion | 5.57 | 0.31 | 17.93 | 0.000 | 5.52 | 0.31 | 17.79 | 0.000 |
| Gun Control | -3.62 | 0.15 | -24.31 | 0.000 | -3.62 | 0.15 | -24.31 | 0.000 |
| Crime | 1.94 | 0.19 | 10.08 | 0.000 | 1.93 | 0.19 | 10.04 | 0.000 |
| Party Money | 2.11 | 0.35 | 6.06 | 0.000 | 2.16 | 0.35 | 6.21 | 0.000 |

| | | | | | | | | |
|---|---|---|---|---|---|---|---|---|
| Election Finance | 2.87 | 0.20 | 14.18 | 0.000 | 2.86 | 0.20 | 14.15 | 0.000 |
| Gay Jobs | -1.02 | 0.15 | -6.80 | 0.000 | -1.01 | 0.15 | -6.75 | 0.000 |
| Black Jobs | -2.02 | 0.17 | -11.57 | 0.000 | -2.00 | 0.17 | -11.43 | 0.000 |
| Poverty | -0.59 | 0.20 | -2.92 | 0.002 | -0.55 | 0.20 | -2.71 | 0.004 |
| Taxes | 4.34 | 0.16 | 26.97 | 0.000 | 4.32 | 0.16 | 26.84 | 0.000 |
| SSI Spend | -1.68 | 0.23 | -7.25 | 0.000 | -1.65 | 0.23 | -7.13 | 0.000 |
| TV Days | -0.04 | 0.06 | -0.55 | 0.579 | -0.04 | 0.06 | -0.77 | 0.442 |
| Cable Days | 0.30 | 0.05 | 5.61 | 0.000 | 0.30 | 0.05 | 5.62 | 0.000 |
| Local TV Days | 0.25 | 0.06 | 4.06 | 0.000 | 0.26 | 0.06 | 4.18 | 0.000 |
| Newspaper Days | -0.10 | 0.05 | -1.86 | 0.062 | -0.11 | 0.05 | -2.08 | 0.037 |
| Radio Days | -0.52 | 0.06 | -8.87 | 0.000 | -0.52 | 0.06 | -8.84 | 0.000 |
| Constant | -2.04 | 1.83 | -1.11 | 0.266 | -1.98 | 1.83 | -1.07 | 0.283 |
| N | 41145 | | | | 41145 | | | |
| $R^2$ / ADJ. $R^2$ | 0.44 | 0.44 | | | 0.44 | 0.44 | | |

\* Also includes controls for month, December 1999–January 2001.

† One-tailed tests, except for TV Days, Cable Days, Local TV Days, and Newspaper Days, which are two-tailed because no direction is predicted.

‡ One-tailed tests, except for TV Days, Cable Days, Local TV Days, and Newspaper Days, which are two-tailed because no direction is predicted. Also, two-tailed test for Tone-Minor Papers because the sign is wrong.

*Source:* 2000 National Annenberg Election Study. See text for details on specific variables.

Other research has found strong local community and interpersonal network effects on voting (Beck et al., 2002). The variable, as measured here, is likely tapping into many of these local community and interpersonal interaction effects. People may also decide to live in communities that better reflect their cultural and political attitudes and orientations, which this variable may also tap. Thus, it should not be too surprising that the variable has the strong impact that it does. Yet, this is to my knowledge the first time that such community and interpersonal network effects have been found for attitudes toward the president.

Partisan and ideological identification also display pronounced effects on the presidential feeling thermometer. Party identification may be the most potent variable in the estimation in terms of both substantive impact and statistical significance. Each one-unit change in party identification on the 7 point scale indicates a shift of nearly 6.9 degrees of warmth. A strong Democrat will be about 41 degrees warmer toward Clinton than a strong Republican. Similarly, self-identified strong liberals will be about 7.6 degrees warmer than strong conservatives; each step unit shift in ideological identification leads to a 1.9-degree swing in warmth.

Demographic factors are also statistically significant in most instances, although they vary widely in substantive impact. Women are 4.1 degrees warmer to Clinton than are men, a smaller than expected impact considering the literature on the gender gap and the apparently high level of support for Clinton among women compared to men during the Lewinsky scandal period. Older people are surprisingly, and counter to expectations, cooler to Clinton than are younger people. Each additional year leads to a tiny 0.06-degree shift in warmth. Thirty-year-olds will then be some 0.6 degrees cooler to Clinton than twenty-year-olds, whereas seventy-year-olds will be about 3 degrees cooler to Clinton than twenty-year-olds. The mildness of the gender and age effects may be in part a result of the correlation between these demographics and other factors that also affect attitudes toward Clinton and that the estimated model controls.

Education, too, affects warmth toward Clinton; as expected, the more educated are cooler to Clinton. Each unit increase in education produces a 0.4-degree shift in warmth, but the overall effect is substantively tiny. From the least to the most highly educated person, we can expect a decline in warmth of about 3.2 degrees.

Racial effects are often quite potent in presidential evaluations. I used as the criterion category those who did not indicate their race. From these estimates, being White has no significant impact on warmth toward Clinton, but Blacks, Hispanics, and Asians are all more positively disposed toward Clinton than those who fail to designate a race. Here we find that Blacks are 20 degrees warmer, Hispanics 16 degrees, and Asians 10 degrees warmer toward Clinton, all significant and substantively meaningful effects.

All but one of the issue variables, support for school vouchers, is statistically significant. Supporters of abortion rights are 5.6 degrees warmer to Clinton than to opponents. Those who support increased aid for health care are 4.5 degrees warmer than those who do not support such increases. Individuals who do not see taxes as a problem are about 13 degrees warmer to Clinton than those who see taxes as an extremely serious problem; whereas voters who want to spend more on Social Security are about 5 degrees warmer to Clinton than those who prefer to spend less on Social Security. Supporters of gun control are about 11 degrees warmer to Clinton than those who oppose gun control, and individuals who want more federal aid for crime are nearly 6 degrees warmer to Clinton than those who do not want a greater federal role here. Supporters of greater federal antipoverty efforts, protections of gay job rights, and protections of Black job rights feel warmer to Clinton by 1.8, 3, and 6 degrees, respectively, than their policy opponents. Finally, those who support regulation of party money in elections and election finance in general feel more warmly toward Clinton by 4 and 9 degrees, respectively, than those who opposed such election finance regulations.

Last, media exposure, in addition to news tone, affects warmth toward Clinton in some instances. All four media exposure variables are statistically significant, although they vary in substantive impact. The number of days that one reads a newspaper has the smallest impact. Everyday readers are only 0.7 degrees cooler to Clinton than individuals who never read a newspaper. Yet, each additional day per week that one watches local television news increases warmth to Clinton by 0.25 degrees, a difference of 1.75 degrees between someone who does not watch local television and someone who watches every day. Cable television viewing effects are slightly larger, at 0.3 degrees per day. Everyday watchers of cable television will be about 2.1 degrees warmer to Clinton than non–cable watchers.

Talk radio had the largest effect of any of the four media exposure variables, and as expected, increased exposure to talk radio reduces warmth toward Clinton by 0.5 degrees for each additional day of exposure. Those who listen to talk radio every day of the week will be 3.5 degrees cooler to Clinton than individuals who do not listen to talk radio. These results for talk radio confirm Barker's (1999, 2002) findings that talk radio has more than reinforcement or self-selection effects. The self-selection idea suggests that conservatives seek out talk radio because its hosts are conservative. Like Barker, we control for ideological self-identification, and talk radio still produces significant effects on attitudes toward Clinton.

## TESTS OF THE CONDITIONAL HYPOTHESES

Table 8.1, Model 2, turns to a test of Hypothesis 2: that news tone impacts should be greater for those who read major versus minor newspapers, with major newspapers defined here as having their own Washington news bureau. Based on this definition of major/minor newspapers, 9,823 (16.7%) respondents read a major newspaper that made an endorsement, and 12,646 (21.6%) read a minor newspaper that made an endorsement.

Results of this estimation strongly support the major newspaper hypothesis. Reading a major newspaper affects assessments of Bill Clinton ($b = 1.9$, $t = 5.95$, $p < 0.000$), but reading a minor newspaper does not. In fact, the minor newspaper variable points in the wrong direction. The substantive effect is quite small, however, slightly more than 1 percent when comparing Democratic and Republican newspapers. But for major newspapers, findings indicate that a person who reads a Democratic-endorsing newspaper will be about 3.8 degrees warmer toward Clinton than someone who reads a Republican-endorsing newspaper. If we had a better measure of newspaper credibility with respect to presidential news – for instance, a survey item asking people whether they viewed their newspaper as a credible source of news about the president – we might find even stronger results. It is

TABLE 8.2. *Impact of interaction between type of newspaper and how much respondent follows public affairs**

|  | b | SE | t | p |
|---|---|---|---|---|
| *News Tone-Major Papers* |  |  |  |  |
| Consistently Follows Public Affairs | 2.18 | 0.49 | 4.48 | 0.000 |
| Moderately Follows Public Affairs | −0.82 | 0.52 | −1.57 | 0.116 |
| Occasionally Follows Public Affairs | 7.36 | 0.77 | 9.61 | 0.000 |
| Rarely Follows Public Affairs | 0.37 | 1.43 | 0.26 | 0.800 |
| *News Tone-Minor Papers* |  |  |  |  |
| Consistently Follows Public Affairs | −0.04 | 0.51 | −0.08 | 0.938 |
| Moderately Follows Public Affairs | −1.59 | 0.48 | −3.32 | 0.001 |
| Occasionally Follows Public Affairs | 0.69 | 0.64 | 1.07 | 0.284 |
| Rarely Follows Public Affairs | −0.86 | 0.84 | −1.02 | 0.306 |
| N | 41071 |  |  |  |
| $R^2$ | 0.44 |  |  |  |
| Adj. $R^2$ | 0.44 |  |  |  |

* Controls for all variables used in Table 8.1 plus the Follows Public Affairs variable.
*Source:* 2000 National Annenberg Election Study. See text for details on variables.

heartening that we were able to find any supportive evidence for this hypothesis given the indirect measurement of newspaper credibility.

Table 8.2 presents results testing Hypothesis 3, which states that news tone effects will vary across types of people. That hypothesis states, first, that one must be directly exposed to the newspaper before newspaper tone effects can occur. Among the exposed, those who need help interpreting events will be more receptive to tone effects than those who do not need help interpreting events.

I used how much a person follows public affairs in general to distinguish individuals' ability to interpret events. The guiding assumption is that those who generally follow public affairs will be better able to interpret events on their own than those who follow public affairs less frequently or regularly. Those who pay greater attention to public affairs will usually possess greater stores of knowledge about politics, which they can use to interpret events. Those who pay less attention, but still some attention, possess shallower bases of knowledge about politics. These individuals should be more likely to turn to newspapers (and other sources) to help them interpret events and the implications of those events on presidential performance.

The specific NAES variable on attention to public affairs classifies people into four groups: those who say that they follow government and public affairs "most of the time" (Consistent Followers), "some of the time" (Moderate Followers), "now and then" (Occasional Followers), and "hardly at all" (Rare Followers). Hypothesis 3 predicts that Consistent Followers generally will resist tone, possessing sufficient political information and knowledge to interpret events independently. Similarly, Rare Followers will not receive news tone messages enough for there to be news tone effects. (It is important to note that rare and consistent followers of public affairs might or might not read a newspaper, a condition that must hold if we are to isolate the effects of newspaper tone exposure and distinguish respondents according to Hypothesis 3.) It is unclear whether Moderate Followers will feel news tone effects. Their political knowledge base may or may not be developed enough for them to independently interpret events. The strongest news tone effects should be found for Occasional Followers, who presumably do not possess a sufficiently well-developed political knowledge base to independently interpret events and, thus, should seek help in such interpretation from newspapers.

To test this hypothesis, I interacted each of the four types of public affairs followers with the tone of the newspaper they read, distinguishing between major and minor newspapers, for a total of eight dummy variables: (Tone of major newspaper that respondent reads) × (Consistent public affairs followers); (Tone of minor newspaper that respondent reads) × (Occasional public affairs followers). In the following analysis, the criterion case is respondents who do not read a newspaper.

First, as hypothesized, for those who read minor newspapers, the type of individual with regard to following public affairs has no impact on evaluations of Bill Clinton. All of these interactions are statistically insignificant except for the interaction with Moderate Followers of public affairs, but that sign points in the wrong direction. The effect, however, is modest, at 3.2 degrees between those who read Democratic-endorsing versus Republican-endorsing newspapers.

Turning to those who read major newspapers, as expected, we see no effect of tone for Rare and Moderate followers of public affairs, as hypothesized. But contrary to expectations, Consistent followers seem somewhat receptive to the tone of presidential news when they read major newspapers. The effect, although statistically significant ($t = 4.48$, $p < 0.000$) is modest, with those who read a

Democratic-endorsing newspaper about 4.7 degrees warmer toward Clinton than those who read a Republican-endorsing newspaper.

However, Occasional Followers who read a major newspaper are highly receptive to the tone of news about the president. Of these occasional followers, readers of a Democratic-endorsing newspaper will be 14.6 degrees warmer to Bill Clinton than those who read a Republican-endorsing newspaper, a substantively massive effect that is even more impressive given the crudeness of the measures used in the analysis. The impact of news tone in a major newspaper for occasional followers is about 40 percent of the standard deviation on the Bill Clinton thermometer. For occasional followers of public affairs, changing their newspaper from one that favors one party to one that favors the other is slightly more potent than shifting two units on the 7-point party identification scale, or nearly 4 steps on the 5-point NAES ideology identification scale (e.g., very conservative to moderately liberal). For occasional followers of public affairs, reading a major newspaper has among the strongest effects on evaluations of the president of any variable used in this analysis.

## CONCLUSIONS

This chapter presents evidence that the tone of news affects public evaluations of the president, a finding with implications for presidential leadership of public opinion. By pooling all of the cross-sections of the 2000 NAES, we can disentangle news tone from event effects on public thermometer ratings of the president. Pooling the cross-sections allows events to vary randomly across respondents. The "random assignment" of respondents across cross sections, along with a host of other control variables, enables us to disentangle event from reporting effects, providing us with evidence that news tone affects evaluations of the president.

Before accepting this finding and its implications too readily, one must recognize an assumption underlying this analysis. The analysis used an indirect measure of the tone of news toward the president, endorsement behavior, based on the assumption that Democratic-endorsing newspapers in the 2000 election will be more likely to publish positive or favorable news on Bill Clinton in 2000 than newspapers that endorsed the Republican. Several other studies provide evidence in support of the assumption linking endorsing behavior with the tonality of news (Kahn and Kenney, 2002; Barrett and Barrington, 2005; Peake, 2007). The endorsement indicator is limited in another sense – it crudely distinguishes among Democratic, Republican, and nonendorsing newspapers. Thus, it cannot discriminate gradations of tonality, for instance, between highly and somewhat (un)favorable news. Nor does it tell us which types of news items (e.g., news stories, editorials) most greatly affect people when they evaluate the president.

Despite these limitations in measurement, the analysis finds strong effects of news tone on evaluations of the president under certain circumstances. The results indicate stronger news tone effects for credible than less credible newspapers and for individuals who need help in interpreting events compared with those who do not need such help, assuming exposure to a newspaper. Most impressive, for individuals who occasionally follow public affairs, and thus may need some help in interpreting some events, switching from a Republican-endorsing to a Democratic-endorsing newspaper will raise warmth to Clinton by more than 14 degrees on the 101-degree thermometer scale. Not only is this result substantively impressive in its own right, it also stands as one of the strongest influences on an individual's evaluation in the analysis.

These findings hold important implications for presidential leadership and present us with the final piece of evidence regarding the going local leadership strategy. If presidents can affect the tone of the news that newspapers publish about them, which previous chapters demonstrate, then presidents can possibly affect public opinion, in particular, public support for them. A leadership strategy that targets local newspapers may have pay-offs for the president and may help compensate for the barriers to national public leadership that polarized politics and the fragmented news media erect. Thus, the findings of this chapter not only reflect on the role of the news media in shaping public opinion, but also speak to issues of presidential leadership style and effectiveness in the late twentieth and early twenty-first centuries. The evidence presented here that the tone of local reporting affects assessments of the president coupled with previous findings on the presidential ability to influence local news coverage suggests pay-offs to the going local leadership strategy that presidents now employ in the post-broadcast age.

## APPENDIX 8.1: VARIABLES FROM THE 2000 NATIONAL ANNENBERG ELECTION STUDY (NAES) USED IN THE ANALYSIS

The following is a list of variables used in the analysis in Chapter 8, with the following details on each variable in this order: NAES variable number, variable name, variable description, and codes used in the analysis. Exact question wordings can be obtained from the NAES codebook.

Ca52 **CLINTON** Clinton Thermometer rating, 0–100.

Cba01 **NATECON** Economic condition in country today: 1 = Excellent, 2 = Good, 3 = Fair, 4 = Poor.

Cba02 **PERSECON** Personal Economic Condition today: 1 = Excellent, 2 = Good, 3 = Fair, 4 = Poor.

Cbb01 **TAXES** Taxes a problem: 1 = extremely serious, 2 = serious, 3 = not too serious, 4 = not a problem.

Cbc01 **SSISPEND** Social Security spending: 1 = more, 2 = same, 3 = less, 4=none.

Cbd02 **VOUCHERS** Federal government should give school vouchers: 1 = yes, 2 = no.

Cbe02 **HEALTHSPEND** Spending on health care: 1 = more, 2 = same, 3 = less, 4 = none.

Cf02 **ABORTION** Government should restrict abortion: 1 = yes, 2 = no.

Cbg06 **GUNS** Government effort to restrict gun purchases: 1 = more, 2 = same, 3 = less, 4 = none.

Cbg12 **CRIME** Not enough criminals being punished is a problem? 1 = extremely serious, 2 = serious, 3 = not too serious, 4 = not a problem.

Cbh01 **PARTYMONEY** Limit money that can be given to political parties: 1 = yes, 2 = no.

Cbh07 **ELECTION** Federal government should provide public money for election campaigns: 1 = more, 2 = same, 3 = less, 4 = none.

Cbl05 **GAYJOBS** Federal effort to stop job discrimination against homosexuals: 1 = more, 2 = same, 3 = less, 4 = none.

Cbm01 **BLACKJOBS** Federal effort to stop job discrimination against Blacks: 1 = more, 2 = same, 3 = less, 4 = none.

Cbp01 **POVERTY** Is poverty a problem: 1 = extremely serious, 2 = serious, 3 = not too serious, 4 = not a problem

Ce01 **TVDAYS** Number of days watched network television news last week: 0–7.

Ce02 **CABLEDAYS** Number of days watched cable news last week: 0–7.

Ce06 **LOCALTVDAYS** Number of days watched local television news last week: 0–7.

Ce13 **PAPERDAYS** Number of days last week read daily newspaper: 0–7.

Ce14 Which newspaper does respondent read.

Ce18 **RADIODAYS** Number of days listened to talk radio last week 0–7

Ck01 **PUBAFFAIRS** How much does respondent follow government and public affairs: 1 = most of the time, 2 = some of the time, 3 = now and then, 4 = hardly at all.

**PID:** Party Identification is created from cv01, cv02, and cv03 below to create the standard 7-point scale with Strong Democrat = 7, Strong Republican = 1 and Pure Independent = 4. Due to the large number of people on cv01 who were coded 4 = verbatim, and to preserve cases for analysis, I coded these respondents as 4 = Pure Independents.

Cv01 PID 1 = R, 2 = D, 3 = I, 4 = verbatim.

Cv02 Strength of PID 1 = strong, 2 = not strong.

Cv03 Leaners 1 = R, 2 = D, 3 = neither.

Cv04 **IDEOLOGY** Self-identification: 1 = Very Conservative, 2 = Conservative, 3 = Moderate, 4 = Liberal, 5 = Very Liberal.

Cw01 **SEX** 1 = male, 2 = female.

Cw02 **AGE** 18–97.

Cw03 **BLACK, WHITE, ASIAN** dummy variables, such that category = 1, otherwise = 0, based on these NAES codes, 1 = White, 2 = Black, 3 = Asian, 4 = verbatim. White is defined as non-Hispanic Whites.

Cw04 **HISPANIC**, 1 = yes, 2 = no.

Cw06 **EDUC** education 1 = 8 or less, 2 = some HS, 3 = HS, 4 = technical or vocational school, 5 = some college, 6 = AA degree, 7 = BA, 8 = Some grad school, 9 = MA degree or more.

Cw23 **COUNTY** Fips code.

Cw28 **INCOME** 1 = less than 10k, 2 = 10–15K, 3 = 15–25K, 4 = 25–35K, 5 = 35–50K, 6 = 50–75K, 7 = 75–100K, 8 = 100–150K, 9 = 150K+.

# CHAPTER 9

# Conclusions: Presidential Leadership in the Post-Broadcast Age

This book began with a puzzle. Why are presidents going public so much more than in the recent past if doing so has proven ineffective as a method of mobilizing public support? The answer to this puzzle begins with distinguishing between going national and going narrow. In going national, presidents aim at moving national public opinion. In going narrow, presidents target segments of the political order, in particular their party base, interest groups, and localities. Because of the rise of polarized parties and fragmented media, going national is no longer as effective a leadership strategy as it once was. In place of going national, presidents now use a going narrow leadership approach. The research in this book demonstrates the effectiveness of this strategy – presidents seem to be able to move or influence narrow groups. Of course, the research presented here is limited, demonstrating these effects primarily for readers of local newspapers. One direction for future research would be to see if other narrow targets of presidential leadership efforts similarly respond.

Along the way to the conclusion that going narrow may be an effective strategy, the research presented herein made several other contributions. First, I offered and tested a theory of presidential news management. Second, in conjunction, I conducted a large content analysis, which has implications for how we understand and study media bias. Third, I offered a context theory of presidential leadership, which tells us why presidents replaced the going national approach with going narrow. In the concluding pages of this book, I discuss the implications of each of these contributions.

## PRESIDENTIAL NEWS MANAGEMENT
## AND LOCAL NEWS COVERAGE

Presidents care about the news coverage that they receive for its sup-
posed impact on public support. They would like the optimal amount
and the proper tone in their news coverage. The administration develops a news management strategy to ensure that the president receives
the kind of news coverage he needs and wants.

But numerous factors affect the production of news; the president's
news management strategy is only one. Economic considerations are
a pervasive influence underlying the news production process. If news
organizations cannot make a profit, they cannot stay in business. A
second major influence on the production of news is the professional orientations of news production personnel, such as reporters
and editors. Thus, the president's news management strategy does
not directly affect presidential news coverage but operates through
these two mechanisms, economic decisions and professional orientation. Effective presidential news management, from the economic
perspective, stimulates demand for news about the president and/or
helps contain news organizations' cost of news production. From the
news professionalism perspective, effective president news management leads journalists to view the president and his actions as newsworthy.

Identifying a president's news management strategy is as difficult
as specifying the causal mechanisms through which it operates. Many
presidential news management decisions are hidden from public view,
and the White House does not pronounce what its news management
strategy will be other than the hollow proclamation that it will run
an "open administration." We can, however, observe the behavioral
manifestations of the news management strategy in the president's
public activities. (This, of course, assumes that the news management
strategy dictates or drives much of the president's public activities.)
Empirically, the question that I addressed in this study was whether the
president's public activities affect the quantity and tone of coverage
in local newspapers, and whether tone affected public evaluations of
the president.

Chapters 5 and 6 addressed the question of the quantity of presidential news using two data sets, a sample of news stories about the president across a random set of days and newspapers in 2000 used in Chapter 5 and a monthly time series from 1990 through 2007 in Chapter 6. Both analyses found that presidential public activities affect the quantity of presidential news, but so do some nonpresidential factors. Several specific findings stand out from that analysis. First, the number of presidential speeches affects news coverage, but nonlinearly. I offered the distraction hypothesis to account for why presidents would engage in such a volume of activity that each successive public announcement after reaching a certain level would begin to reduce the amount of news coverage. The distraction hypothesis argues that presidents want to divert attention from controversial decisions and actions by overloading journalists with activities on which to report. Second, the Saturday presidential radio address seems to lead to more news coverage in local newspapers.

Chapter 7 turned to the question of the tone of presidential news, again finding that presidential activities may affect this important aspect of presidential news coverage. That analysis also revealed additional support for distraction effects. Because presidential actions and decisions can meet with criticism and negative news coverage, presidents can to some degree mitigate bad news by speaking more frequently in public. This overloads reporters with decisions and activities to cover and perhaps reduces the amount of news attention to particularly controversial decisions.

The analysis also found that when newspapers quote the president, he is more likely to receive positive news coverage, or at least neutralize criticism in the news. Frequently, however, when the president is quoted in a story, his voice stands alone and uncontested. Moreover, by speaking about foreign affairs, presidents can increase the likelihood that they will be quoted. This causal chain gives us some understanding of the importance of foreign policy to positive news coverage and why presidents may turn to foreign affairs.

All of the empirical analyses found that the president's public activities – the public face of the president's news management strategy – can affect these characteristics of presidential news coverage. But does news coverage matter? Does the type of news coverage that presidents receive in local newspapers affect public evaluations of the president, what I argue is a major rationale behind the president's news management strategy?

According to the analysis in Chapter 8, it appears that news coverage, in particular tone, can affect voters' thermometer ratings of the president. In other words, it matters whether someone reads a newspaper that on balance provides supportive or critical news coverage of the president. Yet, the analysis in Chapter 8 also found that the tone of news coverage does not affect everyone. The impact of tone is greater for readers of major than of minor local newspapers and for citizens who need help in interpreting events reported by their newspapers. All of the analyses emphasize the value of a presidential leadership strategy in the current age that targets newspapers to reach the mass public living in localities served by those newspapers.

This study should not, however, be viewed as the last word on these topics. For example, most of the analysis of newspaper coverage of the president used a sample of stories for 2000. Although I built a random sample of news for 2000, that year may be unique because it was a lame duck year for a popular president, Bill Clinton. Obviously, we need to perform similar analyses for other presidents and other time periods.

Second, the content analysis of news stories was somewhat crude. Because I found that presidential activities seem to affect the amount and tone of news coverage, it would be worthwhile to content analyze news stories for other characteristics of presidential news. Did the story mention the president's geographic location or communication venue (e.g., radio address, news conference), when the president and/or administration spokesperson was quoted, how long was the quote, what was the topic of the quote, and where was the quote placed in the text of the story? Answers to such detailed questions will help us tighten the linkage between what presidents do and the type of news coverage they receive.

The content analyses used here included all types of newspaper mentions of the president, from straight news stories to editorials and op-ed pieces to even letters to the editor. I justified this decision to content analyze all such mentions because we know so little about presidential news coverage. Future research should discriminate across types of news items. Do presidential public activities have greater affect on some types of news items, like straight news, than on other types, such as editorials and opinion columns?

Furthermore, we know little about how voters process news about the president. In evaluating the president, do voters rely more heavily on some types of news than on others? For instance, does foreign policy news affect public evaluations more than domestic policy news? Does coverage of ceremonies and other non-policy events matter for public evaluations? When presidents are criticized or praised, does the type of criticism or acclaim, such as policy versus personality, matter? Finally, which types of news items matter most in public evaluations? Does the public rely on editorials as they do straight news? Clearly, the research here raises numerous unanswered questions.

## STUDYING BIAS AND TONE IN PRESIDENTIAL NEWS

In this book, I spent considerable time looking at the tone of news about the president in local newspapers and the impact of that tone on voters' assessments of the president. The analysis found several factors that affect the tone of presidential news, most important, presidential public activities, the public face of the president's news management strategies. It also found that the tone of news about the president can affect public evaluations of him.

Throughout this book, I favored the term news tone, avoiding a related term, media bias, for several reasons. First, there tends to be a lack of clarity or consistency when using the term media bias. Different writers use the term in different ways; often media bias is used to make a political point, rather than to guide research. News tone, by contrast, is a more neutral term and may be more easily measured in a reproducible and reliable manner.

Second, media bias may conflate the news production process with the outcome of that process, the news product. News tone refers to a characteristic of the news product itself. We can test hypotheses about the impact of aspects of the news production processes on the tone of news. For example, in this study I looked at whether presidential activities (news management strategies), the economics of the news production process, and news media political agendas affect the tone of news on the president. In this sense, news tone is a dependent variable, distinguishable from factors that affect the tone of the news, independent variables. News tone can also be used as an independent variable when we ask what impact the tone of the news has on, for instance, voters' attitudes. I used news tone as both a dependent and an independent variable in separate analyses. Still, the research reported here has implications for the burgeoning literature on media bias.

## The Many Meanings of Media Bias

Robert Entman's (2007) review of the literature on media bias helps us sort through the many ways writers have used the term. First, some define media bias as news that distorts or falsifies reality, what Entman calls "distortion bias." Others use media bias as the equivalent treatment of both (or more) sides to an argument, "content bias." Third, media bias may refer to the motivations and mindsets of journalists, "decision making bias." Decision making bias may affect how news producers write news stories and comes closest to my approach, which distinguishes news media political agendas (decision making bias) from news tone.

Those who claim distortion bias tend to lament that the news media fail to treat their side fairly or accurately. These claimants often are pushing a political point or an agenda – for example, conservatives who argue that the press is liberal, or liberals who argue the reverse. For the most part, the distortion bias debate cannot be resolved. First, "no 'objective' standard of unbiased coverage exists against which actual coverage can be compared" (Gilens and Hertzman, 2000, 371; also D'Alessio and Allen, 2000; Druckman and Parkin, 2005; Groeling and Kernell, 1998; Kahn and Kenney, 2002). Second, by definition, news distorts reality because news reporting must simplify reality. Reality is just too complex and voluminous to be reported in its entirety. News condenses reality, reporting some facts and filtering out others. Reasonable people may disagree about which facts should be included and the emphasis they should receive because they hold differing values. Insofar as people hold different values, there will be disagreement about whether the news "got it right."

The only headway that we can make with regard to the distortion bias is to assess whether the news media "got the *facts* right." I am making a distinction here between news and facts. Facts, such as what a political leader said, when the leader said it, and to whom he or she spoke, are verifiable and are important elements of news stories, especially news that aims to be "objective." Factcheck.org, of the Annenberg Public Policy Center of the University of Pennsylvania, provides one example of dealing with this aspect of news distortion, but Factcheck.org focuses more on what politicians and campaigns say publicly than on news reports. To my knowledge, there has yet to be a systematic study of how often the news media "gets the *facts* wrong," which types of facts and news outlets report facts most accurately, and what circumstances increase the likelihood of getting the facts right or wrong.

"Content bias" has been given the most sustained attention by scholars, especially in the realm of election reporting (see D'Alessio and Allen, 2000). Election contests pose a natural standard for assessing the degree of equality of treatment of candidates. For instance, do candidates receive the same amount of news space and attention? Still, one can criticize the equality standard. In an election between an incumbent and a challenger, is it best for voters if they are presented with equal amounts of news reporting on the two candidates? Would they be better served by receiving more news about the challenger, who is likely less well-known than the incumbent? Or should more attention be paid to incumbents because of their records in office? These too are normative questions, but they relate to the theory and practice of democracy.

It is not clear to me, however, what standard to apply for content bias when discussing presidents in office. With two candidates competing for office, the fifty–fifty time standard at least presents a baseline against which to judge news reporting of campaigns. In a situation with only one official, the president, equality has no such meaning.

"Decision making bias" comes closest to a concept I used in this research, news media political agendas. Detecting whether a news organization has a political agenda becomes the tricky part. First, news organizations, unlike nations, rarely, if ever, announce policies. Even news organizations that have reputations for being on the left or right, Democratic or Republican, often try to hide or deny such political proclivities, instead arguing that their news product is more objective, reliable, credible, and truthful than its competitors.

Second, we should not equate the individual political attitudes and preferences of news personnel with a news organization being politically tilted or aligned. Doing so may raise the issue of the ecological fallacy and disregard differences in the political outlook of news organization personnel. Studies show that reporters tend to lean in a liberal-Democratic direction, but editors in a more conservative-Republican direction (Weaver and Wilhoit, 1991). In many instances, journalists and editors negotiate their political (and other) differences in producing the news, but sometimes a critical decision maker, such as an editor or owner, puts his or her political and/or ideological stamp on the news product.

Perhaps the best we can do in assessing decision-making bias is, as I have done, to look at the endorsement behavior of news organizations as an indirect measure of that organization's political agenda or look at the newspaper's editorials to see if there is any systematic partisan or ideological pattern. Critically, these indicators are not direct measures of decision-making bias in news organizations. A newspaper may endorse a candidate because he or she is better than the competitor, for instance, more knowledgeable or experienced or has a history of not being corrupt. If one party has been embroiled in corruption and other scandals, but the other party has not, a newspaper may consistently endorse the candidates from the uncorrupt party, not because of partisan preferences or leanings. Furthermore, other newspapers may refrain from endorsing candidates, but because of their political agenda, their news may tilt for or against candidates and politicians of one party over the other systematically. Finally, some newspapers might not break the wall of separation between news and opinion. They may endorse a candidate and over time demonstrate an endorsement preference for one party over the other, but their straight news coverage may be evenhanded and not toned in either direction. Thus, we must be careful in using endorsements as an indicator of the partisan or ideological preferences of a newspaper.

## Tone and Presidential News

Rather than focus on bias, perhaps a more useful way of assessing presidential news is to ask whether presidential news is positive or negative, good or bad, for the president, that is, look at tone or valence, as I have done in this study. Tone is important because presidents, politicians, commentators, and some scholars believe that positive news enhances presidential leadership, whereas negative news undercuts it. Moreover, presidents often believe that the media are biased against them by being more likely to run a negative than a positive news story. A key task of White House media operations is to ensure positive news coverage and mitigate the harm of negative news through what is generally referred to as "spin control" (Kumar, 2007; Kurtz, 1998; Maltese, 1992; Rozell, 1993, 1995). This leads to two critical questions that I spent much time addressing in this study: What is the tone of presidential news, and what determines that tonality?

We may be able to define tone in such a way that we can reliably and reproducibly measure it. For instance, one can define positive news as stories that present the president as a strong, successful, prudent leader, backed by the public and other political leaders, and define negative news as stories that portray the president as weak, indecisive, unsuccessful, beset by opponents, and lacking high levels of public support. Coding news according to such a definition is admittedly difficult but possible (also see Brody, 1991; Farnsworth and Lichter, 2005; Grossman and Kumar, 1981; Erikson, MacKuen, and Stimson, 2002).

One of the primary concerns of the research reported here is whether presidents can affect their news coverage, including its tone, and whether news tone influences public thinking about the president. From this perspective, it is important to distinguish the sources of news tone – whether it is merely a function of events reported in the news or whether the decisions of journalists affect the tone of the news independent of events. Those who subscribe to a model that news tone reflects an event accurately assume, often without stating overtly, the "mirror" model of journalism. A second model, that a story's tone is, in part, a function of journalistic interpretation of the event, raises the issue of decision-making bias and allows for the possibility that presidential news management efforts can affect the tone of news. Decision-making bias suggests that reporters and editors interpose their own interpretations of an event into the news, for instance, by selectively excluding or including information in stories. In other words, news is a social or journalistic construction.

Presidents subscribe to this second way of viewing story tone. The White House expends a massive amount of resources to "news management" or "spin control" because they believe that they can alter the tone of a story. The analysis presented here suggests that presidents may indeed be able to affect the tone of their news coverage, as well as other attributes, which, in turn, may affect public evaluations of the president, a key presidential goal.

Separating the event from journalistic (and other) influences on news tone is difficult. Druckman and Parkin (2005) present one type of design that holds the event constant, allowing only news tone to vary in their effort to isolate the event from news effects on voters. In this study, I used a different approach, which has events vary randomly over time and over survey respondents. Actual content analyses of presidential news that are sensitive to this concern may be necessary to distinguish the effects of events and news on voters' behavior and opinion. Such a research task surely will be daunting given the cost of such data collection, as well as the difficulty of determining a coding scheme that may be able to make such a distinction. Experimental studies, which can vary the event and reporting on the event, may prove a more efficient design for resolving this issue, which is important for our understanding of the ability of presidents, candidates, and journalists to affect citizens. This leads to the other major concern of the research reported here – presidential leadership.

## UNDERSTANDING PRESIDENTIAL LEADERSHIP

> [P]residents typically do not succeed in their efforts to change public opinion. Even "great communicators" usually fail to obtain the public's support for their high-priority initiatives.... [T]he bully pulpit has proved ineffective not only for achieving majority support but also for increasing support from a smaller base.... [P]residents usually fail to move the general public and are frustrated in their attempts to move those who should be most attuned to their messages. –George Edwards, *On Deaf Ears*, 2003, 241.

"[P]residential words are a powerful instrument of economic leadership that can affect consumer and business perceptions of current and future economic conditions.... [P]residents' public relations efforts with respect to the economy affect public attitudes . . . –B. Dan Wood, *The Politics of Economic Leadership*, 2007, 159, 167.

The research presented in this book concentrates its analysis on local news coverage of the president, but this book's larger concern centers on *presidential leadership* in the post-broadcast age. If "leading the public is at the core of the modern presidency," (Edwards, 2003, 4), can presidents lead in the face of polarized politics and a fragmented media, key attributes of the political environment in the post-broadcast era?

The quotes at the beginning of the section by two of our most distinguished and eminent scholars of the presidency and public opinion, George Edwards and B. Dan Wood, present starkly different answers to this question. Edwards is pessimistic about the president's ability to lead public opinion, whereas Wood offers a more affirmative answer. These two scholars' studies come to different conclusions in part because the methodology, data, and the policy areas that they look at differ. But they also look at the question from different theoretical orientations.

Edwards is most concerned with the direct effects of presidential rhetoric on public attitudes on issues of importance to the president, heavily relying on recent political psychology in addressing why presidents seem so unable to move public opinion. Presidents may have difficulty in focusing public attention, a prerequisite for leadership, because the political environment presents voters with many messages in addition to the president's, and the president does not always have the luxury to talk repeatedly about one or a few issues because of his various policy responsibilities. These barriers, as well as public misperception, may frustrate presidential attempts to frame an issue conducive to his leadership efforts. The public also is notorious for its disinterest in politics and public affairs, meaning that many people will not receive or be exposed to presidential communications efforts, and people's political predispositions may erect a barrier against the president's message.

Unlike Edwards, Wood looks at one salient issue, the economy, for which the public holds the president responsible. Presidents possess incentives to continually refer to the economy, which is not the case with most issues. Thus, in the case of the economy, although no one

speech may affect public thinking, repetitive and continual presidential speaking on the economy may cumulate to affect public opinion.
Furthermore, in contrast with Edwards, who focuses on direct presidential effects on public opinion, Wood suggests that indirect effects
of presidential rhetoric on the economy as mediated through the news
media may have a larger impact on public opinion.

The research in this study integrates insights from both Edwards and
Wood. As the analysis in Chapter 8 shows, only a subset of the public
is susceptible to potential leadership efforts, consistent with Edwards's
focus on mass political psychology. Other analysis in this study showed
that presidents may be able to influence news coverage, much as Wood
argues that presidential rhetoric, and the presidential public relations
apparatus, affects news coverage of the economy (162).[1]

By integrating the views of Edwards and Wood, we arrive at a more
nuanced understanding of presidential leadership of public opinion,
which, for many of the reasons that Edwards offers, is always problematic. Yet, presidents may be able to influence the thinking of some
people some of the time. The analysis in Chapter 8 begins to specify
whom and when: People who need help interpreting events because
they only occasionally follow public affairs but tend to read credible,
major newspapers, that is, newspapers they look to for news about the
president.

Furthermore, presidential leadership effects have a greater influence on public opinion when the content of the news people receive
is targeted than when a president speaks directly to the entire mass
public. In explaining why presidents persist in going public so much
for so little, Edwards recognizes that a major target of presidential
communications efforts is the mass media (245). Edwards laments,
"Although we have rich descriptions of these efforts, we know very
little about their success in influencing the media" (245); however,
the analyses in Chapters 5 through 7 present evidence that presidents
may indeed be successful in affecting the quantity and tone of their
news coverage.

[1] Wood does not have a direct measure of news coverage, but relies on the survey of
consumers of the University of Michigan, which asks people if they have recently
heard anything negative about the economy.

The context in which presidents find themselves affects their opportunities for leading, the style of leadership that they will pursue, the effectiveness of leadership efforts, and the targets of presidential leadership efforts. For instance, in his seminal study, *Going Public* (2006), Samuel Kernell argued that changes in the congressional environment from institutional to individual pluralism forced presidents to go public if they wanted to influence congressional support for their policies. Much research on presidential leadership proceeds as though nothing fundamental has changed in the presidential environment since the period for which Kernell was writing, the 1960s through the early 1980s. This may lead scholars to look for leadership effects where they should not exist or be as potent as they once were. In this study, I updated Kernell's key insights regarding presidential leadership, arguing that instead of going national, presidents in the post-broadcast age rely more heavily on a going narrow leadership approach.

This study also differs from the work of Edwards and Wood by arguing that political and media structures may affect the style of presidential leadership and thus tell us where to look for which kinds of presidential leadership effects. Political and media arrangements influence the effectiveness of different leadership styles or approaches.

To understand the type of leadership approach or style that presidents adopt as well as its potential effectiveness, we need to know about the political and media context the president confronts. As this study shows, despite the barriers to effective leadership that the polarized parties and a fragmented media of the post-broadcast age erect, by going narrow, and in particular by going local, presidents can influence the political opinions of targeted segments of the political system. The going local strategy is effective in influencing public opinion, even if it does not build as much public support as going national did for presidents in the "golden age of broadcasting." Yet, this may be the best that current presidents can do given the contextual hand they have been dealt.

# Bibliography

Aberbach, Joel D. 2005. "The Political Significance of the George W. Bush Administration." *Social Policy & Administration* 39 (April): 130–149.

Achen, Christopher H. 2000. "Why Lagged Dependent Variables Can Suppress the Explanatory Power of Other Independent Variables." Presented at the Annual Meeting of Political Methodology, Los Angeles.

Adatto, Kiku. 1990. *Sound Bite Democracy: Network Evening News Presidential Campaign Coverage, 1968 and 1988.* Research Paper R-2. Cambridge: Harvard University, Joan Shorenstein Barone Center.

Althaus, Scott. 2001. "Presidential Influence over Evening News Content: Assessing the Effects of Strategic Communication on News Coverage of the Gulf Crisis." Paper presented at the annual meeting of the American Political Science Association, Washington, DC.

Althaus, Scott L., and Young Mie Kim. 2006. "Priming Effects in Complex Information Environments: Reassessing the Impact of News Discourse on Presidential Approval." *Journal of Politics* 68 (November): 960–976.

Ansolabehere, Stephen, Rebecca Lessem, and James M. Snyder, Jr. 2006. "Research Note: The Orientation of Newspaper Endorsements in U.S. Elections, 1940–2002." *Quarterly Journal of Political Science* 1 (October): 393–404.

Ansolabehere, Stephen, Jonathan Rodden, and James M. Snyder, Jr. 2005. "Purple America." Typescript, Massachusetts Institute of Technology.

Arnold, R. Douglas. 2004. *Congress, the Press, and Political Accountability.* Princeton, NJ: Princeton University Press.

Balutis, Alan P. 1976. "Congress, the President, and the Press." *Journalism Quarterly* 59 (Autumn): 509–505.

Balutis, Alan P. 1977. "The Presidency and the Press: The Expanding Public Image." *Presidential Studies Quarterly* 7 (Fall): 244–251.

Balz, Dan, and Mike Allen. 2004. "Four More Years Attributed to Rove's Strategy Despite Moments of Doubt, Adviser's Planning Paid Off." *Washington Post*, Sunday, November 7, 2004, A01.

Barabas, Jason. 2008. "Presidential Policy Initiatives: How the Public Learns about State of the Union Proposals from the Mass Media." *Presidential Studies Quarterly* 38 (May): 195–222.

Barber, James David. 2009. *The Presidential Character*, 4th ed. New York: Pearson Longman.

Barker, David C. 1999. "Rushed Decisions: Political Talk Radio and Vote Choice, 1994–1996." *Journal of Politics* 61 (May): 527–539.

Barker, David C. 2002. *Rushed to Judgment: Talk Radio, Persuasion, and American Political Behavior*. New York: Columbia University Press.

Barker, David, and Kathleen Knight. 2000. "Political Talk Radio and Public Opinion." *Public Opinion Quarterly* 64 (Summer): 149–170.

Barnhurst, Kevin G., and Steele, Catherine A. 1997. "Image-bite News: The Visual Coverage of Elections on U.S. Television, 1968–1992." *Harvard International Journal of Press/Politics* 2 (1): 40–58.

Barrett, Andrew. 2004. "Gone Public: The Impact of Going Public on Presidential Legislative Success." *American Politics Research* 32 (May): 338–370.

Barrett, Andrew. 2005. "Going Public as a Legislative Weapon: Measuring Presidential Appeals Regarding Specific Legislation." *Presidential Studies Quarterly* 35 (February): 1–10.

Barrett, Andrew W. 2007. "Press Coverage of Legislative Appeals by the President." *Political Research Quarterly* 60 (December): 655–668.

Barrett, Andrew W., and Lowell W. Barrington. 2005. "Bias in Newspaper Photograph Selection." *Political Research Quarterly* 58 (December): 609–618.

Barrett, Andrew W., and Jeffrey S. Peake. 2007. "When the President Comes to Town: Examining Local Newspaper Coverage of Domestic Presidential Travel." *American Politics Research* 35 (January): 3–31.

Bartels, Larry M. 2000. "Partisanship and Voting Behavior, 1952–1996." *American Journal of Political Science* 44 (January): 35–50.

Baum, Matthew A. 2002. "The Constituent Foundations of the Rally-Round-the-Flag Phenomenon." *International Studies Quarterly* 46 (June): 263–299.

Baum, Matthew A., and Samuel Kernell. 1999. "Has Cable Ended the Golden Age of Presidential Television?" *American Political Science Review* 93 (March): 99–114.

Beck, Paul Allen, Russell J. Dalton, Steven Greene, and Robert Huckfeldt. 2002. "The Social Calculus of Voting: Interpersonal, Media, and Organizational Influences on Presidential Choices." *American Political Science Review* 96 (March): 57–73.

Bennett, W. Lance. 1990. "Toward a Theory of Press–State Relations in the United States." *Journal of Communications* 40 (Spring): 103–127.

Bergan, Daniel E., Alan S. Gerber, Donald P. Green, and Costas Panagopoulos. 2005. "Grassroots Mobilization and Voter Turnout in 2004." *Public Opinion Quarterly* 69 (5): 760–777.

Bishop, Bill with Robert G. Cushing. 2008. *The Big Sort: Why the Clustering of America is Tearing Us Apart.* New York: Houghton-Mifflin.

Black, Amy E., Douglas L. Koopman, and David K. Ryden. 2004. *Of Little Faith: The Politics of George W. Bush's Faith-Based Initiatives.* Washington, DC: Georgetown University Press.

Blood, Deborah J., and Peter C. B. Phillips. 1995. "Recession Headline News, Consumer Sentiment, the State of the Economy and Presidential Popularity: A Time Series Analysis 1989–1993." *International Journal of Public Opinion Research* 7 (Spring): 2–22.

Bond, Jon R., and Richard Fleisher. 2001. "The Polls: Partisanship and Presidential Performance Evaluations." *Presidential Studies Quarterly* 31 (3): 529.

Bovitz, Gregory L., James N. Druckman, and Arthur Lupia. 2002. "When Can a News Organization Lead Public Opinion? Ideology versus Market Forces in Decisions to Make News." *Public Choice* 113 (October): 127–155.

Brody, Richard. 1991. *Assessing the President: The Media, Elite Opinion, and Public Support.* Stanford, CA: Stanford University Press.

Brooks, David. 2001. "One Nation, Slightly Divisible." *Atlantic Monthly* 288 (December): 53–65.

Bucy, Erik P., and Maria Elizabeth Grabe. 2007. "Taking Television Seriously: A Sound and Image Bite Analysis of Presidential Campaign Coverage, 1992–2004." *Journal of Communication* 57 (4): 652–675.

Burden, Barry C., and Anthony Mughan. 2003. "The International Economy and Presidential Approval." *Public Opinion Quarterly* 67 (Winter): 555–578.

Canes-Wrone, Brandice. 2005. *Who Leads Whom? Presidents, Policy Making and the Mass Public.* University of Chicago Press.

Canes-Wrone, Brandice. 2001. "A Theory of Presidents' Public Agenda Setting." *Journal of Theoretical Politics* 13 (2): 183–208.

Canes-Wrone, Brandice, William Howell, and David E. Lewis. 2008. "Toward a Broader Understanding of Presidential Power: A Reevaluation of the Two Presidencies Thesis." *Journal of Politics* 70 (January): 1–16.

Clayman, Steven E., and Anne Reisner. 1998. "Gatekeeping in Action: Editorial Conferences and Assessments of Newsworthiness." *American Sociological Review* 63 (April): 178–199.

Clayman, Steven E., Marc N. Elliott, John Heritage, and Laurie L. Mc-
Donald. 2006. "Historical Trends in Questioning Presidents, 1953–
2000." *Presidential Studies Quarterly* 36 (December): 561–583.

Clayman, Steven E., John Heritage, Marc N. Elliott, and Laurie L. McDon-
ald. 2007. "When Does the Watchdog Bark? Conditions of Aggressive
Questioning in Presidential News Conferences." *American Sociological
Review* 72 (February): 232–241.

Cohen, Jeffrey E. 1982. "The Impact of the Modern Presidency on Presidential Success in the U.S. Congress." *Legislative Studies Quarterly* 7
(November): 515–532.

Cohen, Jeffrey E. 1995. "Presidential Rhetoric and the Public Agenda,"
*American Journal of Political Science* 1995 39 (February): 87–107.

Cohen, Jeffrey E. 1997. *Presidential Responsiveness and Public Policy Making:
The Public and the Policies that Presidents Make.* Ann Arbor: University of
Michigan Press.

Cohen, Jeffrey E. 2004. "If the News Is So Bad, Why Are Presidential Polls
So High? Presidents, the News Media, and the Mass Public in an Era of
New Media." *Presidential Studies Quarterly* 34 (3): 493.

Cohen, Jeffrey E. 2006. "The Polls: The Coalitional President from a Public Opinion Perspective." *Presidential Studies Quarterly* 36 (September):
541–550.

Cohen, Jeffrey E. 2008. *The Presidency in an Era of 24-Hour News.* Princeton,
NJ: Princeton University Press.

Cohen, Jeffrey E. Forthcoming. "The Presidency and the Mass Media." In
*Oxford Handbook of the American Presidency,* edited by George C. Edwards
III and William Howell. New York: Oxford University Press.

Cohen, Jeffrey E., Richard Fleisher, and Paul Kantor, eds. 2001. *American
Political Parties: Decline or Resurgence?* Washington, DC: CQ Press.

Cohen, Jeffrey E., and John A. Hamman. 2003. "The Polls: Can Presidential Rhetoric Affect the Public's Economic Perceptions?" *Presidential
Studies Quarterly* 33 (June): 408–422.

Cohen, Jeffrey E., and John A. Hamman. 2006. "Presidential Ideology and
the Public Mood." In *In the Public Domain: Presidents and the Challenge of
Public Leadership,* edited by Diane Heith and Lori Cox Han, 141–162.
Albany, NY: SUNY Press.

Cohen, Jeffrey E., Michael A. Krassa, and John A. Hamman. 1991. "The
Impact of Presidential Campaigning on Midterm U.S. Senate Elections." *American Political Science Review* 85 (March): 165–178.

Cohen, Jeffrey E., and Richard J. Powell. 2005. "Building Public Support
from the Grassroots Up: The Impact of Presidential Travel on State-
Level Approval." *Presidential Studies Quarterly* 35 (March): 11–27.

Comstock, George, and Erica Scharrer. 2005. *The Psychology of Media and
Politics.* Burlington, MA: Elsevier.

Cook, Timothy E. 1998. *Governing With the News: The News Media as a Political Institution.* Chicago: University of Chicago Press.

Cook, Timothy E., and Lyn Ragsdale. 1998. "The President and the Press: Negotiating Newsworthiness in the White House." In *The Presidency and the Political System,* 5th ed., edited by Michael Nelson, 323–357. Washington, DC: CQ Press.

Coombs, Steven L. 1981. "Editorial Endorsements and Election Outcomes." In *More Than News: Media Power in Public Affairs,* edited by Michael B. MacKuen and Steven L. Coombs, 147–226. Beverly Hills, CA: Sage Publications.

Corley, Pamela C. 2006. "Avoiding Advice and Consent: Recess Appointments and Presidential Power." *Presidential Studies Quarterly* 36 (December): 670–680.

Cornwell, Elmer E., Jr. 1957. "Coolidge and Presidential Leadership." *Public Opinion Quarterly* 21 (Summer): 265–278.

Cornwell, Elmer E., Jr. 1959. "Presidential News: The Expanding Public Image." *Journalism Quarterly* 36 (Summer): 275–283.

Cornwell, Elmer E., Jr. 1960. "The Presidential Press Conference: A Study in Institutionalization." *Midwest Journal of Political Science* 4 (November): 370–389.

D'Alessio, Dave, and Mike Allen. 2000. "Media Bias in Presidential Elections." *Journal of Communication* 50 (4): 133–156.

Dalton, Russell J., Paul A. Beck, and Robert Huckfeldt. 1998. "Partisan Cues and the Media." *American Political Science Review* 92 (March): 111–126.

Davies, Philip, and Bruce I. Newman, eds. 2006. *Winning Elections with Political Marketing.* New York: Haworth Press.

Davis, Richard, and Diana Owen. 1998. *New Media and American Politics.* New York: Oxford University Press.

Dixon, Travis L., and Cristina L. Azocar. 2006. "The Representation of Juvenile Offenders by Race on Los Angeles Area Television News." *Howard Journal of Communications* 17 (2): 143–161.

Dixon, Travis L., and Daniel Linz. 2000. "Race and the Misrepresentation of Victimization on Local Television News." *Communication Research* 27 (October): 547–573.

Doherty, Brendan. 2007. "The Politics of the Permanent Campaign: Presidential Travel, Fundraising, and the Electoral College, 1977–2004." Paper presented at the Midwest Political Science Association, April 12, 2007, Chicago.

Dowler, Kenneth. 2006. "Sex, Lies, and Videotape: The Presentation of Sex Crime in Local Television News." *Journal of Criminal Justice* 34 (4): 383–392.

Druckman, James N., and Michael Parkin. 2005. "How Editorial Slant Affects Voters." *Journal of Politics* 67 (November): 1030–1049.

Edwards, George C., III. 2000. "Building Coalitions." *Presidential Studies Quarterly* 30 (March): 47–78.

Edwards, George C., III. 2003. *On Deaf Ears: The Limits of the Bully Pulpit.* New Haven, CT: Yale University Press.

Edwards, George C., III. 2008. *Governing by Campaigning: The Politics of the Bush Presidency.* New York: Pearson Longman.

Edwards, George C., III, William Mitchell, and Reed Welch. 1995. "Explaining Presidential Approval: The Significance of Issue Salience." *American Journal of Political Science* 39 (February): 108–134.

Edwards, George C., III, and B. Dan Wood. 1999. "Who Influences Whom? The President, Congress, and the Media." *American Political Science Review* 93 (June): 327–344.

Entman, Robert M. 2007. "Framing Bias: Media in the Distribution of Power." *Journal of Communication* 57 (March): 163–173.

Entman, Robert, and Benjamin Page. 1994. "The Iraq War Debate and the Limits to Media Independence." In *Taken by Storm: Media, Public Opinion, and U.S. Foreign Policy in the Gulf War,* edited by W. L. Bennett. Chicago: University of Chicago Press.

Erikson, Robert S. 1976. "The Influence of Newspaper Endorsements in Presidential Elections: The Case of 1964." *American Journal of Political Science* 20 (May): 207–233.

Erikson, Robert S., Michael MacKuen, and James A. Stimson. 2002. *The Macro Polity.* New York: Cambridge University Press.

Eshbaugh-Soha, Matthew. 2003. "Presidential Press Conferences over Time." *American Journal of Political Science* 47 (April): 348–353.

Eshbaugh-Soha, Matthew. 2008a. "Local Newspaper Coverage of the Presidency." *Harvard International Journal of Press/Politics* 13 (April): 103–119.

Eshbaugh-Soha, Matthew. 2008b. "The Tone of Local Presidential News Coverage." Paper presented at the annual meeting of the Western Political Science Association, March 20, 2008, San Diego.

Eshbaugh-Soha, Matthew, and Jeffrey S. Peake. 2006. "The Contemporary Presidency: 'Going Local' to Reform Social Security." *Presidential Studies Quarterly* 36 (December): 689–704.

Farnsworth, Stephen J., and S. Robert Lichter. 2005. *The Mediated Presidency: Television News and Presidential Government.* Lanham, MD: Rowman and Littlefield.

Farris, Anne, Richard P. Nathan, and David J. Wright. 2004. *The Expanding Administrative Presidency George W. Bush and the Faith-Based Initiative.* Albany, NY: Nelson A. Rockefeller Institute of Government.

Fiorina, Morris P., with Samuel J. Abrams and Jeremy C. Pope. 2005. *Culture War? The Myth of a Polarized America.* New York: Pearson Longman.

Fleisher, Richard, and Jon R. Bond. 2004. "The Shrinking Middle in the U.S. Congress." *British Journal of Political Science* 34 (July): 429–451.

Foote, Joe S. 1990. *Television Access and Political Power: The Networks, the Presidency, and the "Loyal Opposition."* Westport, CT: Greenwood.

Fowler, Erika Franklin. 2007. "Missing Messages? Elections on Local Television News." Ph.D. diss., University of Wisconsin-Madison.

Froomkin, Dan. 2005. "Bush, Deep Throat, and the Press." Washingtonpost.com, June 3, 2005. http://www.washingtonpost.com/wp-dyn/content/blog/2005/06/03/BL2005060300818_pf.html (accessed May 5, 2008).

Gentzkow, Matthew, and Jesse M. Shapiro. 2006a. "Media Reputation and Bias." *Journal of Political Economy* 114 (2): 280–316.

Gentzkow, Matthew, and Jesse M. Shapiro. 2006b. "What Drives Media Slant? Evidence from U.S. Daily Newspapers." Unpublished manuscript. http://ssrn.com/abstract=947640.

Gershtenson, Joseph. 2003. "Mobilization Strategies of the Democrats and Republicans, 1956–2000." *Political Research Quarterly* 56 (September): 293–308.

Gilens, Martin. 1988. "Gender and Support for Reagan: A Comprehensive Model of Presidential Approval." *American Journal of Political Science* 32 (February): 19–49.

Gilens, Martin, and Craig Hertzman. 2000. "Corporate Ownership and News Bias." *The Journal of Politics* 62 (2): 369–386.

Gillespie, Mark. 2004. "Media Credibility Reaches Lowest Point in Three Decades," *Gallup Tuesday Press Briefing*, September 23, 2004, p. 12.

Gilliam, Franklin D., Jr., and Shanto Iyengar. 2000. "Prime Suspects: The Influence of Local Television News on the Viewing Public." *American Journal of Political Science* 44 (July): 560–573.

Gladney, George Albert. 1996. "How Editors and Readers Rank and Rate the Importance of Eighteen Traditional Standards of Newspaper Excellence." *Journalism and Mass Communication Quarterly* 73 (Summer): 319–331.

Goidel, Robert K., Todd G. Shields, and Mark Peffley. 1997. "Priming Theory and RAS Models: Toward an Integrated Perspective on Media Influence." *American Politics Quarterly* 25 (July): 287–318.

Golan, Guy. 2006. "Inter-Media Agenda Setting and Global News Coverage: Assessing the Influence of the *New York Times* on Three Network Television Evening News Programs." *Journalism Studies* 7 (2): 323–333.

Graber, Doris. A. 1976. "Press and TV as Opinion Resources in Presidential Campaigns." *Public Opinion Quarterly* 40 (Autumn): 285–303.

Graber, Doris. 2001. *Mass Media and American Politics*, 6th ed. Washington, DC: CQ Press.

Greene, Stephen. 2001. "The Role of Character Assessment in Presidential Approval." *American Politics Research* 29 (March): 196–210.

Greenstein, Fred I., 2000. *The Presidential Difference: Leadership Style from FDR to Clinton.* New York: Free Press.

Greenstein, Fred I. 2008. "Understanding Presidential Personality." In *Presidential Leadership: The Vortex of Power*, edited by Bert A. Rockman and Richard W. Waterman, 261–275. New York: Oxford University Press.

Groeling, Tim. Forthcoming. *Singing from the Same Hymnbook: Party Cohesion in the Media.* New York: Cambridge University Press.

Groeling, Tim, and Samuel Kernell. 1998. "Is Network News Coverage of the President Biased?" *Journal of Politics* 60 (November): 1063–1087.

Gronke, Paul, and Brian Newman. 2003. "FDR to Clinton, Mueller to? A Field Essay on Presidential Approval." *Political Research Quarterly* 56 (December): 501–512.

Grossman, Michael Baruch, and Martha Joynt Kumar. 1981. *Portraying the President: The White House and the News Media.* Baltimore: Johns Hopkins University Press.

Hacker, Jacob S., and Paul Pierson. 2005. "Abandoning the Middle: The Bush Tax Cuts and the Limits of Democratic Control." *Perspectives on Politics* 3 (March): 33–53.

Hager, Gregory L., and Terry Sullivan. 1994. "President-Centered and Presidency-Centered Explanations of Presidential Public Activity." *American Journal of Political Science* 38 (November): 1079–1103.

Hallin, Daniel. 1986. *The "Uncensored War."* Berkeley: University of California Press.

Hallin, Daniel C. 1992. "Sound Bite News: Television Coverage of Elections, 1968–1988." *Journal of Communication* 42 (June): 5–24.

Hallin, Daniel, and Todd Gitlin. 1994. "The Gulf War as Popular Culture and Television Drama." In *Taken by Storm: Media, Public Opinion, and U.S. Foreign Policy in the Gulf War*, edited by W. L. Bennett. Chicago: University of Chicago Press.

Hamilton, James T. 2003. *All the News That's Fit to Sell.* Princeton, NJ: Princeton University Press.

Han, Lori Cox. 2006. "New Strategies for an Old Medium: The Weekly Radio Addresses of Reagan and Clinton." *Congress & the Presidency* 33 (Spring): 25–45.

Hart, Roderick P. 1987. *The Sound of Leadership: Presidential Communication in the Modern Age.* Chicago: University of Chicago Press.

Hart, Roderick P. 2002. *Campaign Talk: Why Elections are Good for Us.* Princeton, NJ: Princeton University Press.

Herrnson, Paul S., and Irwin L. Morris. 2007. "Presidential Campaigning in the 2002 Congressional Elections." *Legislative Studies Quarterly* 32 (November): 629–648.

Hertsgaard, Mark. 1988. *On Bended Knee:* The Press *and the Reagan Presidency*, rev. ed. New York: Schocken Books.

Hetherington, Marc J. 2001. "Resurgent Mass Partisanship: The Role of Elite Polarization." *American Political Science Review* 95 (September): 619–631.

Hill, Kim Quaile. 1998. "The Policy Agendas of the President and the Mass Public: A Research Validation and Extension." *American Journal of Political Science* 42 (October): 1328–1334.

Hillygus, D. Sunshine, and Todd G. Shields. 2008. *The Persuadable Voter: Wedge Issues in Presidential Campaigns.* Princeton, NJ: Princeton University Press.

Hoddie, Matthew, and Stephen R. Routh. 2004. "Predicting the Presidential Presence: Explaining Presidential Midterm Elections Campaign Behavior." *Political Research Quarterly* 57 (June): 257–265.

Hoffman, Donna R., and Alison D. Howard. 2006. *Addressing the State of the Union: The Evolution and Impact of the President's Big Speech.* Boulder, CO: Lynne Rienner.

Hollander, Sidney. 1979. "On the Strength of a Newspaper Endorsement." *Public Opinion Quarterly* 43 (Autumn): 405–407.

Holmes, Lisa M. 2008. "Why 'Go Public'? Presidential Use of Nominees to the U.S. Courts of Appeals." *Presidential Studies Quarterly* 38 (January): 110–122.

Horvit, Beverly, Adam J. Schiffer, and Mark Wright. 2008. "The Limits of Presidential Agenda Setting: Predicting Newspaper: Coverage of the Weekly Radio Address." *Harvard International Journal of Press/Politics* 13 (1): 8–28.

Howell, William G. 2003. *Power without Persuasion: The Politics of Direct Presidential Action.* Princeton, NJ: Princeton University Press.

Hurd, Robert E., and Michael W. Singletary. 1984. "Newspaper Endorsement Influence on the 1980 Presidential Election Vote." *Journalism Quarterly* 61 (Summer): 332–338.

Iyengar, Shanto, and Donald Kinder. 1987. *News That Matters.* Chicago: University of Chicago Press.

Jacobson, Gary C. 2008. *The Politics of Congressional Elections*, 7th ed. New York: Longman.

Jacobson, Gary C. 2006. "The Polls: Polarized Opinion in the States: Partisan Differences in Approval Ratings of Governors, Senators, and George W. Bush." *Presidential Studies Quarterly* 36 (4): 732–757.

Jacobson, Gary C. 2007. *A Divider, Not a Uniter: George W. Bush and the American People: The 2006 Election and Beyond.* New York: Longman.

Jacobson, Gary, Samuel Kernell, and Jeffrey Lazarus. 2004. "Assessing the President's Role as Party Agent in Congressional Elections: The Case of Bill Clinton in 2000." *Legislative Studies Quarterly* 29 (May): 159–184.

Johnston, Richard, Michael G. Hagen, and Kathleen Hall Jamieson. 2004. *The 2000 Presidential Election and the Foundations of Party Politics.* New York: Cambridge University Press.

Just, Marion, Ann Crigler, and Tami Buhr. 1999. "Voice, Substance, and Cynicism in Presidential Campaign Media." *Political Communication* 16 (1): 25–44.

Just, Marion R., Dean E. Alger, and Montague Kern, eds. 1996. *Crosstalk: Citizens, Candidates, and the Media in a Presidential Campaign.* Chicago: University of Chicago Press.

Kahn, Kim Fridkin, and Patrick J. Kenney. 2002. "The Slant of the News." *American Political Science Review* 96 (June): 381–394.

Kaniss, Phyllis. 1991. *Making Local News.* Chicago: University of Chicago Press.

Keele, Luke, Brian Fogarty, and James Stimson. 2004. "Presidential Campaigning in the 2002 Congressional Elections." *PS: Political Science and Politics* 37 (October): 827–832.

Keele, Luke, and Nathan J. Kelly. 2006. "Dynamic Models for Dynamic Theories: The Ins and Outs of Lagged Dependent Variables." *Political Analysis* 14 (Spring): 186–205.

Kernell, Samuel. 1986. *Going Public: New Strategies of Presidential Leadership.* Washington, DC: CQ Press.

Kernell, Samuel. 2006. *Going Public: New Strategies of Presidential Leadership,* 4th ed. Washington, DC: CQ Press.

Kernell, Samuel, and Gary C. Jacobson. 1987. "Congress and the President as News in the Nineteenth Century." *Journal of Politics* 49 (November): 1016–1035.

Klite, Paul. 1995. "Tabloid Fever." *Television Quarterly* 27 (4): 25–32.

Krosnick, Jon A., and Laura A. Brannon. 1993a. "The Impact of the Gulf War on the Ingredients of Presidential Evaluations: Multidimensional Effects of Political Involvement." *American Political Science Review* 87 (December): 963–975.

Krosnick, Jon A., and Laura A. Brannon. 1993b. "The Media and the Foundations of Presidential Support: George Bush and the Persian Gulf Conflict." *Journal of Social Issues* 49 (Winter): 167–182.

Krosnick, Jon A., and Donald R. Kinder. 1990. "Altering the Foundations of Support for the President through Priming." *American Political Science Review* 84 (June): 497–512.

Kumar, Martha Joynt. 1997. "The White House Beat at the Century Mark." *Harvard International Journal of Press/Politics* 2 (3): 10–30.

Kumar, Martha Joynt. 2003. "Source Material: "Does This Constitute a Press Conference?" Defining and Tabulating Modern Presidential Press Conferences." *Presidential Studies Quarterly* 33 (March): 221–237.

Kumar, Martha Joynt. 2007. *Managing the President's Message: The White House Communications Operation*. Baltimore: Johns Hopkins University Press.

Kurtz, Howard. 1998. *Spin Cycle: Inside the Clinton Propaganda Machine*. New York: Free Press.

Lawrence, Adam B. 2004. "Does It Matter What the Presidents Say? The Influence of Presidential Rhetoric on the Public Agenda, 1946–2003." Ph.D. diss., Department of Political Science, University of Pittsburgh.

Light, Paul C. 1999. *The President's Agenda: Domestic Policy Choice from Kennedy to Clinton*, 3rd ed. Baltimore: Johns Hopkins University Press.

Long, Marilee, Michael D. Slater, Greg Boiarsky, Linda Stapel, and Thomas Keefe. 2005. "Obtaining Nationally Representative Samples of Local News Media Outlets." *Mass Communication & Society* 8 (4): 299–322.

Lowi, Theodore J. 1985. *The Personal President: Power Invested, Promise Unfulfilled*. Ithaca, NY: Cornell University Press.

Lowry, Dennis T., and Jon A. Shidler. 1995. "The Biters and the Bitten: An Analysis of Network TV News Bias in Campaign '92." *Journalism & Mass Communication Quarterly* 69 (Spring): 33–44.

Lowry, Dennis T., and Jon A. Shidler. 1998. "The Sound Bites, the Biters, and the Bitten: A Two-campaign Test of the Anti-incumbent Bias Hypothesis in Network TV News. *Journalism & Mass Communication Quarterly* 75 (Winter): 719–729.

MacKuen, Michael B. 1983. "Political Drama, Economic Conditions, and the Dynamics of Presidential Popularity." *American Journal of Political Science* 27 (May): 165–192

Maltese, John Anthony. 1992. *Spin Control: The White House Office of Communications and the Management of Presidential News*, 2nd ed. Chapel Hill: University of North Carolina Press.

Manheim, Jarol B. 1994. *Strategic Public Diplomacy and American Foreign Policy: The Evolution of Influence*. New York: Oxford University Press.

Martin, Howard H. 1984. "President Reagan's Return to Radio." *Journalism Quarterly* 61 (4): 817–821.

Mayer, Kenneth R. 2001. *With the Stroke of a Pen: Executive Orders and Presidential Power*. Princeton, NJ: Princeton University Press.

McManus, John T. 1994. *Market-Driven Journalism: Let the Consumer Beware?* Thousand Oaks, CA: Sage.

Mermin, Jonathan. 1999. *Debating War and Peace: Media Coverage of U.S. Intervention in the Post-Vietnam Era*. Princeton, NJ: Princeton University Press.

Milkis, Sidney M., and Jesse H. Rhodes. 2007. "George W. Bush, the Republican Party, and the 'New' American Party System." *Perspectives on Politics* 5 (September): 461–488.

Miller, Joanne M., and Jon A. Krosnick. 2000. "News Media Impact on the Ingredients of Presidential Evaluation: Politically Knowledgeable Citizens Are Guided by a Trusted Source." *American Journal of Political Science* 44 (April): 295–309.

Miroff, Bruce. 1982. "Monopolizing the Public Space: The President as a Problem for Democratic Politics." In *Rethinking the Presidency*, edited by Thomas Cronin, 218–232. Boston: Little, Brown.

Mueller, John E. 1970. "Presidential Popularity from Truman to Johnson." *American Political Science Review* 64 (March): 18–34.

Mutz, Diana C. 1992. "Mass Media and the Depoliticization of Personal Experiences." *American Journal of Political Science* 36 (May): 483–508.

Mutz, Diana C. 1994. "Contextualizing Personal Experience: The Role of the Mass Media." *Journal of Politics* 56 (August): 689–714.

Nadeau, Richard, Richard G. Niemi, David P. Fan, and Timothy Amato. 1999. "Elite Economic Forecasts, Economic News, Mass Economic Judgments, and Presidential Approval." *Journal of Politics* 61 (February): 109–135.

Nelson, Michael A. 1988. "The President and the Court: Reinterpreting the Court-packing Episode of 1937." *Political Science Quarterly* 103 (Summer): 267–293.

Neustadt, Richard E. 1960. *Presidential Power.* New York: Wiley.

Neustadt, Richard E. 1990. *Presidential Power and the Modern Presidents: The Politics of Leadership from Roosevelt to Reagan.* New York: Free Press.

Newman, Brian. 2003. "Integrity and Presidential Approval, 1980–2000." *Public Opinion Quarterly* 67 (Fall): 335–367.

Nicholson, Stephen P., Gary M. Segura, and Nathan D. Woods. 2002. "Presidential Approval and the Mixed Blessing of Divided Government." *Journal of Politics* 64 (August): 701–720.

Page, Benjamin I., Robert Y. Shapiro, and Glenn R. Dempsey. 1987. "What Moves Public Opinion?" *American Political Science Review* 81 (March): 23–44.

Paletz, David L., and Entman, Robert M. 1980. "Presidents, Power, and the Press." *Presidential Studies Quarterly* 10 (Summer): 416–426.

Paletz, David L., and Richard J. Vinegar. 1977–1978. "Presidents on Television: The Effects of Instant Analysis." *Public Opinion Quarterly* 41 (Winter): 488–497.

Pan, Zhongdang, and Gerald M. Kosicki. 1997. "Priming and Media Impact on the Evaluations of the President's Performance." *Communication Research* 24 (February): 3–30.

Panagopoulos, Costas, and Peter Wielhouwer. 2008. "The Ground War 2000–2004: Strategic Targeting and Mobilization in Grassroots Presidential Campaigns." *Presidential Studies Quarterly* 38 (2): 347–362.

Patterson, Thomas E. 2000. "Doing Well and Doing Good: How Soft News and Critical Journalism are Shrinking the News Audience and Weakening Democracy – And What News Outlets Can Do About It." Joan Shorenstein Center for Press, Politics, and Public Policy, John F. Kennedy School of Government, Harvard University, Boston.

Peake, Jeffrey S. 2001. "Presidential Agenda Setting in Foreign Policy." *Political Research Quarterly* 54 (March): 69–86.

Peake, Jeffrey S. 2007. "Presidents and Front-page News: How America's Newspapers Cover the Bush Administration." *Harvard International Journal of Press/Politics* 12 (October): 52–70.

Peterson, Mark A., and Jack L. Walker. 1986. "Interest Group Responses to Partisan Change: The Impact of the Reagan Administration upon the National Interest Group System." In *Interest Group Politics,* 2nd ed., edited by Allan J. Cigler and Burdett A. Loomis, 162–182. Washington, DC: C.Q. Press.

Poindexter, Paula M., Laura Smith, and Don Heider. 2003. "Race and Ethnicity in Local Television News: Framing, Story Assignments, and Source Selections." *Journal of Broadcasting & Electronic Media* 47 (4): 524–536.

Powell, Richard J. 1999. "'Going Public' Revisited: Presidential Speechmaking and the Bargaining Setting in Congress," *Congress & the Presidency* 26 (Fall): 153–170.

Powell, Richard J., and Dean Schloyer. 2003. "Public Presidential Appeals and Congressional Floor Votes: Reassessing the Constitutional Threat." *Congress & the Presidency* Autumn (30): 123–138.

Prior, Markus. 2007. *Post-Broadcast Democracy: How Media Choice Increases Inequality in Political Involvement and Polarizes Elections.* New York: Cambridge University Press.

Protess, David, and McCombs, Maxwell. 1991. *Agenda Setting: Readings on Media, Public Opinion, and Policymaking.* Hillsdale, NJ: Lawrence Earlbaum.

Ragsdale, Lyn. 1984. "The Politics of Presidential Speechmaking, 1949–1980." *American Political Science Review* 78 (December): 971–984.

Ragsdale, Lyn. 1987. "Presidential Speechmaking and the Public Audience: Individual Presidents and Group Attitudes." *Journal of Politics* 49 (August): 704–736.

Ragsdale, Lyn. 1998. *Vital Statistics on the Presidency: Washington to Clinton,* rev. ed. Washington, DC: CQ Press.

Ragsdale, Lyn. 2009. *Vital Statistics on the Presidency: Washington to Clinton,* 3rd ed. Washington, DC: CQ Press.

Riffe, Daniel, and Alan Freitag. 1997. "A Content Analysis of Content Analyses: Twenty-five Years of 'Journalism Quarterly'." *Journalism and Mass Communication Quarterly* 74 (Autumn): 515–524.

Riffe, Daniel, Stephen Lacy, and Frederick Fico. 2005. *Analyzing Media Messages: Using Quantitative Content Analysis in Research*, 2nd ed. Mahwah, NJ: Lawrence Erlbaum.

Romer, Daniel, Kate Kenski, Paul Waldman, Christopher Adasiewicz, and Kathleen Hall Jamieson. 2004. *Capturing Campaign Dynamics: The National Annenberg Election Study*. New York: Oxford University Press.

Rosenstone, Steven J., John Mark Hansen, and Keith Reeves. 2003. *Mobilization, Participation and Democracy in American*, 4th ed. New York: Longman.

Rowland, Robert C., and John M. Jones. 2002. "'Until Next Week': The Saturday Radio Addresses of Ronald Reagan." *Presidential Studies Quarterly* 32 (1): 84–110.

Rozell, Mark J. 1990. "President Carter and the Press: Perspectives from White House Communications Advisers." *Political Science Quarterly* 105 (Autumn): 419–434.

Rozell, Mark J. 1993. "The Limits of White House Image Control." *Political Science Quarterly* 108 (Fall): 453–480.

Rozell, Mark J. 1995. "Presidential Image-Makers on the Limits of Spin Control." *Presidential Studies Quarterly* 25 (Winter): 67–90.

Russomanno, Joseph A., and Stephen E. Everett. 1995. "Candidate Sound Bites: Too Much Concern Over Length?" *Journal of Broadcasting & Electronic Media* 39 (3) 408–415.

Schier, Steven E. 2009. *Panorama of a Presidency: How George W. Bush Acquired and Spent His Political Capital*. Armonk, NY: M. E. Sharpe.

Seligman, Lester G., and Cary R. Covington. 1989. *The Coalitional Presidency*. Chicago: Dorsey Press.

Sellers, Patrick J., and Laura M. Denton. 2006. "Presidential Visits and Midterm Senate Elections." *Presidential Studies Quarterly* 36 (August): 410–432.

Shah, Dhavan V., and Mark D. Watts. 1999. "News Coverage, Economic Cues, and the Public's Presidential Preferences, 1984–1996." *Journal of Politics* 61 (November): 914–943.

Shah, Dhavan V., Mark D. Watts, David Domke, and David P. Fan. 2002. "News Framing and the Cueing of Issue Regimes: Explaining Clinton's Public Approval in Spite of Scandal." *Public Opinion Quarterly* 66 (Fall): 339–370.

Shaw, Darren R. and Bartholomew H. Sparrow. 1999. "From the Inner Ring Out: News Congruence, Cue-Taking, and Campaign Coverage." *Political Research Quarterly* 52 (June): 323–351.

Shoemaker, Pamela J., and Stephen D. Reese. 1996. *Mediating the Message: Theories of Influences on Mass Media Content*. White Plains, NY: Longman.

Shull, Steven A., ed. 1991. *The Two Presidencies: A Quarter Century Assessment.* Chicago: Nelson-Hall.

Sigelman, Lee, and Cynthia Whissell. 2002a. "The Great Communicator' and 'The Great Talker' on the Radio: Projecting Presidential Personas." *Presidential Studies Quarterly* 32 (March): 137–146.

Sigelman, Lee, and Cynthia Whissell. 2002b. "Projecting Presidential Personas on the Radio: An Addendum on the Bushes." *Presidential Studies Quarterly* 32 (September): 572–576.

Skinner, Richard M. 2008–2009. "George W. Bush and the Partisan Presidency." *Political Science Quarterly* 123 (Winter): 605–622.

Stanley, Harold W., and Richard G. Niemi. 1998. *Vital Statistics on American Politics, 1997–1998.* Washington, DC: CQ Press.

Stovall, James Glen. 1984. "Incumbency and News Coverage of the 1980 Presidential Election Campaign." *Western Political Quarterly* 37 (December): 621–631.

Stevens, Daniel, Dean Alger, Barbara Allen, and John L. Sullivan. 2006. "Local News Coverage in a Social Capital Capital: Election 2000 on Minnesota's Local News Stations." *Political Communication* 23 (1): 61–83.

Tedin, Kent. 1986. "Change and Stability in Presidential Popularity at the Individual Level." *Journal of Politics* 40 (Winter): 1–21.

Tidmarch, Charles M., and John J. Pitney. 1985. "Covering Congress." *Polity* 17 (Spring): 463–483

Ubertaccio, Peter. 2006. "Machine Politics for the Twenty-First Century? Multilevel Marketing and Party Organizations." In *The State of the Parties: The Changing Role of Contemporary American Parties,* 5th ed., edited by John C. Green and Daniel J. Coffey. Lanham, MD: Rowman & Littlefield.

Underwood, Doug. 1998. "Market Research and the Audience for Political News." In *The Politics of News: The News of Politics,* edited by Doris Graber, Denis McQuail, and Pippa Norris, 171–192. Washington, DC: CQ Press.

Valentino, Nicholas. 1999. "Crime News and the Priming of Racial Attitudes During Evaluations of the President." *Public Opinion Quarterly* 63 (Autumn): 293–320.

Walker, Jack L. 1991. *Mobilizing Interest Groups in America: Patrons, Professions, and Social Movements.* Ann Arbor: University of Michigan Press.

Wang, Jian, and Tsan-Kuo Chang. 2004. "Strategic Public Diplomacy and Local Press: How a High-profile "Head-of-State" Visit Was Covered in America's Heartland." *Public Relations Review* 30 (March): 11–24.

Wanta, Wayne, and Joe Foote. 1994. "The President–News Media Relationship: A Times Series Analysis of Agenda-Setting." *Journal of Broadcasting & Electronic Media* 38 (Fall): 437–448.

Waterman, Richard G., and Hank C. Jenkins-Smith. 1999. "The Expectations Gap Thesis: Public Attitudes toward an Incumbent President." *Journal of Politics* 61 (November): 944–966.

Waterman, Richard W., Gilbert St. Clair, and Robert Wright. 1999. *The Image-Is-Everything Presidency: Dilemmas in American Leadership.* Boulder, CO: Westview Press.

Wattenberg, Martin, P. 2004. "The Changing Presidential Media Environment." *Presidential Studies Quarterly* 34 (3): 557–572.

Weaver, David H., and G. Cleveland Wilhoit. 1991. *The American Journalist: A Portrait of U.S. News People and Their Work,* 2nd ed. Bloomington: Indiana University Press.

West, Darrell M. 1991. "Television and Presidential Popularity in America." *British Journal of Political Science* 21 (April): 199–214.

White, Graham J. 1979. *FDR and the Press.* Chicago: University of Chicago Press.

Wielhouwer, Peter W. 2006. "Grassroots Mobilization." In *The Electoral Challenge: Theory Meets Practice,* edited by Stephen Craig. Washington, DC: CQ Press.

Wielhouwer, Peter W., and Brad Lockerbie. 1994. "Party Contacting and Political Participation, 1952–90." *American Journal of Political Science* 38 (February): 211–219.

Wildavsky, Aaron. 1966. "The Two Presidencies." *Trans-Action* 4 (1): 7–14.

Winfield, Betty Houchin. 1990. *FDR and the News Media.* Urbana: University of Illinois Press.

Wood, B. Dan. 2007. *The Politics of Economic Leadership: The Causes and Consequences of Presidential Rhetoric.* Princeton, NJ: Princeton University Press.

Wood, B. Dan, and Jeffrey S. Peake. 1998. "The Dynamics of Foreign Policy Agenda Setting." *American Political Science Review* 92 (March): 173–184.

Young, Garry, and William B. Perkins. 2005. "Presidential Rhetoric, the Public Agenda, and the End of Presidential Television's 'Golden Age'." *Journal of Politics* 67 (November): 1190–1205.

Zaller, John R. 1992. *The Nature and Origins of Mass Opinion.* Cambridge, UK: Cambridge University Press.

Zaller, John R. 1998. "The Rule of Product Substitution in Presidential Campaign News." *Annals of the American Academy of Political and Social Science* 560 (November): 111–128.

Zaller, John, and Dennis Chiu. 2000. "Government's Little Helper: U.S. Press Coverage of Foreign Policy Crises, 1946–1999." In *Decisionmaking in a Glass House: Mass Media, Public Opinion, and American and European Foreign Policy in the 21st Century,* edited by Brigitte L. Nacos, Robert

Y. Shapiro, and Pierangelo Isernia, 61–84. New York: Rowman and Littlefield.

Zeidenstein, Harvey G. 1984. "News Media Perceptions of White House News Management." *Presidential Studies Quarterly* 14 (Summer): 391–398.

# Index